Ethical and Legal Issues in School Counseling

Edited by

Wayne C. Huey

and

Theodore P. Remley, Jr.

A division of the
American Counseling Association

The American School Counselor Association, a division of the
American Counseling Association (formerly AACD)
5999 Stevenson Avenue
Alexandria, Virginia 22304

Library of Congress Cataloging-in-Publication Data

Ethical and legal issues in school counseling.

    1. Personnel service in education—United States.
    2. Student counselors—Professional ethics—United States.
    3. Personnel service in education—Law and legislation—United
      States.
I. Huey, Wayne C.
II. Remley, Theodore Phant, 1947–
LB1027.5.E84   1988   371.4'0973   88-34273
ISBN 1-55620-055-2

Printed in the United States of America (Fifth Printing)
Cover design by Sarah Jane Valdez

CONTENTS

FOREWORD

As professional school counselors, we all tend to operate under a personal and professional code of ethics. We must also be concerned and knowledgeable about the law and legislative issues as we carry out our work. At times, we may wonder whether what we are doing is consistent with professional standards of ethical behavior, the law, and legislative issues. This monograph will provide the reader with guidelines and information that will help facilitate the decision making process as to whether one is doing the "right" thing.

The American School Counselor Association supports and encourages the education of its membership and all school counselors to be aware, to understand, and to have knowledge about ethical, legal, and legislative issues to effectively carry out their work in the schools. Membership in local, state, and national professional associations that work to promote the improvement of school guidance and counseling is encouraged as a base of support and information for school counselors.

School counselors are in a position to have positive impact on society by appropriately enhancing the potential, dignity, worth, and uniqueness of each student. Guidelines on the pages that follow will strengthen that opportunity for positive impact.

—Jim Whitledge, President
American School Counselor Association

CONTRIBUTORS

Helen Aiello, Counselor, Glasgow Intermediate School, Alexandria, Virginia.

Patrick Callanan, Private Practitioner, Santa Ana, California.

Lanthan D. Camblin, Jr., Assistant Professor, Departments of Educational Leadership and Early Childhood/Special Education, University of Cincinnati.

Susan E. Cayleff, Assistant Professor, Institute for the Medical Humanities, University of Texas Medical Branch, Galveston, Texas.

John H. Childers, Jr., Associate Professor, Department of Counselor Education, University of Arkansas, Fayetteville.

Eli Coleman, Assistant Professor and Associate Director, Program in Human Sexuality, Department of Family Practice and Community Health, Medical School, University of Minnesota, Minneapolis.

Gerald Corey, Professor of Human Services, California State University, Fullerton.

Marianne Schneider Corey, Private Practitioner, Idyllwild, California.

Michael A. Crabbs, Consultant, Estes Park, Colorado.

Susan K. Crabbs, Consultant, Estes Park, Colorado.

Kathleen L. Davis, Professor, University of Tennessee, Knoxville.

Mary E. DePauw, Director of Counseling and Career Development, Saint Mary's College, Notre Dame, Indiana.

Patricia A. Ferris, Coordinator of Guidance and Counseling, Center School District, Kansas City, Missouri.

Kevin Geoffroy, Professor of Counselor Education, College of William and Mary, Williamsburg, Virginia.

Edwin R. Gerler, Jr., Associate Professor, Department of Education, North Carolina State University, Raleigh.

Douglas R. Gross, Associate Professor, Department of Counselor Education, Arizona State University, Tempe.

Barbara Herlihy, Assistant Professor of Counselor Education, University of Houston—Clear Lake.

Janet Howell-Nigrelli, Counselor, Fort Allen Elementary School, Hempfield Area School Distsrict, Greensburg, Pennsylvania.

Wayne C. Huey, Director of Counseling, Lakeside High School, Dekalb County School System, Decatur, Georgia.

Charles W. Humes, Associate Professor, Virginia Polytechnic and State University, Northern Virginia Graduate Center, Falls Church.

Leslie S. Kaplan, Director of Guidance, York County Schools, Grafton, Virginia.

John R. Klenowski, Associate Executive Director, Community Mental Health Services, St. Clairsville, Ohio.

Jeffrey A. Kottler, Clinical Director, Huron Valley Counseling Services, Farmington Hills, Michigan.

Richard D. Krugman, Associate Professor of Pediatrics, University of Colorado Health Sciences Center, Denver.

Marva J. Larrabee, Associate Professor, Department of Educational Psychology, College of Education, University of South Carolina.

James L. Levenson, Assistant Professor, Department of Psychiatry and Medicine, Medical College of Virginia, Richmond.

Malcolm E. Linville, Professor of Counseling and Teacher Education, School of Education, University of Missouri—Kansas City.

Alan R. Mabe, Associate Professor and Chair, Department of Philosophy, Florida State University, Tallahassee.

William Marchant, Associate Professor, College of Education, University of Nevada, Las Vegas.

Naomi M. Meara, Associate Professor, University of Tennessee, Knoxville.

H. Thompson Prout, Assistant Professor, Department of Educational Psychology and Statistics, State University of New York, Albany.

K Richard Pyle, Director of Advising, Counseling, and Career Development, Alma College, Alma, Michigan.

Theodore P. Remley, Jr., Director of Department of Counselor Education, Mississippi State University.

Sharon E. Robinson, Chair and Associate Professor, Department of Counselor Education, Arizona State University, Tempe.

Stephen A. Rollin, Associate Professor, Department of Human Services, Florida State University.

J. Michael Russell, Professor, Departments of Philosophy and Human Services, California State University, Fullerton.

James P. Sampson, Jr., Assistant Professor, Department of Human Services and Studies, Florida State University, Tallahassee.

David N. Sandberg, Attorney and Judge, New Hampshire.

Susan Schaefer, Private Practitioner, Minneapolis, Minnesota.

Vernon L. Sheeley, Professor, Department of Educational Leadership, Western Kentucky University, Bowling Green.

Lawrence D. Spiegel, Clinical Psychologist and Visiting Lecturer, Rutgers University, New Brunswick, New Jersey.

Lou Culler Talbutt, Research Associate, College of Education, Virginia Polytechnic Institute and State University, Blacksburg.

Cynthia K. Terres, Director of Counseling Services, University of South Carolina—Coastal Carolina College.

Margaret M. Walker, Counselor, Allendale County Schools, Allendale, South Carolina.

Joseph C. Zingaro, Doctoral Student, Division of Counseling and Educational Psychology, The Pennsylvania State University.

INTRODUCTION

For a number of years we, the editors of this book, have been intensely involved in ethical and legal issues relative to the counseling profession. In addition to our roles as counselor educators, one of us (Huey) has served as chair of the American School Counselor Association (ASCA) Ethics Committee and directed the writing of the ASCA *Ethical Standards for School Counselors* (1984), and the other (Remley) is a practicing attorney who has worked closely with ASCA and its Ethics Committee. From our experiences as counselors, educators, professional association leaders, and workshop presenters, we have been acutely aware of the concerns of practicing school counselors about whether they are responding appropriately to ethical dilemmas. For the past 6 years, we have participated as panelists on the ASCA Ethics Program at AACD conventions. Program attendance has averaged between 75–125 people each year. Practicing school counselors have asked questions such as, "What should I have done in that situation?" or "Did I do the right thing?" This desire for information and feedback regarding difficult cases was reiterated by respondents to the ASCA Membership Survey conducted in 1988, wherein the need for ethics information was ranked among the top concerns. Why are we seeing this ongoing interest in legal and ethical issues? Why are we seeing an increase in the literature in these areas? It is hoped that the counseling profession as a whole is becoming more aware of, and sensitive to, the need for ethical practice; that is, the importance of practicing ethically within the law. Perhaps the increase in litigation involving educators and mental health practitioners is a factor. Certainly the laws are changing or at least are being interpreted differently, requiring counselors to stay up-to-date. A common concern, for instance, relates to the impact of the Hatch Amendment on school counseling programs.

Ethical decisions are usually not clear cut; they tend to be in the gray areas rather than in black and white. Furthermore, the "right" answer in one situation is not necessarily the "right" answer in a similar case at another time. As society changes, the issues change; and, indeed, as counselors change, their perspectives change. If we understand and accept the fact that ultimately counselors will have to struggle with themselves to determine the appropriate action in each situation, then we realize the importance of ethical and legal awareness and sensitivity. We then also understand the need for periodic reexamination of the issues throughout our professional lives.

Ethical and Legal Issues in School Counseling was prepared primarily for practicing school counselors. It could also serve, however, as a supplementary text in counselor education courses or provide an invaluable resource for counselor supervisors, guidance and counseling units of state departments of education, professional associations, and workshop presenters.

A young counselor-in-training recently asked, "Aren't the ethical standrds sufficient to guide me in making decisions?" We might respond that the ethical standards serve about as well in that capacity as does the U.S. Constitution or various religious canons. Any document that attempts to set standards or principles of behavior for a given population will, of necessity, be general and subject to human interpretation.

This volume was purposefully restricted in an attempt to keep the cost of purchase as low as possible, and at the same time, produce a valuable resource. An attempt was made to carefully select articles from AACD journals that were timely and well written to represent the most controversial and relevant issues. Although AACD has published a casebook (currently being revised) to assist with the interpretation of the AACD *Ethical Standards*, and some school situations are included among the dilemmas presented, a single body of information focused on ethical and legal issues in the school setting does not exist. School counselors' need for ready access to more detailed information and resources motivated ASCA to sponsor this publication. School counselors have a responsibility to practice ethically and to keep up-to-date on ethical and legal issues, and ASCA has a major responsibility to assist them in this pursuit. This book is an excellent resource, but it is not intended to stand alone. More current controversies and issues will appear in the journals, and readers must use those resources as well.

Although the editors have attempted to group articles in the most useful manner, there is necessarily some content overlap among chapters and articles. For example, an article in one section, such as legal issues, may contain information on a topic covered in another section, such as confidentiality. In some cases, readers will find conflicting information or recommendations in various articles. Again, this highlights the role of the individual counselor in interpreting ethical standards. Our hope is that this collection of articles will assist readers to respond more competently and comfortably to ethical or legal dilemmas.

The Appendices include documents with which school counselors should be familiar. It should be noted that ethics codes and position statements are periodically revised. The 1988 revision of the AACD *Ethical Standards* is included; the revision of the ASGW *Ethical Guidelines for Group Leaders*, however, was not completed when this publication went to press. Readers are encouraged to use the references at the end of each article for a supplementary bibliography.

The editors solicit reader comments about this book. Suggested responses might include the reader's work setting; reasons for purchasing the book; parts of the book that were most helpful and least helpful; and suggestions about which parts should be expanded and what new material might be added in a second volume. We visualize another edition on this topic in 5 to 6 years.

In our opinion, an interactive dialogue about ethical dilemmas provides the best framework for learning and professional growth. We recommend that state school counselor associations, guidance and counseling units in state departments of education, local school systems, and counselor education departments periodically offer courses, workshops, and programs on ethical and legal issues. The ASCA Ethics Committee is availalble as a resource to help plan and implement such programs. Inquiries should be addressed to the ASCA Ethics Committee, American School Counselor Association, 5999 Stevenson Avenue, Alexandria, VA 22304.

ABOUT THE EDITORS

Wayne C. Huey, PhD, is director of counseling at Lakeside High School in the Dekalb County school system and part-time instructor in the Department of Counseling and Psychological Services at Georgia State University.

Theodore P. Remley, Jr., JD, PhD, is director of the Department of Counselor Education at Mississippi State University.

1

ETHICAL STANDARDS

The importance of knowing the contents of professional codes of conduct and the purposes and limitations of such codes is explained in the first two articles in this chapter. Huey (1987) presents a quiz to help school counselors assess their current levels of awareness and understanding of their ethical standards. Although detailed memorization of the ethical codes is not required, school counselors should have at least a basic understanding of their ethical responsibilities as defined in these documents.

Mabe and Rollin (1986) discuss the purposes of ethical codes and their limitations. The ethical standards of ASCA and AACD present school counselors with the behaviors to which they should aspire and give general guidelines for addressing difficult issues. They do not, however, necessarily provide answers to the many specific dilemmas that practitioners will face. When the standards do not provide enough direction, counselors are encouraged to consult with colleagues, professional experts, and perhaps their administrative supervisors before taking action.

Ferris and Linville (1985) explore the school counselor's responsibility to respect and protect the rights of minors. In many instances, school counselors must serve as parental substitutes in a child's life. As the more powerful party in the relationship, school counselors must be careful to respect the privacy of students and at the same time take any necessary steps to protect them from harm.

The difficult question of whether adolescents have a right to seek or refuse counseling services is explored by Klenowski (1983). Legally, counselors are responsible to the parents or guardians for the care of any minors they counsel. Parents have the right to initiate or terminate counseling relationships for their children. As a result, school counselors need to understand the rights of parents and include them in the counseling process to the degree appropriate in each case.

A discussion of ethical issues from the inception of the counseling relationship through its termination is offered by DePauw (1986). School counselors need to be aware of their ethical responsibilities early in the counseling relationship, particularly regarding informed consent, and they need to watch for other issues in subsequent stages.

Almost all professionals, at some point in their career, suspect or become aware of a colleague's unethical behavior. School counselors are obligated to address any conduct by a colleague that could cause harm to clients. Counselors should: (a) try to resolve the issue by confronting the colleague directly, if possible; (b) report the behavior to a superior, professional association, or credentialing authority if a direct confrontation is not possible or is not effective; and (c) take steps to protect any vulnerable clients. Levenson (1986) discusses some of the problems with this process and Marchant (1987) responds to his suggestions.

Huey (1986) presents a common ethical dilemma confronting high school counselors and reminds them that they will always be called upon to exercise good judgment no matter how explicit ethical standards might seem.

Ethical Standards for School Counselors: Test Your Knowledge

Wayne C. Huey

School counselors have expressed varying degrees of dissatisfaction with the perceived adequacy of the *Ethical Standards* (1981) of the American Association for Counseling and Development (AACD) and their applicability to counseling children and youth (Wagner, 1981). In 1983, the American School Counselor Association (ASCA) acknowledged the need for a code of ethics that specifically addressed ethical issues confronting school counselors. The *Ethical Standards for School Counselors* (1992) were not intended to replace the AACD *Ethical Standards* but were "developed to complement the AACD standards by clarifying the nature of ethical responsibilities of counselors in the school setting" (ASCA, 1992, p. 1).

Counselors can test their knowledge of the ASCA *Ethical Standards for School Counselors* by responding to the cases described in the following test and then studying the standards that are keyed by section and item number to each test situation. Moreover, counselors can increase their levels of awareness and understanding of the standards and thus become more competent and comfortable in making ethical decisions.

The ASCA standards address counselor responsibilities to pupils, parents, colleagues and professional associates, school and community, self, and the profession. Conflicts among these responsibilities are inevitable, because ethical standards are general guidelines for professional behavior, not laws, and must be interpreted by each counselor in each context. Factors affecting the interpretation of ethical standards include the counselor's personal needs, values, beliefs, and attitudes.

Experienced school counselors know that it is not always easy to interpret ethical standards; however, counselors can enhance this process by engaging in an honest self-examination, keeping

abreast of current issues by reading professional journals, participating in continuing education activities, and consulting with
professional colleagues (Corey, Corey, & Callanan, 1984). Even
with these resources, situations will continue to arise for which
there are no obvious answers. Counselors will have to struggle with
themselves to find the best way to assist their clients. The positive
side of the struggle is that it allows counselors the freedom to
exercise their good judgment within the general framework of the
ethical standards.

The following test is similar in format to Bailey's (1980) ethics
test. Counselors are encouraged to complete both assessments as
part of a self-examination.

Ethical Standards for School Counselors: Test Your Knowledge

Each of the following cases has been selected to stimulate your
thinking about specific ethical standards. In each situation, determine whether you *agree* (A) or *disagree* (D) with the counselor's
decision and place the appropriate letter (A or D) in the blank. For
each dilemma, a citation to the American School Counselor Association (ASCA) *Ethical Standards for School Counselors* (1992)
is provided.

_____1. The principal of an affluent suburban high school
was under community pressure to ensure that the majority of graduates enrolled in college. As a result of this pressure, the counselors
were instructed to "do a little arm twisting" with any students who
were reluctant to apply to college. The counselors agreed to cooperate because they also believed that a college education was a
worthy goal for everyone. (Preamble, Items 2 and 3; Section A-1)

_____2. A 16-year-old girl reported that she was pregnant
and wanted a referral to an abortion clinic. The counselor suggested
that the teenager discuss the situation with her parents before
making a decision and offered to provide assistance if the girl chose
to follow the recommendation. (B-1)

_____3. A counselor learned that several students had ob-
tained copies of a final examination for an English class. The situation was reported to the English teacher without revealing the
students' names. (D-2)

_____4. A counselor noticed that the secretary frequently
left student records in full view on top of the desk when she was

out of the office. Students had been observed looking at the records. The counselor decided to remind the secretary of the confidentiality guidelines, even though she had ignored previous reminders and had resented the counselor's suggestions. (C-2)

_____5. A counselor with a strong aversion to homosexuality was confronted by a gay student who confessed to a physical attraction to the counselor. The counselor attempted to conceal personal feelings and decided to try and counsel the student toward a heterosexual orientation. (E-3, A-4)

_____6. Based on information provided by a second-grade student, an elementary school counselor reported a case of suspected child abuse, even though no physical signs of abuse were evident on the child. It turned out that the child had made up the whole story, and the parents were furious with the counselor because they had not been contacted before the report was filed. The counselor still believed that the correct procedure was followed. (A-5, F-4)

_____7. Parents with strict fundamentalist religious beliefs asked the counselor to help them get their daughter "right with God" so that she would stop getting into trouble at school. The counselor, who held very liberal religious beliefs, did not believe that an objective perspective could be maintained and therefore referred the parents to another counselor whose beliefs were more closely aligned with those of the parents. (A-7, E.2)

_____8. A counselor attempted to get professional colleagues involved in the state counseling association. They informed the counselor that they already had too many obligations and did not need the affiliation. The counselor told them that professional involvement was an ethical responsibility. (F-3)

_____9. A student was discouraged by low mathematics scores on the Scholastic Aptitude Test (SAT). In an effort to boost the student's morale, the counselor named several former students who had also scored low on the mathematics section but were currently performing well in college. (A-8)

_____10. An assistant principal for discipline demanded that the counselor conduct a group for disruptive students to "straighten them out." The students were to be required to attend under threat of suspension. Unable to change the assistant principal's mind, the counselor made an appointment with the principal to explain why leading a group under those conditions would not be appropriate. (D-3)

_____11. A counselor attended a workshop on hypnosis and excitedly returned to school to use the newly learned techniques in helping students cope with test anxiety. When questioned by a colleague, the counselor insisted that the benefits would far outweigh any possible risks. (E-1)

_____12. The 15-year-old daughter of a counselor's close friend confided that she was sexually involved with her boyfriend and wanted to know where to obtain contraceptive information. The counselor provided the referral information and then informed the girl's mother of her activities. (A-9)

_____13. A young boy's parents expressed their concerns about his effeminate appearance and behavior. They asked for the counselor's assistance in determining whether their son was a homosexual. In interviewing the client, the counselor told him that his parents were afraid that he was gay. (B-4)

_____14. Upon receipt of Preliminary Scholastic Aptitude Test scores, the counseling department chairperson suggested that a meeting be scheduled with students to interpret test results. A colleague believed that such a meeting was unnecessary because an interpretive booklet was provided for each student with the score report. The department chairperson insisted that an interpretive session would be more beneficial. (A-12)

_____15. A counselor repeatedly turned down opportunities to attend professional conferences. The counselor stated that being away from school was a waste of valuable time and that extensive graduate training had provided more than adequate preparation for the job. (E-4)

_____16. A male counselor held daily counseling sessions behind closed doors with an attractive female student. To save the reputation of the counseling department, a colleague reported to the principal that "something is going on in there." (C-3)

_____17. The counselor informed a senior that he would not graduate because of a failing grade in his English class. The angry student, who had a history of violent behavior, threatened to kill the English teacher. The counselor told the student that the teacher, an administrator, and the student's parents must be informed of the threat. (A-10)

_____18. A counselor routinely encouraged students to be liberal free thinkers and not to conform to the dictates of parents and society. Using personal experiences for references, the counselor encouraged students to explore all of life, including experimentation with drugs and sex, if they so desired. (A-4)

_____19. A counselor used reality therapy in working with students who had attendance problems. When the principal asked for some evidence of the program's effectiveness, the counselor stated that there was not enough time to do an evaluation. The counselor then told the principal where to go for information on reality therapy's effectiveness. (F-2, D-4, C-1)

_____20. A counselor solicited students for a leadership training group. After the second session, the counselor noted that six of the eight group members were having severe family problems because their parents were either divorced, separated, or thinking about getting a divorce. Without announcing a change, the counselor shifted the focus of the group to address the more immediate needs of the students. (A-3)

_____21. Believing that humor would ease student anxiety during administration of the SAT, a counselor developed and used several jokes pertinent to testing and college admissions. The counselor carefully worked the jokes into the reading of the standardized test directions, and the students seemed to appreciate the attempt to humanize the test administration. (A-13)

_____22. Although local school guidelines prohibited long-term family counseling, the counselor continued to provide these services for families in need. The counselor stated that the local mental health center was understaffed and that the mental health counselors were not trained any better than the school counselor. (B-6)

_____23. A counselor worked with members of the school track team in an effort to improve athletic performance. Several colleagues criticized the use of the counselor's time, citing the need for more academically oriented programs. The counselor believed that this program was an appropriate service for the student athletes. (A-2)

_____24. An elementary school student was referred to a mental health clinic because of severe emotional problems. Although the student resisted the change in counselors, the parents supported the referral. The student demanded that the school counselor not reveal anything they had discussed. Because the counselor had discussed the possible need for consultation before working with the student and because the parents supported the referral, the counselor felt comfortable in disclosing complete client data to the mental health agency counselor. (C-4)

_____25. A counselor repeatedly observed a colleague violating an ethical standard in working with students. Concerned about harmful effects on the students, the counselor filed a report with the ASCA Ethics Committee. (G-2, G-3, G-4)

Suggested Responses

Agree (A): 2, 3, 4, 6, 7, 8, 10, 14, 17, 23, 24

Disagree (D): 1, 5, 9, 11, 12, 13, 15, 16, 18, 19, 20, 21, 22, 25

Score Interpretation By Number of Correct Answers

24–25: Apply for a position on the ASCA Ethics Committee.

21–23: An experienced, well-educated, ethical counselor.

20: Passing score. Consult with colleagues on questionable cases.

18–19: Attend programs and workshops on ethical issues and read professional counseling journals.

15–17: Explore your values in relation to those of more ethical school counselors.

13–14: Obtain and read the *Ethical Standards for School Counselors*.

12 and below: Ask your counselor educator to read and explain the Ethical Standards for School Counselors to you.

The author will respond to written inquiries about the interpretation of any of these cases for 6 months after date of publication. Readers should refer to the ASCA *Ethical Standards for School Counselors* (1984) before requesting an interpretation. The ASCA standards may be obtained by writing ASCA Headquarters, 5999 Stevenson Avenue, Alexandria, VA 22304. For additional case studies with more detailed interpretations, counselors are referred to Corey et al. (1984), Callis, Pope, and DePauw (1982), and Stude and Goodyear (1975).

References

American Association for Counseling and Development. (1981). *Ethical standards.* Alexandria, VA: Author. (Originally published by American Personnel and Guidance Association).

American School Counselor Association. (1992). *Ethical standards for school counselors.* Alexandria, VA: Author.

Bailey, J.A. (1980). School counselors: Test your ethics. *School Counselor, 27,* 285–293.

Callis, R., Pope, S.K., & DePauw, M.E. (1982). *APGA ethical standards casebook* (3rd ed.). Falls Church, VA: American Personnel and Guidance Association.

Corey, G., Corey, M., & Callanan, P. (1984). *Issues and ethics in the helping professions* (2nd ed.). Monterey, CA: Brooks/Cole.

Stude, E.W., & Goodyear, D.L. (1975). *Ethics and the counselor: A situational case study approach.* Fullerton: California Personnel and Guidance Association.

Wagner, C.A. (1981). Confidentiality and the school counselor. *Personnel and Guidance Journal, 59,* 305–310.

The Role of a Code of Ethical Standards in Counseling

Alan R. Mabe and *Stephen A. Rollin*

The authors focus on the role of a code of professional ethics as a basis for articulating the responsibilities of a member of a profession. Although concentrating on the AACD Ethical Standards, they attempt to provide some of the lessons learned in other professions, particularly medicine, regarding the role of the code and the problems and limitations involved in constructing and using a code of ethics.

Counseling practitioners, researchers, and educators are well aware of the need to address ethical questions that arise in their work. One way of addressing this need is through a code of professional ethics. A revised document on ethical standards (American Association for Counseling and Development, 1981) was approved by the Executive Committee of the American Personnel and Guidance Association.

Medicine has been the focus of contemporary debate regarding what the content of an ethical code should be, who should decide that content, and what role the code should have in the profession and in society (Beauchamp & Childress, 1983). Given the unrest and the problems encountered in the area of medical ethics and the changing content and role of medical codes, it is important to examine carefully the advantages and difficulties that will be encountered by the practitioner in using the counseling code. In this article we discuss the importance of having a set of standards and the problems and limitations in a code of professional ethics.

The kinds of codes under discussion are codes of professional ethics. The primary types of items to be found in a code are (a) the specific duties or rights that differ from ordinary ethical requirements, (b) the specific duties or rights that may simply be the application of general ethical principles in a particular professional area, (c) a reiteration of certain ordinary ethical requirements that

10

need emphasis for some reason, (d) aims or general goals that the profession should aspire to realize, (e) requirements that relate to coordinating or protecting the interest of members of the profession, and (f) a statement of the responsibility of members of the profession for reporting code violations or other violations. Items (a), (c), and (f), in particular, make a code necessary for the profession.

Although its primary function is to establish a framework for professional behavior and responsibility, the code also serves as a vehicle for professional identity and a mark of the maturity of the profession. A responsible member of the counseling profession must look to various sources for guidance. We fear that many professions may see a code of ethics as the sole basis for explicating responsibility for its members. The code is clearly a central part, but only a part, of the basis for the explication of professional responsibility. A professional code is necessary but not sufficient for the exercise of professional responsibility. An awareness of a code's limitations is a key element in developing an adequate account of professional responsibility. A proper appreciation of the strengths and limits of codes is directly related to the wise use by the profession of its autonomy.

In the discussion and practice of medical ethics in the past 25 years, there has been a dramatic shift from a paternal model of physician-patient relations to what many refer to as a "rights" model of that relationship. The movement has been from a situation in which physicians had virtually complete autonomy to set the standards for their behavior and interaction with patients to a situation in which their behavior is significantly circumscribed by patients, courts, regulatory agencies, and institutional lay boards (Beauchamp & Childress, 1983). In the process, practitioners' autonomy to set the standards for their profession was attacked and to a significant degree lessened. There are many complex factors that account for this development; however, here we can only identify the general structure of what happened. A profession renders a service to society, and traditionally society has been willing to grant a large degree of autonomy to that profession to set the terms and ethical standards for its activities (Bayles, 1981). A profession can use that grant of autonomy well or poorly. If the public judges that a profession does not use its autonomy well, it will withdraw the grant of autonomy and become an active participant in setting standards for that profession's services.

If the profession's autonomy is to be used wisely, then there must be a careful and critical scrutiny of the strengths and limitations of the use of a code of ethics. We will concentrate on selected problems and limitations in the use of a code, not because there are not strong arguments for a code but because we want to articulate the pitfalls based in part on the experience of the use of codes of ethics in other professions. We have selected the following six issues that constitute either problems or limitations in the use of a code to explicate professional responsibility:

1. There are some issues that cannot be handled in the context of a code.
2. There are some difficulties with enforcing the code, or at least the public may believe that enforcement committees are not tough enough on their peers.
3. There is often no way to systematically bring the interests of the client, patient, or research participant into the code construction process.
4. There are parallel forums in which the issues in the code may be addressed with the results sometimes at odds with the findings of the code (e.g., in the courts).
5. There are possible conflicts associated with codes: between two codes, between the practitioner's values and code requirements, between the code and ordinary morality, between the code and institutional practice, and between requirements within a single code.
6. There is a limited range of topics covered in the code, and because a code approach is usually reactive to issues already developed elsewhere, the requirement of consensus prevents the code from addressing new issues and problems at the "cutting edge."

Issues That Cannot Be Handled in the Code Context

One issue that cannot be handled in the context of the code is the conflict between autonomy and welfare. This issue is at the core of competing moral and political conceptions, and although a code may make reference to these ideas, it cannot provide a definitive result. An emphasis on autonomy stresses self-direction and the rights of the individual; an emphasis on welfare stresses satisfaction or benefit over self-direction. In Section B.1 of the AACD (1981) *Ethical Standards*, a member's primary obligations are identified: "to respect the integrity and promote the welfare of the client(s) . . . " (1981). Integrity is closely related to autonomy. What is one to do if there is a conflict between the welfare of a person and the autonomy of a person? This is a difficult question that is not susceptible to a "code" solution. The issue of the conflict between welfare and autonomy is at the core of the disputes between utilitarians and Kantians in applied and technical ethical discussions. It is difficult to articulate a code without invoking ideas or concepts that are significantly contested in moral, political, or legal thought. These issues cannot be settled by fiat, so a code is always at the mercy of the continuing debate in other domains.

Problems With Enforcement

Defensible and enforcible standards are important in the exercising of autonomy. There is always the possibility that the public or members of the profession will attach different degrees of seriousness to violations of the code or to behavior judged to be unacceptable in other ways. It is highly likely that the public's perception that medical societies were not willing to punish their own members to the degree the public thought justified led to the attack on the autonomy of the medical profession. The code must communicate to the public that it is more than just a paper document, that it is enforced, and that members who violate the code are disciplined. Currently AACD does not have a provision for publication of the names of those who are disciplined for violating the standards of the professional code. In contrast, the American Psychological Association (APA) provides a list to its members of those who have been disciplined along with a notation of the specific area of the code that has been violated. There are two problems: (a) whether sufficient penalities are imposed for violations, and (b) whether the public perceives that the profession is really regulating iteself. A profession must successfully deal with both problems or the code and the profession will come under attack by the public through its various institutions.

Interest of Clients

Although there are several issues involved in a code, practitioner-client interaction is at the core of any code. The professional code gives the members of that profession the right to set the standards for interacting with clients. It is natural to wonder how the interests and rights of clients are to enter the code construction process. In counseling, people are oriented toward helping others, so one may presume there is a basic regard for the interest of clients and patients. One could argue that those responsible for the construction and administration of the code will have the best interests of patients in mind in their work (and there is no reason to doubt that they do), but clients do not have an opportunity to represent their interests directly in a process in which they have any degree of control. The paternal medical model, which operated under the rationale of benefiting the patient, came under severe attack by individuals and organized consumer groups for not giving due regard to the needs and rights of patients. To maintain autonomy of the profession, ethical standards must function to protect clients. The nature of an autonomous code approach is to have a profession regulate itself without client participation in the regulatory process. The problem here is the risk of seriously misrepresenting the interests, needs, or rights of clients. The profession could attempt to systematically bring the point of view of clients and research participants into the process by some type of lay participation or by more effective ways of anticipating how patients and clients understand their interests and rights.

Parallel Forums

There are problems and limitations in the code approach because there are alternative forums in which applicable standards may be set. Later in the article we discuss the problem of conflicting code requirements for those who may be members of more than one professional association. One might argue that because of similar professional tasks and problems the developments are likely to closely parallel each other. But there are other forums in which this is not as likely to be the case—the courts and state and federal regulatory agencies. One formal way to approach this problem is to include a code requirement to obey the law. The problem, however, particularly with court cases in which clients or third parties have a forum for equal participation, is that outcomes rather different than those anticipated in the code may occur. *Tarasoff v. Regents of the University of California* provides an illustration of this point (Applebaum, 1981). In this milestone case the question was raised of whether counselors have a duty to warn third parties against whom their clients have made threats during sessions that are expected to be held in confidence. The courts ruled there was such a duty to warn. The code is silent on the issue of a duty to warn. The formal requirement to obey the law does not provide a sufficient basis for reconciling the issue of confidentiality as expressed in the code and the developments in the Tarasoff case. As the Tarasoff case shows, codes cannot be definitive even when they speak precisely about a topic, because a parallel but overriding legal forum may arrive at a different position. Codes cannot preclude this from happening, so those bound by a code must be alert to the possibility of other forums reaching conclusions different from the code requirements.

Those other forums are not immune from advice and influence from professional associations. If the professional code reflects a well-conceived position on a particular issue, the profession may be successful in influencing the outcome in parallel forums.

Conflicting Codes

There are numerous kinds of conflicts that may be experienced by a member of a profession governed by a code. Many members of AACD may also belong to APA, the American Association for Marriage and Family Therapists (AAMFT), or the American Association of Sex Educators, Counselors, and Therapists (AASECT), just to name a few. If one receives different guidance from different codes, what is one to do? An example can be found in the section on assessment and testing in the respective codes of AACD and APA. The AACD (1981) *Ethical Standards* have references in Section C to the codes of APA, the Association for Measurement and Evaluation in Counseling and Development (AMECD, formerly AMEG), and the National Council on Measurement in Education (NCME) and to an article, "Responsibilities of Users of Standardized Tests" (APGA, 1978). On the other hand, the APA code has six paragraphs dealing with assessment that are much more general and therefore seem to offer more latitude to the APA members in use of tests. What if this more general statement is at odds with the more specific view of the AACD Code? Which is to be followed? Who should decide this?

A practitioner may have code requirements that conflict with personal or moral values. An obvious example is the issue of abortion. Section B.1 of the AACD (1981) *Ethical Standards* states, "The member's *primary* obligation is to . . . the welfare of the

client." What should happen when a counselor's religious preferences or moral position lead to a view that abortion is wrong, yet
from the client's perspective it is in her best interest to have an
abortion? Does the counselor state his or her position, disqualify
himself or herself, argue against abortion, or give advice based on
the values of the client? Can the counselor, if he or she holds a
strong belief against abortion, operate ethically and in the best
interest of the client without stating his or her position?

Although the very point of a code of responsibility is to establish a set of standards that may be different from the requirements of ordinary morality, in cases in which there are differences
between the code and ordinary morality, practioners may experience conflicts. Ordinarily, one should warn another person if one
has reason to believe that someone is about to harm that person,
but the code requirement of confidentiality seems to override this
concern. Obviously, as the Tarasoff case illustrates, there are good
arguments for both duties. Although the code addresses conflicts
between institutional practices and the code, this remains a trou-
blesome area. Also, as our discussion of integrity and welfare above
indicated, there can be conflicting ideas or requirements within a
single code.

Finally, there can be situations of conflict that involve more
than one of the above examples in a specific situation, making the
resolution even more complicated. Of course, conflicts are a part
of life and one must be careful not to attribute all these problems
solely to the code. After all, there are deep conflicts within and
among different approaches to ethical theory. Some of the conflicts
within a code simply represent conflicts in the broader culture.
Our view is that one must be aware of the problems that remain
even when a code is in place and that some of the problems are a
function of the use of a code.

Limited Range

A code is a finite document that can cover only a limited
number of issues. To some extent historical factors influence the
selection of the content of a code. If particular issues are pressing
at the time that a code is being constructed, then those issues are
likely to be given more attention in the code. There can be oversights and omissions even of important issues. Significant changes
in society can result in a code being out of step with the social

consensus. These matters can be addressed by revision committees that meet periodically to bring the code up to date. Many problems of omission or emphasis can be remedied over time. There are, however, some problems that cannot be resolved so easily.

First, the issue of generality versus specificity is a persistent one. If the statement is too general, little actual guidance is provided; if the statements are too specific, the rationales for the specific conclusions may be missing and some issues may be omitted through oversight. Codes attempt to solve this conflict in a variety of ways, most successfully perhaps by a statement of general principles combined with more specific statements of application and supplemental case studies to illustrate the application of principles to specific cases.

Second, for the most part a code must gain wide acceptance in the profession so that it represents the distilled wisdom about which there is a consensus in the profession. It is difficult for a code to be in the forefront of solving issues at the "cutting edge." For example, how should the code respond to issues such as the developments in information technology? More particularly, what impact will new systems for storage and retrieval of information have on the issue of confidentiality? Each specific issue can be worked out over time, but there will always be new issues for which the code is without a response.

Third, many new problems find their earliest resolution in the courts. As our discussion above of parallel forums indicated, there will frequently be court decisions to which the code must react.

Finally, the code, by its nature, is a limited document set in the context of a broader ethical tradition. A code is not meant to cut itself off from that tradition but to carry the values of that tradition into a specialized area. Thus, a code is limited in the sense that it cannot replicate the tradition out of which it grows. That is not a deficiency, but it must be recognized or else there will be a tendency to place too much weight on the code as opposed to the broader ethical traditions and ethical debates out of which the code arises.

The broader ethical tradition can provide considerable insight to constructing and operating a code. There are not precise and agreed upon definitions even of key terms in ethical theory, but there are two distinct and different components of an ethical theory. There is a theory of value and a theory of morality. In a theory of value there is an attempt to identify what is valuable in some fundamental sense (e.g., in the nature of things, for humankind, for one society or tradition, for an individual). In a theory of morality there is an attempt to establish principles for how people are to treat one another. A social morality will have a set of principled limitations on how people can treat one another. Certain things are simply ruled out, such as murder, rape, coercion, and serious deceit. A code may be more successful in identifying clearly un-acceptable behavior in terms of practitioner-client interactions. It is somewhat more difficult to articulate values that should be pro-moted. In general, rooting code construction in the broader ethical traditions out of which they arise is likely to be beneficial to both the code and the tradition. The broader tradition of ethical theory provides a background out of which many of the ideas in the code have arisen. Awareness of this background is very helpful in in-terpreting and understanding the code. If the code is silent on an issue or if significant conflicts exist between the code and other directives, the broader ethical tradition can provide a source of guidance and a basis for evaluating practice. And probably most important of all, broader ethical principles can be a source for approaching new problems that are not yet familiar enough for inclusion in the code.

The various problems and limitations of codes can be mitigated to some extent, as we have suggested throughout this article. The solution to the basic problem articulated here—the possibility of overreliance on a code of professional ethics for explicating profes-sional responsibility—is greater understanding of the role and func-tion of a code of ethics in relation to the broader tradition of ethical theory and practice. For example, greater understanding of the debate between Kantians and utilitarians will make theorists and practitioners better able to solve conflicts between autonomy and welfare within the code (Frankena, 1973; Kant, 1964; Mill, 1979). Counselors are not alone—being an ethical professional is not in-dependent of being an ethical person.

Our view is that a code of ethical standards is necessary, but, as we have tried to articulate above, there are many problems and limitations to constructing and following a code. These problems also arise in the educational process when the code approach is communicated to students. A full understanding of the code re-quires an understanding of the strengths, limitations, problems, and functional context of the code. People all strive to be respon-sible members of their professions. To be a fully responsible profes-sional, one must rely on more than a code of ethical standards in resolving difficulties. Our discussion of the limitations of profes-sional codes has demonstrated that.

References

American Association for Counseling and Development. (1981). *Ethical standards.* Alexandria, VA: Author. (Originally published by American Personnel and Guidance Association)

American Personnel and Guidance Association. (1978, October 5). Responsibilities of users of standardized tests. *Guidepost*, pp. 5–8.

American Psychological Association. (1981). *Ethical principles of psychologists* (Rev. ed.). Washington, DC: Author.

Applebaum, P. (1981). Tarasoff: An update on the duty to warn. *Hospital and Community Psychiatry, 32*, 14–15.

Bayles, M.D. (1981). *Professional ethics.* Belmont, CA: Wadsworth.

Beauchamp, T.L., & Childress, J.F. (1983). *Principles of biomedical ethics* (2nd ed). New York: Oxford University Press.

Frankena, W.K. (1973). *Ethics* (2nd ed.). Englewood Cliffs, NJ: Prentice-Hall.

Kant, I. (1964). *Groundwork of the metaphysics of morals* (H.J. Paton, Trans.). New York: Harper & Row.

Mill, J.S. (1979). *Utilitarianism.* Indianapolis: Hackett Publishing Co. Tarasoff v. Regents of the University of California, 529 P.2d 533 (Cal. 1974); 551 P.2d 334, 331 (Cal. 1976).

The Child's Rights: Whose Responsibility?

Patricia A. Ferris and *Malcolm E. Linville*

An elementary or middle school counselor might look at the theme of this special issue and ask: "Why another discussion of ethics? I am familiar with the *Ethical Standards* of the American Association for Counseling and Development (AACD, formerly American Personnel and Guidance Association [APGA]) (APGA, 1981), and the *Position Statements* of the American School Counselor Association (ASCA) (1983). I have seen a copy of *Ethical Standards for School Counselors*, also from ASCA (1984). In addition, I have on my desk a copy of the educational amendments made in 1974 to PL 92-380, the Elementary and Secondary Education Act of 1965. These documents provide a firm basis for ethical conduct on the part of the counselor. So why go over established positions again?"

This seems to be a legitimate question, especially with recent articles by Zingaro (1983) and Wanger (1981) that offer interpretations of these basic guidelines. So why not file away another discussion of these subjects?

There are several good reasons not to file this issue. One reason involves a changing conception of the primary role of the counselor that may profoundly affect the functions and responsibilities of elementary and middle school counselors. If the counselor's role changes, as some people predict, then many of our present ethical guidelines become obsolete.

Ethics and Changing Roles of Counselors

The changing roles of counselors are clearly reflected in a recent survey of perceptions of what a counselor should be doing.

Based on a questionniare sent to principals and counselors in upper elementary and middle schools, both principals and counselors believed that individual counseling should receive the greatest emphasis in a counseling program (Bonebrake & Borgers, 1984). Although the researchers who conducted the survey classified this top-priority activity as a counseling function, the next three functions ranked by counselors apparently were not in the category of counseling. They were what the authors classified as *consultation* functions (teacher consultant, student assessment consultant, parent consultant). Ranks given by counselors were similar to those given by principals. It is significant that a major counseling function, group counseling, was ranked in the middle of the list by both groups.

You might say, "But counselors are expected to talk to teachers and parents, and they have always done this." Indeed, they have, but the term *consultant* is beginning to have more specific meaning in the counseling field. Umansky and Holloway (1984) stated: "Traditionally, counseling services have concentrated on direct service to the individual student . . . Student administrators have been largely unimpressed with the 'individual-adjustment' treatment model because of the high cost per service ratio and its lack of accountability to the school community" (p. 329). The authors concluded bluntly: "Unfortunately, most counselors have failed to adopt the consultant role as their main function in the schools" (p. 330).

The Consultant Role

The consultant role, as it is now defined, removes the counselor from his or her therapeutic role with the student. Rather, in one possible model, the counselor interviews a student who is having difficulties and then prescribes techniques for intervention to be carried out by teachers or parents. The counselor may have little or no direct contact with the student after the initial interview.

A less rigidly defined form of consultation has always been part of the counselor's role but was rarely seen as the counselor's primary function. Yet, a formal change in the role of counselors would raise certain ethical questions that have rarely been addressed.

The present ethical guidelines, from whatever source, are largely based on the assumption that the counselor's primary function is to establish a therapeutic relationship. This is expressed in the ASCA *Position Statements* (1983) as a relationship that "requires an atmosphere of trust and confidence between the client and the counselor" (p. 6).

In the ASCA *Statements*, the definition of consultation differs greatly from current usage. ASCA's definition is: "The counselor reserves the right to consult with other professionally competent persons when this is in the interest of the client. Confidentiality assures that disclosures made will not be divulged to others except when authorized by the client" (p. 6).

How relevant are these guidelines if elementary counselors begin to see consultation with teachers and parents as a major function involving little direct contact with children? The guidelines are based on the establishment of a close and continuing relationship with a student that emphasizes the student's welfare as the counselor's primary consideration. How can the counselor take responsibility for a student's welfare if he or she is working only indirectly with the student, literally one person removed from the student? How can confidentiality be preserved in such a setting? What are the ethical implications of giving major responsibility for intervention and treatment to an individual who is not professionally trained as a counselor?

The various ethical standards clearly state that counselors have the right to consult with other professionally competent persons when it is in the best interest of the client. Because teachers and parents may not have received such counseling training, they can seldom be considered professionally competent as defined in the standards. Yet the word *consultation*, as used in some of the newer models of counseling, seems to assume parents and teachers are as professionally competent in specific helping techniques as counselors with master's degrees in the field.

In practice, of course, most elementary counselors define consultation much less formally. The counselor has direct contact with the child and also works with the teacher or with the parent when this is desirable. Such consultation involves talking over the situation with the teacher or parent and considering positive solutions together. Yet, even these limited forms of consultation may lead to ethical dilemmas. In the *Position Statements* (ASCA, 1983) it is clearly asserted:

> A client has the right to privacy—and to expect confidentiality. . . . Confidentiality assures that disclosures made will not be divulged to others except when authorized by the client. . . . The main purpose of privileged communication is to offer counselees a relationship in

which they will be able to deal with what concerns them without fear of disclosures. . . . In reality, it is the client who is privileged. It is the client's own information and the client has the right to say who shall have access to it and who shall not. (p. 6)

Confidentiality in Practice

Suppose the elementary school counselor is working with a child such as Aletha Lindstrom described in the real-life account, "Billy, I Won't Forget You" (1983). Billy came from an unstable home and other children avoided him. If anything was missing in the classroom, they immediately accused Billy of taking it. One day a child could not find her dime and insisted that Billy had stolen it. The teacher lost control of herself and ordered Billy to give back the dime. When he didn't respond, the teacher made him turn out his pockets, take off his shoes, and then empty his desk. But the dime was not found anywhere. Billy put the things back in the desk without saying a word. He put his arms on his desk and buried his face in them. Later, the dime was found by the pencil sharpener, where Billy's accuser had laid it.

What if there had been a counselor in the school to whom Billy could feel free to express his humiliation, shame, and anger? What could the counselor do to help the teacher and Billy without breaking confidentiality? How could he or she let the teacher know how Billy really felt?

If counselors are to honor ASCA's guidelines, then before counseling they must tell a child that they will not divulge specific things said by the child without his or her permission, but that they may share a sense of the child's feelings about a situation with a teacher or parent. The counselor might add: "Sometimes it helps other people if they understand how you feel. Your feelings are important, too."

Of course there are times when a counselor cannot ethically keep a child's disclosures confidential. According to the ASCA *Position Statements* (1983), confidentiality may be abridged if the child imparts information that suggests "there is a clear and present danger to the client and to other persons" (p. 6).

It may be difficult, especially with young children, to distinguish between fact and fantasy or between genuine intentions and half-formed wishes. Making such distinctions necessitates that the counselor use careful judgment and possess well-developed in-

terpretive skills. These qualities must supplement the requirements found in ethical guidelines if the counselor is to observe
more than the bare framework for ethical conduct.

Ethical Dilemmas in School

Many of the ethical dilemmas a counselor confronts are associated with when and how to report child abuse, the use and
reporting of test scores, and informal communications within the
school community. Concern and caring for the student is not enough.
Professional organization standards and public law, integrated with
the counselor's beliefs concerning the welfare of the student and
the family, are essential to the process of ethical resolution of the
dilemmas counselors face in schools.

Child Abuse

Careful evaluation is especially important when the counselor
encounters a suspected case of child abuse or neglect. Although
laws regarding reports of child abuse differ from state to state, the
principal in many schools has the actual responsibility of reporting
suspected cases of abuse to the designated authorities. Because
counselors are often asked to make the initial evaluation in these
cases, related ethical issues need to be considered by all elementary
and middle school counselors.

The ASCA *Position Statements* (1983) provide several criteria
for deciding whether child abuse may have occurred, and they
suggest that the counselor use more than one of the criteria in
making a decision. Only some of the criteria, however, have obvious implications for child abuse, such as patterns of bruises caused
by a particular instrument (e.g., a belt buckle or coat hanger).
Other criteria are more difficult to interpret, such as lacerations
and abrasions. The counselor should be extremely careful in reporting suspected child abuse on the basis of limited and uncertain
evidence. The involvement of at least two parties in the situation
(such as the counselor and the principal) is helpful. Individual
schools need clearly written guidelines for handling such cases.

Reporting of Test Scores and Other Information

Another area that requires deliberate and careful judgment is
deciding the appropriate use and reporting of test scores. The

counselor may have to decide whether to use test scores in a consultation. In certain cases the counselor has no choice. The Educational Amendments of the Elementary and Secondary Education Act of 1965 (1974) state unequivocally that no federal funds will be made available to schools that deny parents "the right to inspect and review any and all official records, files and data directly related to their children" (p. 3). Such data specifically include "scores on standardized intelligence, aptitude, and psychological tests, interest inventory results, [and] teacher or counselor ratings and observations" (p. 3).

Many counselors are aware that parents have a legal right to obtain test scores but do not realize that a counselor's ratings and observations are also legally open to parental inspection. The provisions of the amendments immediately made obsolete an ethical standard issued by APGA in 1974 (the same year as the amendments): "The examinee's welfare and explicit prior understanding should be the criteria for determining the recipients of the test results" (p. 6). Law supersedes ethical standards, and confidentiality of test scores is no longer protected as it was before 1974. The problem of whether to give parents test scores with or without interpretation has generally been left to individual schools. The AACD *Ethical Standards* state: "The member must see that adequate interpretation accompanies any release of individual or group test data" (APGA, 1981, p. 3).

At this point, a counselor might say, "The law has begun to make *confidentiality* a hollow word." Legally a parent can obtain not only a child's scores on aptitude and achievement tests but also the results of personality inventories and the data a counselor has obtained from observations. In view of the broader ethical questions involved, it seems irrelevant that most parents are not going to ask for such information.

What can counselors do if they do not believe it is in the best interest of the client for parents to obtain this information? Perhaps counselors should avoid recording certain sensitive materials that may be open for inspection. In addition, taping counseling sessions may be unwise unless tapes are immediately listened to and erased. The ASCA *Position Statements* (1983) warn counselors to be especially careful with recorded information. In the past, clear distinctions were made in ethical standards between official school records and the counselor's personal records, which included scores on personality inventories and the counselor's notes on sessions with a client. Unfortunately, the 1974 amendments blurred this distinction, and there is still no adequate legal interpretation of the phrase "data directly related to their children" (p. 452). The words could be interpreted as almost any data obtained in school. The words "any and all," which directly precede "official records, files and data," should immediately signal greater caution by the counselor. A counselor may be wise to keep two "Beware" signs posted in his or her mind. These signs would read: "Beware of Tape Recorders" and "Beware of Computer Data Banks." Unfortunately, the blessings of modern technology are hardly blessings for the counselor confronting ethical concerns.

Of course, the constraints of confidentiality apply only if a parent requests information. Perhaps the most difficult dilemmas arise when a parent calls a counselor and says, "My child tells me you gave him a test in which there were questions about whether he still wets the bed and whether the sight of blood makes him sick. What did you ask him those kinds of questions for?" The counselor can explain that he or she wanted to learn more about the child's perception of the world around him. Then the parent may ask: "Did the test show he was crazy or something?" The counselor can state that this inventory was not designed to determine whether people are crazy and that it really cannot be intepreted properly without further observation of the child. The counselor can add: "I honestly cannot say much about Johnny on the basis of this test score." Such an answer may satisfy the parent.

Laws, standards, and position statements all have bearing on consultations in which a teacher or parent does not directly ask for test scores. According to the ASCA *Position Statements*, unless a child has previously given the counselor permission, a counselor cannot discuss test scores even if the scores are relevant to the discussion or support what the counselor wants to communicate. If the child has given permission and test scores are presented, any discussion of the test scores should include an adequate interpretation of their meaning by the counselor.

When giving and interpreting tests, the counselor should select tests with norm groups that are representative of the child's socioeconomic, racial, and ethnic background. If the norm groups do not include appropriate representation, however, an explanation should be included in the interpretation.

It seems that test scores are becoming synonymous with education itself; therefore, it is more important for the counselor to stress that test scores are tentative assessments and are not, like the Ten Commandments, chiseled in stone. Indeed, ASCA in its *Position Statements* (1983) expressed opposition to "continued use of standardized group intelligence tests . . . until a time when the problems with the tests and their users can be corrected" (p. 8).

Informal Communications

Much of the discussion about formal consultation also applies to the ethical dilemmas associated with more informal communication in a school. Each school is a small social organization, a little community, and as such has a web (sometimes a tangle) of social interrelationships. These relationships, if they are to be productive, require a set of ethical assumptions that help regulate how individuals attempt to live together.

An important aspect of day-to-day contacts involves the counselor's relationship to the leader of the small society, the principal. Of course, according to AACD guidelines, the principal should be informed if the counselor receives information from a client that indicates possible harm or injury to the child or others (APGA, 1981). But what if the principal asks for information that the counselor believes is protected and confidential? What if the principal flatly demands such information? There are certainly principals who are demanding and insistent. What if the child has told the counselor that he or she has taken several things from other students in the past and has lied about this, and the counselor is working with the student on these problems? The principal says, "Mrs. Burns thinks he's been stealing. She asked you to talk to Jerry about that. Has he been stealing? What did he tell you?"

The counselor knows the principal is a harsh disciplinarian who attaches labels to a child that will stigmatize the child for the rest of his or her life. What does the counselor answer?

The counselor should have explained to the school staff the function of an elementary school counselor and the implications of confidentiality and privileged communication. The counselor should also have made clear why confidentiality is essential to a helping relationship. A short workshop session with the entire school staff (including secretaries and custodians) might be an effective way for a counselor to clearly communicate these ideas. Perhaps the principal in our example had not understood the concepts. In this kind of situation it may not be wise for the counselor to say, "I cannot tell you what Jerry said. This would be a breach of confidentiality." Such a statement might only increase the principal's determination and hostility. It might be better to say, "Jerry and I have been

working through his problems together. I see some real progress."
Or the counselor could say: "I believe Jerry has been responding
to counseling sessions. We are beginning to develop a good relationship. His teacher has told me he has been getting along better
with other students."

In responding to a demanding principal, the counselor should
always keep two things in mind: "My basic obligation is to the
welfare of the child" and "I am less likely to help a child if basic
trust is broken." If Jerry were to be severely punished as a result
of what the counselor said to the principal, what credibility would
the counselor have in that school's community? There is also the
question of the counselor's personal integrity. That may seem an
old-fashioned word in an age of shifting values and deep uncer-
tainties, but a counselor is lost without it.

Of course, not all principals are like the one we have described,
but all principals and all school personnel will benefit if a school
has its own set of written policies prepared by those who will be
implementing these policies. The policies should, of course, be
compatible with national and state laws, the ethical standards of
professional associations, and the school district guidelines. (See
the article by Walker and Larrabee in this issue of the journal for
information on written policy making.) They should deal with such
matters as child abuse, substance abuse, and the release of information.

Written policies and written requests are essential. In certain
situations, of course, much of the communication in an elementary
school is oral communication. There are casual contacts in the
hallway, in the teachers' lounge, and in the teachers' lunchroom,
and often the counselor is involved in these informal interchanges.
Inevitably, a favorite topic in these situations is students, their
peculiarities, and their behavior. After a rough morning in the
classroom and on the playground, a frustrated teacher may make
some pointed comments that help relieve his or her tensions but
can also initiate equally pointed comments from other sources. The
counselor must avoid being drawn into discussions in which confidential information about a student could slip out. Information
tends to spread as quickly in a school as it would if it were flashed
to a communications satellite. Unfortunately, some of that information could be legally classified as slander.

In one such situation several teachers were talking in a teachers' lounge. This conversation, which could have provided the basis
for a law suit, followed: "Mildred was sent home at 9:30 this morn-

ing," one of the teachers said knowingly, "Guess what? Sick at her stomach."

"You know that family," another teacher said, "All their girls got pregnant. Regular as clockwork." She shook her head. "Poor Mildred. She's only 13." Then she added brightly, "But she is big for her age."

Fortunately, the door of the teachers' lounge was closed, and no students overheard this discussion. It is also fortunate that few teachers are sued for slander. That afternoon the girl had an operation for acute appendicitis.

Of course, it is easy after a tiring day, when the weather has been bad and no one could go outside, to say things that represent only a temporary mood and not actual feelings. Often a counselor may have the most exhausting day of anyone in a school. At these times a counselor must be especially careful that what he or she says does not violate a student's right to confidentiality.

With oral communication, another "Beware" sign needs to be posted: "Beware of the Telephone." The ASCA *Statements* (1983) say flatly, "Counselors must not discuss matters over the telephone" (p. 6). For some, the telephone has become an added appendage to their bodies, but what is said over the telephone can be overheard and can easily be misinterpreted. A disembodied voice on the telephone lacks the facial expressions and gestures that reinforce and clarify the meaning of what is said.

Furnishing information to others from school records requires written permission from students' parents or guardians. The various reasons for using records and the stipulations for sharing the information about students typically are established by school district policy. Requests for records are responded to by the principal or other administrators, but, to comply with the law, counselors must be aware of the conditions under which information may be released, because some school records may be in their custody. In addition to school records, other client information the counselor may have could also be subject to court order; this varies from state to state. A counselor should consult a knowledgeable lawyer if he or she ever becomes involved in such situations. (See Walker and Larrabee's guidelines for school records and Remley's suggestions for interactions with lawyers and legal concerns in this issue). In addition, knowledge of related legislation is essential if counselors are to uphold high ethical and professional standards. Of course, knowledge of ethical standards set by professional organizations and the interpretation of these standards is essential if counselors involve others in the consultation process to help elementary and middle school students.

Counselors must also look within themselves and develop skills for making a reflective anlaysis of specific situations. The counselor should also develop a willingness to withhold judgment that is not based on a reasonable amount of evidence. Finally, and most significantly, the counselor who seeks ethical integrity must respect the child, the child's needs, the child's possibilities, and the child's best interests. As far as possible, these factors should be the basis of decision in ethical matters. When seen from this perspective, ethical guidelines are not just lists of "thou shalt nots." Instead, they point toward trust, confidence, and respect for one another.

References

American Personnel and Guidance Association. (1981). *Ethical standards*. Falls Church, VA: Author.

American School Counselor Association. (1983). *Position statements*. Falls Church, VA: Author.

American School Counselor Association. (1984). *Ethical standards for school counselors*. Alexandria, VA: Author.

Bonebrake, C.R., & Borger, S.B. (1984). Counselor role as perceived by middle school counselors and principals. *Elementary School Guidance & Counseling, 18,* 194–199.

Educational Amendments of 1974, 20 U.S.C. § 1232g (1981).

Lindstrom, A. (1983, February 8). Billy, I won't forget you. *Guidepost,* pp. 2, 4.

Umansky, D.L., & Holloway, E.L. (1984). The counselor as consultant: From model to practice. *School Counselor, 31,* 329–338.

Wagner, C.A. (1981). Confidentiality and the school counselor. *Personnel and Guidance Journal, 59,* 305–310.

Zingaro, J.C. (1983). Confidentiality: To tell or not to tell. *Elementary School Guidance & Counseling, 17,* 261–267.

Adolescents' Rights of Access to Counseling

John R. Klenowski

This article focuses on hindrances and problems confronting the adolescent and counselor when adolescents have to surrender their right to accept or to refuse treatment.

At a time when children and adolescents are being identified as a target population to be served by mental health professionals (Ambrose, 1981), it is important to work toward alleviating hindrances that prevent minors from receiving effective and timely counseling services. In this article reference to the minor is confined to adolescents age 15 to 18.

In reviewing the historical efforts to attain treatment rights for minors, it is apparent that a consistent and major issue in granting adolescents the right to consent to counseling involves their competency to give such consent. The competency of minors to give consent continues to be an issue as evidenced by a 1979 Supreme Court ruling in *Parham v. J.L. and J.R.* (Schwitzgebel & Schwitzgebel, 1980). In this case the Supreme Court observed that most children, including adolescents, are not able to make sound judgments and that their parents can and must make such timely decisions. Comprehensive reviews of developmental research indicate that adolescents 15 years of age and above are as intellectually and psychologically capable in most situations to make competent decisions concerning consent to mental health counseling as most adults (Grisso & Vierling, 1978; Hayes, 1979; Melton, 1981a). Conversely, the ability of minors under 15 years of age to give consent is not as certain because of this age group's constantly changing developmental and dependency needs and questionable ability to distinguish among treatment alternatives (Hayes, 1979; Melton, 1981a). Consent is defined as an act of reason whereby an individual can sort out the advantages and disadvantages of alternatives in a rational manner in order to make competent decisions about one's life (Slovenko, 1978). Such a definition raises the question of when is a child transformed into an adult? The law is not consistent from state to state nor from one area of functioning to another. In order for examples to be specific, the State of Ohio will be used as a reference in this article.

Rights of Adolescents to Treatment

The issue of consent to treatment by minors is a multidimensional problem. The parent or guardian can refuse to give consent when the minor wants counseling or the parent can initiate counseling when the minor does not want it. At most community mental health centers the minor is seldom the applicant (Stewart, 1976). Referral is usually made by parents, schools, doctors, or the courts. If the minor were to be the applicant, the minor would most likely be ineligible for service without parental consent. Most states do not recognize minors as being competent to contract for treatment services. Mature minors in most states do not have the freedom to select the service they believe reasonable to resolve identified problems or concerns. This point is emphasized in an Ohio Department of Mental Health intradepartmental communication (Panico, 1979):

> Whenever any person under the age of eighteen years voluntarily admits himself or arrives at the Center as an "emergency walk-in" desiring treatment because he believes himself to be mentally ill, the parents, guardian, or person having custody of the minor should be notified immediately for the purpose of giving consent in order that the Center may consult with or treat the minor. If the parents, guardian, or person having custody of the minor refuse to give consent the minor may be detained, unless he refuses, only until the parents, guardian, or custodian come to the Center to pick up the minor; however, no treatment or consultation shall be given to the minor during the interim.
>
> In the event that the Center is unable to contact a parent, guardian, or person having custody of a minor for purposes of receiving consent from them to consult or treat a minor under the foregoing circumstances, the Center shall not consult with or treat a minor unless it is a case of grave emergency where a medical staff person

feels that some intervention is necessary to prevent serious consequences or death of the minor. These cases of "grave emergency" should only be considered by a medical staff person, and, if available, at least two medical persons should concur that it is necessary for some type of consultation or treatment to be administered in order to avoid serious consequences or death of the minor.

What effect does the inability to obtain services have on adolescents when they are hurting or concerned? What does denial or postponing of services because of lack of parental consent do in perpetuating the stigma of receiving mental health counseling when the adolescent can make other important decisions, but not one regarding counseling? For example, the adolescent can work, can make purchases, can drive an automobile, or can receive help for a drug problem or venereal disease. In addition, Ohio law recognizes that minor children may be considered emancipated prior to their 18th birthday by marriage or by living independently from their parents. Ohio law also views minors as having the capacity to select their own guardian at age 14 and to select their custodial parent at age 12 (Spohn, 1980). In spite of being able to make such important life decisions, adolescents still cannot apply for counseling on their own in Ohio and many other states. Virginia, a state which implemented a law in 1979 permitting minors to consent to mental health treatment, was the focus of a survey by Melton (1981b) to determine the effects of the law on community mental health clinics. One finding was that although the law does not have an age standard, the only minors who applied for mental health counseling without parental consent were adolescents and not younger children.

Rights of Adolescents to Refuse Treatment

Up to this point focus has been on the right to counseling. If a person has a right to counseling, they should have a corresponding right to refuse counseling. Once again, the adolescent is denied a right by the same law that considers persons under 18 to be incompetent (Everstine, Everstine, Heymann, True, Frey, Johnson, & Seiden, 1980). In many mental health settings the refusal by minors to accept treatment does little to keep them from physically attending counseling sessions. In referring to such situations, Glenn

(1980) uses the concept of informed forced consent. That is, the minor is informed of why he or she is being seen but is not given any choice about participation. It is no surprise that many adolescents initially respond to mental health services in "resistant" ways.

Let us assume that conceptually the best of situations exists where the adolescent assents to treatment and has parental consent. Such a situation is not an indication that there will not be any further hindrances to counseling based on consent. For example, to be in accordance with the law on informed consent, the parents should be informed of the type of treatment their child will receive and aspects of the treatment plan (Glenn, 1980; Nye, 1980). The person giving the consent has to know what they are consenting to, and what alternatives to the proposed counseling process exist. The consentor also needs to know the prognosis and anticipated outcomes. One of a possible number of dilemmas may be that the adolescent, although wanting treatment, may not want the parents to know about the treatment. In some situations, it could even be contraindicated for the parents to know (Melton, 1981a; Nye, 1980). If the therapist is saying "Your parents need to know you are coming in," it can affect the degree of trust the adolescent will be able to invest in the relationship. Such situations can create difficulty in the therapeutic process where trust and a guarantee of privacy are important ingredients. This is documented by studies such as that by Howard and Orlinsky (1978), who concluded that effective therapy is an interpersonal process marked by a number of characteristics, one of which is mutual respect and trust. Barrett-Lennard (1981) also identified a trusting professional relationship as one of the unifying components of the counseling process.

Case Illustrations

To assist in focusing on the various ways treatment can be delayed, denied, or adversely affected by the adolescents' inability to consent to treatment, several vignettes are presented. The vignettes are based on situations that occurred at one mental health setting over a period of several months. To facilitate a problem-solving approach, and to stimulate the reader to ponder how similar situations might be handled in one's own setting, methods of responding are not presented. The implications of each vignette will be dependent on the specific law of each state.

Case One

An adolescent was referred by the school. The person was living with an aunt and uncle. In the course of getting consent, it was determined that the relatives had never received legal custody. Two years ago, when the parents moved to another state, they agreed it would be acceptable for the adolescent to live with the aunt and uncle during the school year so that he could graduate from a particular high school. Because the relatives did not have legal custody, treatment had to be delayed until contact was made with the parents.

Case Two

A call was received from a teacher who wanted to refer an adolescent boy who approached the teacher about his home situation. He was concerned about the fighting between his mom and dad. Could a center staff person see him to help advise him on some actions he could take? He did not want his parents to know as he was concerned it might aggravate the problems at home if the parents knew he had contacted the mental health center.

Case Three

A 15-year-old girl came to the clinic for counseling. Mother gave consent and daughter assented. Both mother and daughter stated they did not want the girl's father to know she was receiving counseling because they were fearful of his reaction. After the adolescent's second session, her father called the clinic and wanted to know if his daughter was a client.

Case Four

A client who was engaged in weekly counseling brought in a 17-year old friend who was "upset" about difficulties in her love relationship with a married man. She wanted to apply for counseling but did not want her parents to know as "it would just kill them."

I think the aforementioned examples demonstrate the range of possibilities and implications for both the adolescent and the therapist. The examples emphasize potential drawbacks to the establishment of a trusting relationship between adolescent and therapist, especially when the therapist must say to the adolescent "You need to have your parents' permission before I can counsel with you."

Rights of Parents

When parents give consent for the treatment of their child, the therapist has to be aware of the parents' rights as well as the adolescent's rights. In some situations it is not always easy for the therapist to determine whether responsibility is to the parent or to the adolescent client. Although most colleagues with whom I have consulted indicate allegiance to their client, and are supported in this position by their professional code of ethics, legal precedence would indicate parental rights usually take precedence over the child's rights (Nye, 1980). The parents are the ones who contract for service and who are responsible for paying for the service. In a situation where the adolescent client may be involved in a constructive and relevant counseling relationship, the parents can withdraw consent because they personally do not like the changes their adolescent is making (Everstine et al., 1980). Does the therapist risk alienating the parents and thus deprive the adolescent of services? Does the therapist go along with the parents' wishes, which may be contrary to the minor's clinical needs, because the therapist believes it is better to have the minor in treatment than to have services completely withdrawn? To accede to the parents' wishes in the aforementioned situation would put the counselor in a position for malpractice charges (Nye, 1980). If the counselor were to offer alternative action plans to the minor that were not of the minor's own making, the counselor might be subject to charges of undue influence (Schwitzgebel et al., 1980). To continue to see the minor after consent had been withdrawn also could lead to charges of contributing to the delinquency of a minor (Henkener, 1981).

The referral of a minor does not always come from the parents. A Children Services Board may threaten to remove a child from the home if the parents do not get the minor into counseling. A school principal may threaten a child with expulsion if parents do not obtain counseling for the child. The referring agency may request to be kept informed of the minor's progress, a practice that is not unusual in many states (Popiel, 1980). Under such circumstances the counselor is confronted with additional blocks to establishing a strong position of confidentiality and for creating a climate of sharing and trust. In certain situations the referral of an adolescent to a mental health facility may be court ordered. Confusion can occur because of the gray area between delinquency and emotional illness. Such adolescents may be referred to appease an upset community system or to serve the needs of some disgruntled parents rather than to meet the needs of the minor. Other minors may have their cases dropped by the court without receiving any consideration for mental health intervention (Melton, 1981a). A mental health therapist was recently confronted by a situation where a 17-year-old was sent for counseling by a court order. The adolescent did not want counseling. The therapist did not believe counseling for the adolescent was appropriate and concluded that it would be more appropriate for the parent to receive mental health services. The parent refused service. The court representative responded to the therapist by saying, "Isn't it true counseling can't hurt anyone? It's either the counseling or I'm going to throw him (adolescent) in jail." The issue of rights for the adolescent regarding mental health counseling becomes more complicated when certain behaviors are accepted for adults (father's refusal) but not for adolescents.

What Can Professionals Do?

It takes time for laws to change and so the issues around adolescents' rights to treatment are likely to continue for some time. There are, however, some ways of dealing with the issues and working toward change. One immediate way of starting is to become familiar with the juvenile laws of your state. Many therapists are unfamiliar with the juvenile laws that affect their work. Melton (1981b), in reporting the results of a survey involving mental health clinics in Virginia, found that approximately 40% of the clinics were unaware of a Virginia state law that permitted minors to consent to psychotherapy. If possible, arrange to have access to a lawyer. An attorney knowledgeable in juvenile and mental health laws can be a valuable and supportive resource. To prevent misunderstandings and to lessen pressure from parents, it can be helpful to structure the ground rules of treatment early. Learn how to mobilize and manipulate resources by knowing when agencies such as schools, child welfare agencies, and courts can be allies. Church organizations and groups such as the League of Women Voters can be good resources when it comes to supporting human services. Work at developing your relationships with court personnel. Find out what the legislature is doing, who is doing it, and who has political connections. Make yourself and your points known to your local state legislators. They usually do not have the staff available to them to be knowledgeable in all areas. If you have made yourself and your areas of expertise known, you will have opened the door for the legislator to contact you.

References

Ambrose, J.P. The omnibus reconciliation bill: What does it mean for CMHS's? *National Council News*, October 1981, 4-5.

Barrett-Lennard, G.T. The empathy circle: Refinement of a nuclear concept. *Journal of Counseling Psychology*, 1981, *28*, 91-100.

Everstine, D.S.; Everstine, L.; Heymann, G.M.; True, R.H.; Frey, D.H.; Johnson, H.G.; & Seiden, R.H. Privacy and confidentiality in psychotherapy. *American Psychologist*, 1980, *35*, 828-840.

Glenn, C.M. Ethical issues in the practice of child psychotherapy. *Professional Psychology*, 1980, *11*, 613-619.

Grisso, T., & Vierling, L. Minors consent to treatment: A developmental perspective. *Professional Psychology*, 1978, *9*, 412-427.

Hayes, M. Rights of the child. In I.N. Berlin & L.A. Stone (Eds.), *Basic handbook of child psychiatry* (Vol. 4). New York: Basic Books, 1979.

Henkener, A *Clients' rights*. Paper presented at the meeting of the Ohio Council of Mental Health Centers, Columbus, March 1981.

Howard, K., & Orlinsky, O. The relationship of process to outcome in psychotherapy. *Handbook of psycotherapy and behavior change*. New York: John Wiley & Sons, 1978, 283-329.

Melton, G.B. Children's participation in treatment planning: Psychological and legal issues. *Professional Psychology*, 1981, *12*, 246-252. (a)

Melton, G.B. Effects of a state law permitting minors to consent to psychotherapy. *Professional Psychology*, 1981, *12*, 647-654. (b).

Nye, S.G. Legal issues in the practice of child psychiatry. In E.P. Benedek & D.H. Schetky (Eds.), *Child psychiatry and the law*. New York: Brunner-Mazel, 1980.

Panico, N. Liability of agency providing mental health treatment to minor child without parental consent. *Intradepartmental Communication, Ohio Department of Mental Health and Mental Retardation*, June 20, 1979.

Popiel, D.J. Confidentiality in the context of court referrals to mental health professionals. *American Journal of Orthopsychiatry*, 1980, *50*, 678-685.

Schwitzgebel, R.K., & Schwitzgebel, R.L. *Law and psychological practice*. New York: Wiley & Sons, 1980.

Slovenko, R. Psychotherapy and informed consent: A search in judicial regulation. In W.E. Barton & C.J. Sanborn (Eds.), *Law and the mental health professions*. New York: International Universities Press, 1978.

Spohn, J.R. Community mental health services opinion number 2: Consent for minor. Personal Communication, October 27, 1980.

Stewart, M.A. Treating problem children with drugs: Ethical issues. In G.P. Koocher (Ed.), *Children's rights and the mental health professions*. New York: John Wiley & Sons, 1976.

Avoiding Ethical Violations: A Timeline Perspective for Individual Counseling

Mary E. DePauw

The author outlines a timeline perspective that helps coun-selors avoid ethical violations and organize the ethical mandates that contribute to effective practice. Ethical considerations are proposed during the initiation phase of counseling, as counseling develops, when a period of crisis arises, and at the termination phase.

In recent years increased attention has been given to ethical issues in counseling. Concerned professionals have (a) explored specific ethical dilemmas such as confidentiality (Denkowski & Denkowski, 1982), (b) addressed the assets and limitations of ethical standards (Talbutt, 1981), and (c) questioned the assumptions of ethical recommendations for psychotherapy (Widiger & Rorer, 1984). The goal of all ethical exploration is to assist professionals in ad-dressing their primary responsibility "to respect the integrity and promote the welfare of the client(s)" (American Association for Counseling and Development [AACD], 1981, Section B.1). The AACD (formerly APGA) *Ethical Standards* (1981) directly chal-lenge members "to stimulate greater concern . . . for their own professional functioning and for the conduct of fellow professionals" (AACD, 1981, Preamble).

Counselors interested in avoiding ethical violations and estab-lishing procedures to address the many ethical mandates that con-tribute to effective practice need an organizing structure. The timeline perspective outlined in this article helps counselors identify the relevant ethical considerations that occur over the course of a coun-seling relationship. The timeline focuses attention on issues that occur (a) during the initiation phase of counseling, (b) as counseling develops, (c) when a period of crisis arises, and (d) at the termi-nation point (see Table 1).

Table 1

TIMELINE ETHICAL CONSIDERATIONS

I. *Initiation Phase Issues*
  A. *Pre-counseling considerations*
    1. Advertising
    2. Avoiding misuse of institutional affiliations
    3. Financial arrangements
    4. Donated services.
  B. *Service provision issues*
    1. Adequacy of counselor skills, experience, and training
    2. Better service option for the client
    3. Concurrent therapist involvement
    4. Conflicting dual relationship
  C. *Informed consent issues*
    1. Structures to educate regarding purposes, goals, and techniques
    2. Explanation of rules of procedure and limitations
    3. Supervision and consultation release concerns
    4. Experimental methods of treatment

II. *Ongoing Counseling Issues*
  A. Confidentiality
  B. Special issues of confidentiality with minors
  C. Consultation
  D. Record keeping

III. *Dangerousness and Crisis Concerns*
  A. Threat to self
  B. Threat to others
  C. Child abuse
  D. Gray areas

IV. *Termination Phase Considerations*
  A. Referral if unable to assist
  B. Professional evaluation

Examples are included to highlight specific ethical issues on the timeline. The *Ethical Standards Casebook, Third Edition* (Callis, Pope, & DePauw, 1982) was sponsored by AACD to provide positive and negative examples that illustrate each operative element of the *Ethical Standards* (AACD, 1981). Interested professionals may refer to this work for further clarification and additional illustrative ethical incidents.

Initiation Phase Considerations

Precounseling Considerations

Most counseling agencies, counseling partnerships, and individual practitioners are involved in publicizing their availability and developing a clientele. Advertising must be done "in such a manner so as to accurately inform the public as to services, expertise, profession, and techniques of counseling in a professional manner" (AACD, 1981, Section F.2). Section F.2 also specifies what members may list in advertisements and stresses clarity and accuracy. A related ethical caveat is the misuse of one's institutional affiliation to recruit clients for one's private practice (AACD, 1981, Section F.6).

Another precounseling consideration involves fee structure and financial arrangements. Although this issue is not addressed in the AACD *Ethical Standards*, the "Ethical Principles of Psychologists" (American Psychological Association [APA], 1981a) specify "advance financial arrangements that safeguard the best interests of and are clearly understood by . . . clients" (p. 636). Psychologists are further charged with contributing "a portion of their services to work for which they receive little or no financial return" (p. 636).

Service Provision Questions

When approached by people seeking counseling services, counselors must answer the question, "Should I provide services?" Section G.1 of the AACD *Ethical Standards* (1981) states that "members must define and describe the parameters and levels of their professional competency." During initial client contacts it is imperative not only to assess clients' needs but to determine the adequacy of counselor skills, experience, and training to provide the services requested or required by the client.

A related consideration is the availability of a better service option for the client. Hare-Mustin, Marecek, Kaplan, & Liss-Levinson (1979) explored examples of alternative helping systems as a safeguard to assure that therapists enact their responsibilities to facilitate client informed choice. In Section F.1 (AACD, 1981) members are urged "to assist the profession by facilitating the availability of counseling services in private as well as public settings."

In determining the appropriateness of establishing a counseling relationship, two additional ethical aspects need consideration—a concurrently established counseling relationship and dual relationships. If the client is already involved in another counseling relationship, then either the client must choose to terminate that relationship or the counselor must obtain consent to contact the other professional to negotiate approval for concurrent counseling (AACD, 1981, Section B.3). Dual relationships with a client may take the form of personal relationships that may "impair . . . objectivity and professional judgment" or a professional relationship of an "administrative, supervisory and/or evaluative nature" (AACD, 1981, Section B.11). Dual relationship difficulties are not confined to the initiation phase and may arise at other stages of the counseling relationship.

Informed Consent Issues

When the counselor determines that it is appropriate to initiate a counseling relationship, a relevant question that must be addressed is, "What does the client need to know?" Section B.7 (AACD, 1981) indicates that "the member must inform the client of the purposes, goals, techniques, rules of procedure and limitations that may affect the relationship at or before the time that the counseling relationship is entered." Widiger and Rorer (1984) explored questions of incompatibility between ethical requisites of informed consent and certain therapeutic orientations and techniques.

Counselors need to determine structures appropriate to the setting of the practice for educating clients regarding basic information: the general counseling approach being proposed, specific techniques to be included, the professional qualifications and orientation of the therapist, and specific goals for the client in the counseling relationship. Gill (1982) discussed professional disclosure statements as they relate to consumer protection in counseling. Many counselors use a general description that appears on the request for services form and then is reviewed and expanded on during discussion with the client. An invitation to raise questions

or concerns about any aspect of the counseling process or relationship at any time is an appropriate addition to such a discussion.

An important aspect of informed consent procedures may involve engaging the client in a mutual decision-making process that
encourages openness and establishes honesty between client and
counselor. Realistic expectations for counseling can be established
and any misconceptions clarified. The counselor can also discuss
possible effects—positive and negative—that the client may not
have considered.

Once consensus is reached with the client regarding the goals
and direction of counseling, rules of procedures and limitations
need to be clearly explained. Examples of issues in this category
are cost factors, maintenance of case records, limits of confidentiality, scheduling, and length and duration of sessions.

A recent action by the APA Committee on Scientific and
Professional Ethics and Conduct (APA, 1984) advises psychologists
to "inform their clients at the beginning of a professional relationship if they intend to share information about their case with a
supervisor or consultant" and to indicate "the nature of the information that will be disclosed" (p. 36). In discussing supervision
and consultation release issues with clients, counselors who focus
on the intent to use these relationships to develop an effective
counseling process may not only minimize resistance but may educate clients to the overall profession's commitment to service.

Section B.12 (AACD, 1981) emphasizes that "all experimental
methods of treatment must be clearly indicated to prospective
recipients and safety precautions are to be adhered to by the member." Two definitions of *experimental* need to be considered (Callis
et al., 1982): (a) "those treatments that at the time of use are
essentially nonstandard practice in the profession, the efficacy of
which are not proven either by research or by usual practice by
members of the profession" and (b) "those treatments which at the
time of use for a specific condition by any given member are novel
in his or her repertoire of treatments for that given condition" (p.
48). An example of methods that could fall into the experimental
category is group or individual counseling experiences for students
with eating disorders. The critical factor in approaching such situations is "the honesty on the part of the practitioners about limitations of the state of the professional knowledge and/or their own
professional experiences in the area of services which they are
negotiating and undertaking to provide" (Callis et al., 1982, p. 49).

Although not an ethical mandate, developing written contracts
with clients may be an effective practice. Hare-Mustin et al. (1979)

and Widiger and Rorer (1984) have discussed issues concerning contracts.

Ongoing Counseling Issues

Confidentiality

Section B.2 (AACD, 1981) indicates that the "counseling relationship and information resulting therefrom be kept confidential, consistent with the obligations of the member as a professional person." Denkowski and Denkowski (1982) concluded that the "professional requirement for safeguarding confidentiality seems to be purely ethical" (p. 373) and that "the extent of confidentiality that can be assured under . . . legal limitations is not absolute and is declining" (p. 374). Counselors need to attend to their professional role definitions, be knowledgeable of applicable state laws, and formulate practice procedures proactively. They also need to develop policies and procedures relative to confidentiality responsibilities that extend to supervision of support staff in counseling settings.

Protection of counseling records in educational settings is the intent of Section B.5 (AACD, 1981). Procedures for disclosure of information must be determined in accordance with the Family Educational and Privacy Rights of 1976. Other relevant state statutes or regulations should be identified and implemented.

A special case involves the treatment of minors with alcohol or drug abuse problems. Maintaining confidentiality of information disclosed about these problems is subject to state statute and may not be possible, without parental involvement, subsequent to the first interview (as mandated in Confidentiality of Alcohol and Drug Patient Records, 1975).

Consultation

Section B.9 (AACD, 1981) indicates that a "member may choose to consult with any other professionally competent person about a client" but must avoid placing the consultant "in a conflict of interest situation." The informed consent procedures described above permit counselors to discuss clients with other professionals when they are unclear about case progress or need additional information to work effectively with clients.

Record Keeping

"Records of the counseling relationship, including interview notes, test data, correspondence, tape recordings, and other documents, are to be considered professional information for use in counseling" (AACD, 1981, Section B.5). The APA "Specialty Guidelines for the Delivery of Services by Counseling Psychologists" (1981b) specify that records should "include, but are not limited to, identifying data, dates of services, types of services, significant actions taken, and outcome at termination" (p. 21). These guidelines also outline that (a) records be completed within a reasonable time, (b) records be retained for the length of time specified, (c) a system be established to protect confidentiality, and (d) special safeguards be used when electronic data systems are involved.

Release of information contained in counseling records "must occur only upon the expressed consent of the client" (AACD, 1981, Section B.5). Counselors need to be aware that many states have enacted statutes specifying the precise nature of release forms for clients of health services providers, including mental health practitioners.

Ethical Considerations Involving Danger

Threat to Self

Section B.4 (AACD, 1981) mandates that counselors act to protect the safety of any client whose condition indicates that there is clear and imminent danger to the client or others by taking reasonable action or by informing responsible authorities. Counselors need to pursue carefully any client suicidal ideation and make a judgment regarding dangerousness. Counselors should be knowledgeable of state statutes and relevant local procedures, including voluntary hospitalization options. Openly discussing counselor concerns and engaging the client in a decision-making process frequently results in client cooperation and voluntary hospitalization, thus avoiding involuntary procedures. The "assumption of responsibility for the client(s) behavior must be taken only after careful deliberation. The client must be involved in the resumption of responsibility as quickly as possible" (AACD, 1981, Section B.4).

Threat to Others

Section B.4 (AACD, 1981) also obligates counselors to pursue threats to others reported by clients. *Tarasoff v. Regents of University of California* (1976) has been interpreted to imply "a duty to warn" the endangered party based on a California statute. It is important for practitioners to know what is permitted or obligated based on local statutes. Denkowski and Denkowski (1982) suggested that counselors "formulate contingency plans for dealing with dangerous clients that are derived in consultation with an informed attorney, a local psychiatric hospital, and area law-enforcement personnel" (p. 374).

Child Abuse

Most states have legislated that actual or suspected child abuse be reported to designated authorities. Counselors should obtain the related specifics for their practice areas. Because of the recent reports of the prevalence of child sexual abuse, counselors who work with children may wish to develop procedures to obtain a comprehensive history to allow for disclosure of such problems.

Gray Areas

An ethical dilemma is raised for practitioners when clients report behaviors that, although not currently endangering, may become so (e.g., failure by a diabetic client to follow a prescribed medical regimen). Extension of the intent of current ethical standards would suggest the need for establishing procedures to enhance client problem resolution before a crisis occurs. For example, clients with eating disorders should be referred to a physician for examination, health education, and follow-up regarding the damaging effects of starvation and repeated purging. Establishing a continuing consultation relationship with the client's physician and having the physician collaborate in outlining actions that might be taken if life threatening behavior develops would also be effective practice strategies.

Termination Phase Considerations

Referral If Unable To Assist

Sections B.10 and F.4 (AACD, 1981) clearly indicate that when practitioners determine that the counseling relationship is no longer productive or that they are unable to assist the client, the relationship must be terminated immediately. Practitioners have an obligation to be knowledgeable of referral sources and to suggest appropriate alternatives. If the client declines the suggested referral, the practitioner is not obligated to continue the relationship.

Professional Evaluation

Section G.5 (AACD, 1981) mandates that "members must submit regularly to professional review and evaluation." The APA "Specialty Guidelines for the Delivery of Services by Counseling Psychologists" (1981b) specify that there "be periodic, systematic, and effective evaluations of counseling psychological services" to assess effectiveness, efficiency, continuity, availability, accessibility, and adequacy (p. 23). The acquisition of client follow-up data from each user of a practitioner's service not only provides evaluative feedback but enables that practitioner to establish a mechanism through which clients can express post-termination concerns.

Conclusion

The counseling profession does not lend itself to "cookbook" practices. The timeline perspective proposed here facilitates practitioner exploration of effective daily practices and procedures to avoid ethical violations. It also offers a valuable structure for teaching ethics to counselors in training and serves as a basic guideline for new practitioners.

References

American Association for Counseling and Development. (1981). *Ethical standards.* Alexandria, VA: Author. (Originally published by American Personnel and Guidance Association)

American Psychological Association. (1981a). Ethical principles of psychologists (revised). *American Psychologist, 36,* 633–638.

American Psychological Association, Committee of Professional Standards. (1981b). *Specialty guidelines for the delivery of services by counseling psychologists.* Washington, DC: Author.

American Psychological Association, Committee on Scientific and Professional Ethics and Conduct. (1984, May). Ethics statement issued. *APA Monitor,* p. 36.

Callis, R., Pope, S.K., & DePauw, M.E. (1982). *Ethical standards casebook* (3rd ed.). Alexandria, VA: American Association for Counseling and Development.

Confidentiality of Alcohol and Drug Abuse Patient Records, 42. C.F.R. § 2 (1975).

Denkowski, K.M., & Denkowski, G.C. (1982). Client-counselor confidentiality: An update of rationale, legal status, and implications. *Personnel and Guidance Journal, 60,* 371–375.

Family Educational and Privacy Rights (Buckley Pell Amendment), 20 U.S.C. § 1232g (1976).

Gill, S.J. (1982). Professional disclosure and consumer protection in counseling. *Personnel and Guidance Journal, 60,* 443–446.

Hare-Mustin, R.T., Marecek, J., Kaplan, A.G., & Liss-Levinson, N. (1979). Rights of clients, responsibilities of therapists. *American Psychologist, 34,* 3–16.

Talbutt, L.C. (1981). Ethical standards: Assets and limitations. *Personnel and Guidance Journal, 60,* 110–112.

Tarasoff v. Regents of University of California, 17 Cal. 3d 425, 551 P.2d 334, 131 Cal. Rptr. 14 (1976).

Widiger, T.A., & Rorer, L.G. (1984). The responsible psychotherapist. *American Psychologist, 39,* 503–515.

When a Colleague Practices Unethically: Guidelines for Intervention

James L. Levenson

When professionals learn of unethical professional practice by a colleague, they have an ethical obligation to intervene through appropriate evaluation and reporting. Sexual activity between a professional and a client is used as an example, and guidelines are provided for initial approach and evaluation, confidentiality, and the rationale for and ways of reporting misconduct. Ambivalence and resistance by both client and professional may interfere with needed intervention and must be worked through.

Dilemma. Ms. B., a 30-year-old single woman, comes to Dr. Jones asking for counseling. She says that she has had chronic fears of getting close to men and has been too anxious to ever date. She had consulted Dr. Smith for the same problem 1 year previously. She began seeing him for regular sessions. She reports that Dr. Smith told her that she would learn to trust other men by learning to trust him. This initially involved embracing each other and progressed to sexual intercourse, which Ms. B. says continued for several months. Ms. B. became increasingly uncomfortable about her sessions with Dr. Smith and recently discontinued seeing him. What should Dr. Jones do?

The many possible permutations of negligent behavior by a psychotherapist constitute an obsessive's nightmare and a scholar's delight. (Gutheil & Appelbaum, 1982, p. 152)

The ethical principles that guide professionals and the ethical dilemmas that they face have received much attention in recent years. When a professional becomes aware of unethical conduct practiced by a colleague, however, there is little literature to consult on how to respond and intervene. Similarly, the impaired professional has become a topic of wide interest. There are many evaluation procedures and treatment programs for professionals who suffer from alcoholism or severe depression, but what of those who suffer from corruption?

Unethical behavior may include violation of confidentiality, negligent practice, sexual activity with a client, certain conflicts of interest, and questionable financial arrangements. Different professional groups have defined ethical guidelines that vary in specificity and mandate. Channels and procedures for processing complaints of unethical behavior may vary not only between professions but also within a particular profession from state to state. The purpose of this article is to describe the options for response when one learns of possible improper actions by a colleague. I focus here on professional sexual misconduct as an example and look at what Dr. Jones should do about Dr. Smith and Ms. B. I write from the vantage point of a psychiatrist, but the principles can be extrapolated to the wider group of mental health and counseling professionals.

Sexual activity between a professional and a client is explicitly considered unethical by the American Psychiatric Association (1984), the American Psychological Association (1981), and the National Association of Social Workers (1980). The American Association for Counseling and Development (AACD, formerly American Personnel and Guidance Association) (1981) cited sexual intimacy with a client as an example of a conflicting dual relationship that must be avoided. Although the Hippocratic oath (cited in Beauchamp & Walters, 1982, p. 121) forbids sexual relations between physician and patient, the American Medical Association's *Principles of Medical Ethics* (1980) and the recent American College of Physicians' "Ethics Manual" (1984) have not directly addressed the issue.

Learning of Misconduct

Learning from the Client: Assessing the Validity of Allegations

How one learns of possible professional misconduct affects the information's credibility and the potential for intervention. One may hear from the client directly as in the case of Ms. B. The professional must first consider whether the client is capable of gross distortion of reality (i.e., that the allegations seem prima facie untrue). Such distortions may derive from an unsuccessful attempt to seduce the counselor, primitive rage and consequent retaliation after a perceived injury or slight, or underlying psychosis in which the client delusionally misinterprets the real relationship.

How can one tell if the client is telling the truth? If Ms. B. is disturbed enough to be lying or delusional about Dr. Smith, then Dr. Jones is almost certain to see gross interpersonal pathology in Ms. B's relationship with him. This may be the same or a different kind of distortion, such as paranoid suspiciousness or extreme idealization involving Dr. Jones or other people in Ms. B.'s life. Such serious pathology in relationships should lead to careful and critical examination of the allegations of sexual abuse but not necessarily to discounting them. After all, such clients are not immune to being taken advantage of by others, and they may be especially vulnerable to an unscrupulous authority figure.

Learning from Colleagues

One may also hear stories about a colleague's misbehavior from other colleagues. Such stories are hearsay evidence, ranging from convincing detail to shadowy rumor. In this case, a professional's prime responsibility is to strongly encourage any professional who has more direct knowledge of the misconduct to report it appropriately as described below. If one knows the accused professional personally, it may even be appropriate to discuss rumors directly with him or her.

Learning Directly From the Errant Professional

More directly, one may observe evidence of a colleague's misconduct, or he or she may confess. If this occurs in a setting in which the impaired colleague is himself or herself a client, confidentiality comes into conflict with the responsibility to intervene against unethical behavior. Many counselors and therapists would feel bound by confidentiality to not "turn in" a client who had confessed to professional misconduct. Confidentiality, however, is not an absolute good outweighing all other principles. If the misconduct poses a very serious threat to others, one must consider competing responsibilities and sometimes break confidentiality. Sexual abuse of child clients is such an example because of the legislation that exists in all 50 states regarding mandatory reporting of child abuse.

Intervention

Consent, Confidentiality, and Clients' Reluctance to Report

Having learned from Ms. B. of Dr. Smith's misconduct and believing that her story is not manifestly false, Dr. Jones must obtain her written consent before taking any other steps. To proceed without her consent is not only a breach of confidentiality but an additional violation of her already injured integrity. Like a victim of rape or incest, the client who has been sexually abused by a trusted professional is likely to be deeply ambivalent about getting involved in reporting him or her for a number of different reasons. Ms. B. may be reluctant because of persistent affection for, dependence on, or fear of Dr. Smith. She may feel too guilty to report him, viewing herself as actively or passively complicit in forbidden behavior. She may fear that she will not be believed and that her own conduct and reputation will be maligned in the process (Burgess, 1981). She may wish to leave a traumatic experience behind as quickly as possible. It is therefore crucial that Dr. Jones carefully explore Ms. B.'s feelings and help her resolve conflicts over whether to proceed with reporting Dr. Smith. As part of this process, Dr. Jones should clearly identify sexual activity between counselor and client as professionally unethical and harmful to Ms. B.

In addition to clarifying the nature of the misconduct, exploring the client's ambivalence, and obtaining consent, the counselor needs to consider when the client is psychologically ready to pursue formal reporting. For most victims, readiness requires that they overcome guilt and self-blame sufficiently to understand that they really have been wronged. This entails awareness and expression of anger at having been victimized. A small number of clients, with more serious underlying psychopathology, may become psychotic, suicidal, or homicidal after having been sexually abused. They must be helped through treatment before the process of reporting and confrontation can be safely initiated.

Director Discussion with the Accused Professional

Given Ms. B.'s readiness and consent, Dr. Jones should first contact Dr. Smith to discuss the allegations directly. This step complies with the AACD "Policy and Procedure for Processing Complaints of Ethical Violations." This gives Dr. Smith an early opportunity to take an active role in either defending himself or if he acknowledges the wrong, confronting and redressing it. In Minneapolis, Dr. Jones could consult the Walk-in Counseling Center, a model program that offers a service for processing complaints of sexual misconduct by therapists. Voluntary sessions would be held with Dr. Smith and Ms. B. both present (Schoener, 1984). Unfortunately, this option is not available in most locations.

Formal Reporting

After discussing the case with Dr. Smith, Dr. Jones should formally report the allegations if he still believes they may be true. Why? The number of professionals who engage in sexual acts with their clients is small, but of those who do, 75% to 80% engage in sexual acts with more than one client (Bouhoutsos, Holroyd, & Lerman, 1983). Clients frequently do not realize that sexual acts between client and counselor are unethical (Bouhoutsos et al., 1983). Reporting of professionals by professionals is necessary to protect a naive and vulnerable public from those few counselors who practice unethically.

Official reporting procedures vary among both professions and states. It is usually indicated but not always sufficient to notify the accused professional's supervisor, if there is one. If the professional is neither licensed nor a member of a professional society, then informing a supervisor is essential. Most professional organizations, including AACD, have ethics committees in most state or local branches, with formal procedures for investigating and ruling on possible misconduct. Dr. Jones should contact the appropriate representative of the committee. Usually, the state professional ethics committee can be reached through the association's president without the necessity of revealing any confidential information.

States license or certify professionals to varying degrees. If a licensing board exists, one must consider whether to file a report there as well. Such a report is indicated if Dr. Jones believes that Ms. B. is one of many clients that Dr. Smith has misused. On the other hand, if there remain doubts about Ms. B.'s allegations, it may be better to defer to the ethics committee's investigation and judgment. Legislation for mandatory reporting has been proposed for professional sexual misconduct but has been rarely adopted. There is a conflict here between competing ethical principles. On the one hand, there is the responsibility to protect the public from unethical practitioners (beneficence and justice). On the other hand, there is the right of the individual client to determine whether he or she wishes to report the practitioner (autonomy). To supersede the right of autonomy would require the abridgement of confidentiality and consequently damage the client's trust. Therefore, legislatures have chosen not to make reporting mandatory when the client is an adult. Children, however, are not in a position to make fully autonomous choices. Sexual activity between a professional and a minor client constitutes child abuse and must be reported like any other form of child abuse.

If the offending professional received third-party payment for services (e.g., Blue Cross-Blue Shield, Medicare), an additional notification responsibility may be present. Some forms of misconduct, including engaging in sexual acts under the pretense of treatment, constitute fraud, and fradulent services should not be reimbursed (Sharfstein, 1985).

Professionals' Reluctance to Report

Given the wide consensus among mental health and counseling professionals that sexual activity between professional and client is unequivocally wrong, why are professionals reluctant to report? Historically, professionals have developed their identity and power partly through forging strong intraprofessional bonds predicated on common interests. Unfortunately, this has sometimes taken the form of an implicit expectation that no member of a professional organization will testify against another (Starr, 1982). If he reports Dr. Smith, Dr. Jones may fear that he will be ostracized by his colleagues as a traitor, becoming professionally isolated and losing referrals. Dr. Jones may be apprehensive that Dr. Smith will respond by suing him for libel, thereby causing Dr. Jones much expense and lost time in defending himself. Dr. Jones may believe that nothing much will happen to Dr. Smith as a result of reporting him and that it therefore is not worth the risks.

Carrying great responsibilities and being humanly fallible, many professionals cannot bring themselves to accuse another. Dr. Jones may believe that his own record is not without mistakes and be reluctant to come forward, thinking, "Who am I to condemn another's behavior?" Especially unfortunate, Dr. Jones may exhibit outright denial and refuse to believe that Ms. B.'s story could be true (Burgess, 1981). Alternatively, Dr. Jones may do nothing because he is not absolutely sure that Dr. Smith is guilty. If so, he fundamentally misunderstands his professional responsibilities. It is not Dr. Jones's role to be detective, judge, and jury. Ethics committees, licensing boards, and the legal process, not individual professionals, are charged with the responsibilities of determining guilt and punishing offenses. In any case, as compelling as one's responsibilities are, reporting a colleague is a very difficult and often lonely step.

Treating the Victim of Unethical Conduct

In addition to Dr. Jones's responsibility to report unethical professional conduct, he has the responsibility of treating Ms. B., the victim, or at least referring her for treatment. In some cases, it may be impossible for Dr. Jones to play both roles. Ms. B. may not believe that sessions with Dr. Jones can remain sufficiently private and confidential if he has reported Dr. Smith and perhaps will formally testify about the case. Stone (1983) has argued that it is preferable to separate what can be conflicting responsibilities and have one professional perform evaluation and intervention for reporting purposes and another treat the client without getting involved in any way in the reporting, thereby preserving confidentiality in the therapeutic relationship.

The specific methods and issues in providing psychotherapy to the victim of professional sexual misconduct are beyond the scope of this article. In referring such a client for therapy, however, the counselor should keep in mind that the client may resist treatment for any of the reasons outlined above. The counselor must also be sensitive to the varying appropriateness of individual, group, or marital therapy for each specific client.

Each practitioner must recognize his or her ethical obligations to clients, individual professions, and society and actively intervene when a colleague practices unethically. This task is not an easy one; it requires that professionals deal with ambivalence and resistance in both clients and themselves while simultaneously respecting clients' confidentiality and autonomy.

References

American Association for Counseling and Development. (1981). *Ethical standards.* Alexandria, VA: Author. (Originally published by American Personnel and Guidance Association)

American College of Physicians. (1984). Ethics manual. *Annals of Internal Medicine, 101*, 129–137, 263–274.

American Medical Association. (1980). *Principles of medical ethics.* Washington, DC: Author.

American Psychiatric Association. (1984). *Principles of medical ethics with annotations especially applicable to psychiatry.* Washington, DC: Author.

American Psychological Association. (1981). Ethical principles of psychologists. *American Psychologist, 36*, 633–638.

Beauchamp, T.L., & Walters, L. (Eds.). (1982). *Contemporary issues in bioethics* (2nd ed.). Belmont, CA: Wadsworth.

Bouhoutsos, J., Holroyd, J., & Lerman, H. (1983). Sexual intimacy between psychotherapists and patients. *Professional Psychology, 14*, 185.

Burgess, A.W. (1981). Physician sexual misconduct and patients' responses. *American Journal of Psychiatry, 138*, 1335–1342.

Gutheil, T.G., & Applebaum, P.S. (1982). *Clinical handbook of psychiatry and the law.* New York: McGraw-Hill.

National Association of Social Workers. (1980). *Code of ethics.* Silver Spring, MD: Author.

Shoener, G.R. (1984, May). *Processing complaints of therapist sexual misconduct.* Paper presented at the meeting of the American Psychiatric Association, Los Angeles.

Sharfstein, S.S. (1985). Fraud committed by psychiatrists. *American Journal of Psychiatry, 142*, 219.

Starr, P. (1982). *The social transformation of American medicine.* New York: Basic Books.

Stone, A.A. (1983). Sexual misconduct by psychiatrists: The ethical and clinical dilemma of confidentiality. *American Journal of Psychiatry, 140*, 195–197.

Reporting Unethical Practices: Revised Guidelines

William Marchant

Professional counselors should interpret with caution Levenson's (January 1986) advice on reporting unethical practice by colleagues. The information is confusing and may be incorrect when reporting to a state licensing board or to the court system.

As an example, Levenson (p. 315) suggests that the counselor must assess the truthfulness of the client who makes an allegation against a colleague and contradicts the point (p. 317) by saying that it is not the counselor's role "to be detective, judge, and jury. Ethics committees, licensing boards, and the legal process, not individual professionals, are charged with the responsibilities of determining guilt and punishing offenses." He is correct on the second point. It is the responsibility of the various boards and committees to investigate a complaint and hold hearings on the allegations before determining guilt and punishment. That process relieves the counselor of the responsibility for determining the truthfulness of a complaint and leaves the counselor in place to continue therapy with the client, no matter what the outcome of the investigation.

Because a disciplinary hearing is adversarial, the burden in proving the case against the accused is held by the complaining party. The pressure is on the client to provide clear, specific testimony during the investigation and hearings. With that pressure, the client is likely to need support, rather than doubt, from the counselor.

Levenson suggests that treatment be concluded, or at least be well along the way, before the complaint can be made. In fact, it is important that the complaint be made as close to the occurrence as possible. Anyone who has been involved in counseling rape or abuse victims is aware of cases that have not been filed because too much time has passed between an event and the report of that event. As a consequence, the counselor has had to deal with the anger of the victim toward the legal system, as well as toward the abuser, thus making the therapy more complicated and lengthy.

The counselor should treat the report or complaint as part of the therapy. Helping the client through the process of reporting an ethics violation and through the investigation and hearings is likely to help the client become stronger in dealing with feelings of vulnerability and, hence, in dealing with the world.

Levenson suggests that the counselor who is concerned with the ethical practices of a colleague should first discuss those concerns with that colleague (p. 316). Although such advice may be consistent with reporting ethical violations to AACD, it is incorrect when reporting to a state licensing board. Such a contact may interfere with a continuing investigation. Putting the offending therapist on guard may delay or otherwise interfere with the investigation.

The client may need information about the different kinds of complaints that may be filed. A criminal complaint should be filed with the local police or with the office of the district attorney. Such a complaint would allege a violation of criminal statutes, such as rape or sexual assault. An administrative complaint should be filed with the state licensing board. This complaint would allege a violation of statutes or regulations created by the board. The client may file a violation of ethical standards complaint with a professional organization. It is also possible to file a civil complaint against the therapist.

The purpose of listing these alternatives is to emphasize that the criminal complaint, the civil complaint, the complaint to the administrative board, and the report to the ethics committee are discrete reporting events. Making a complaint to one creates no guarantee that anything else will occur.

Levenson suggests that the therapist who reports an ethical violation may have difficulty in maintaining the therapeutic relationship because of loss of trust of the client through a violation of confidentiality. But if the therapist has obtained the consent and cooperation of the client in making the complaint, then confidentiality is no longer an ethical concern.

It would be best if the client makes the complaint, because no role confusion will exist. The counselor is free to be counselor and to provide support to the client during the process, which would avoid the confusion anticipated by Levenson of appointing one therapist to be the investigator and complainant and another therapist to be the counselor.

Ethical Concerns in School Counseling

Wayne C. Huey

In this article the author discusses ethical dilemmas inherent in the school setting that result from conflicts in counselor responsibilities to pupils, parents, and school. An ethical dilemma involving a pregnant student who is considering an abortion is described, and some possible counselor responses are discussed.

> *Dilemma.* Janice, a socially mature 16-year-old, confides in her counselor that she is pregnant. Her family is active in the "prolife" movement, and Janice held similar beliefs before the pregnancy. She now wishes to explore the physical and psychological ramifications of an abortion and seeks assurance that, whatever the final decision, the counselor will not reveal any information to her family. The counselor, who is also a strong "pro-lifer," contemplates informing the girl's parents.

The single characteristic that best distinguishes school counselors from other mental health professionals is a direct result of their work setting. School counselors work with minors and thus have certain legal and ethical responsibilities to parents as well as to clients. A potential conflict between allegiances to clients and parents is further compounded by ethical-legal responsibilities to the employing institution. In response to these and other issues in school counseling, the American School Counselor Association (ASCA) adopted the *Ethical Standards for School Counselors* (1984). These standards are not intended to replace the American Association for Counseling and Development (AACD, formerly American Personnel and Guidance Association) *Ethical Standards* (1981) but rather to complement them by clarifying the nature of ethical responsibilities of counselors in the school setting.

The purpose of this article is to provide a brief review of the school counselor's responsibilities to pupils, parents, and school.

An attempt is made to relate these three areas of ethical responsibilities to a specific dilemma, that of a pregnant teenage girl (Janice) considering an abortion, and to generate some realistic options for school counselors.

Responsibilities to Pupils

Duncan and Moffett (1974) cautioned that ethical standards do not give guidelines for every situation. The standards must be interpreted by each counselor in each context. Moreover, interpretation is a function of the counselor's personal values, beliefs, and attitudes. Counselors working with children need to be particularly careful not to promote acceptance of the counselor's values as the "right" ones. Section A.4 of the ASCA standards (1984) states that "The school counselor refrains from consciously encouraging the counselee's acceptance of values, lifestyles, plans, decisions, and beliefs that represent only the counselor's personal orientation." Clients of all ages have the right to choice and self-direction in their beliefs. Talbutt (1983) warned that it is not only unethical for counselors to impose their values and views on minors; it can result in legal action. The school counselor's role is to challenge and assist students to explore their own values on which they can base their own decisions. This task is not always easy. As individuals, counselors feel strongly about values, and such convictions are not readily pushed aside or effectively concealed. Attempting to deny a position or trying to ignore values may undermine the trust necessary for a productive counseling relationship. The school counselor should express his or her values and emphasize that they were accepted and incorporated after much thought and exploration. Although they seem right for the counselor, they are not accepted as right by all people. If a counselor feels so strongly about an issue that his or her effectiveness in the relationship will be impaired, a referral is appropriate.

Responsibilities to Parents

The counselor-client relationship is private and thus requires compliance with confidentiality standards; school counselors, however, work with minors, and their legal responsibility is generally to the parent, whereas their ethical responsibility may be more to the client. Obviously, the legal and ethical requirements are not always in agreement, thus placing the counselor in a precarious position that must be balanced to ensure the rights of clients and at the same time ensure the rights of parents. Wagner (1981) reported that the younger the client, the greater the counselor's allegiance to the parent. She recommended, however, that children should have control over the release of information that results from their choosing to engage in the counseling process. Eberlein (1977) stated that most judges would be sympathetic to a client's request that a counselor not reveal information to the parent, and the counselor should not voluntarily inform parents of content unless the minor makes such a request.

For many school counselors, the issue is whether legal responsibility takes precedence over confidentiality based on professional ethics. Ethical codes do not supersede the law, and they should never be interpreted so as to encourage conduct that violates the law. Counselors must become familiar with local, state, and federal laws, but legal knowledge is not sufficient to determine the best course of action. Each case is unique, and laws are subject to interpretation; consequently, professional judgment will always play a role. Corey, Corey, and Callahan (1984) stated that although counselors need to use caution in legal issues, they must not become useless and paralyzed by ineffectiveness. Counseling is risky, and counselors should not become so involved in legalism that they reduce client welfare to a secondary responsibility.

Responsibilities to the School

Section A.2 of the AACD *Ethical Standards* (1981) states that "The acceptance of employment in an institution implies that the member is in agreement with the general policies and principles of the institution. Therefore the professional activities of the member are also in accord with the objectives of the institution." Counselors should adhere to local school policies, whether determined by the principal or the board of education, to the extent possible without compromising their primary responsibility to the client. Counselors cannot afford to be perceived as more concerned about school rules than about student needs. When a conflict exists between a counselor's loyalty to the client and to the employer, the counselor should always attempt to find a resolution that protects the rights of the client; the ethical responsibility is to the client first and the school second. Information obtained in the counseling relationship should remain confidential if the school's policies are not in the best interest of the client's well-being. When institutional policies exist that hinder the effectiveness of the counseling relationship, the counselor must actively use all available resources to promote a policy change in keeping with ethical standards of behavior.

Discussion

It is not uncommon for adolescents to seek advice about personal issues from school counselors, and a dilemma such as Janice's generates value-laden questions: What do you think about abortion? Should I have one? Where can I go? Will you help me? A counselor who views abortion as a viable alternative could help Janice clarify her choices and, if she wishes, suggest a referral to a family planning clinic. A counselor who accepts abortion provisionally could explore the situation with Janice to determine if referral to another counselor who can be more objective is warranted. If the counselor's values include viewing abortion as murder, then, based on ASCA standard A.9 ("The school counselor informs appropriate authorities when the counselee's condition indicates a clear and imminent danger to the counselee or others. . . ."), the counselor might feel justified in informing Janice that he or she must break confidentiality to prevent the abortion even though the consequences to his or her reputation among students would probably be severe. Whatever the interpretation, the counselor must still consider legal and ethical responsibilities to Janice's parents.

Generally, the courts have ruled that minors have a legal right to obtain abortions without the consent of parents (Talbutt, 1983); Section B.1 of the ASCA standards, however, states that "The school counselor respects the inherent rights and responsibilities of parents for their children and endeavors to establish a cooperative relationship with parents to facilitate the maximum development of the counselee." The counselor in this case should strongly encourage Janice to discuss the issue with her parents. The final decision, however, must rest with Janice.

Regarding institutional responsibilities, the counselor should determine whether the school has a policy concerning adolescent pregnancy and, in particular, the issue of confidentiality. Typically, a policy does not exist, at least not in written form. If, however, reports to the parents or school are required, the counselor needs to consider carefully the full implications of making such a report. Ethical standards should always apply, regardless of the situation, and the counselor's concern for Janice's well-being must be foremost in the counseling relationship.

Applying ethical standards to practical situations is difficult because it involves values and human judgment. In the school setting it is especially difficult because the clients are minors. Moreover, there exists an ethical-legal responsibility to the school. School counselors confronting ethical dilemmas are often unsure where their allegiances lie; nevertheless, they must learn to tolerate the inherent ambiguity in ethical dilemmas. As trained professionals, school counselors have the capacity to take responsibility for their own judgments. Consultation and other resources are readily available through professional associations such as ASCA and AACD.

References

American Association for Counseling and Development. (1981). *Ethical standards.* Alexandria, VA: Author. (Originally published by American Personnel and Guidance Association)

American School Counselor Association. (1984). *Ethical standards for school counselors.* Alexandria, VA: Author.

Corey, G., Corey, M.S., & Callanan, P. (1984). *Issues and ethics in the helping professions* (2nd ed.). Monterey, CA: Brooks/Cole.

Duncan, J., & Moffett, C. (1974). Abortion counseling and the school counselor. *School Counselor, 21,* 188–195.

Eberlein, L. (1977). Counselors beware! Clients have rights! *Personnel and Guidance Journal, 56,* 219–223.

Talbutt, L.C. (1983). Current legal trends regarding abortions for minors: A dilemma for counselors. *School Counselor, 31,* 120–124.

Wagner, C.A. (1981). Confidentiality and the school counselor. *Personnel and Guidance Journal, 59,* 305–310.

2

PRIVACY, CONFIDENTIALITY, AND PRIVILEGED COMMUNICATION

Confidentiality and privileged communication are two related issues that school counselors often confuse. Information clients relate to school counselors should be kept confidential with the following exceptions: (a) the client is a danger to self or others; (b) the client or parent requests that information be related to a third party; or (c) a court orders a counselor to disclose information.

Although all school counselors have a confidentiality responsibility, very few relationships with students are considered privileged. Privileged communication is granted only by statute and guarantees clients that a court cannot compel a counselor to disclose information related in confidence. Such statutory privileges belong to clients rather than to counselors, and most states do not grant privileged communication in school counseling relationships.

Zingaro (1983) takes the position that a child's right to privacy, regardless of the child's age, should be compromised only in the most extreme circumstances. He offers recommendations for school counselors who are asked to disclose information told to them by a child in confidence.

Before the Buckley Amendment was passed in 1974, many students were maligned in school records without their knowledge, and information from their records was often released to third parties without the students' consent. Although the students' privacy is now protected by federal legislation, Walker and Larrabee (1985) encourage school counselors to take responsibility for managing students' records in a manner that assures students of their rights.

Sheeley and Herlihy (1987) report that 20 states have passed statutes that provide some degree of protection of the privacy involved in student and school counselor relationships. The statutes in existence are summarized and implications for practice are discussed.

Confidentiality: To Tell or Not To Tell

Joseph C. Zingaro

Elementary school counselors, school psychologists, and other members of the student personnel team need to be sensitive to the issue of confidentiality with the child-client. Children depend on and have a right to expect security and protection from adults in whose care they are entrusted.

Professionals who work with children are aware of the fine line that often differentiates the rights of children from the rights of adults, especially parents. When does the child's right to confidentiality supersede the parent's right to know? Are there guidelines that school counselors and school psychologists can use to aid them in making decisions about disclosing information received within the privacy of the counselor's or school psychologist's office while doing individual or group counseling?

The American Psychological Association (APA) and the American Personnel and Guidance Association (APGA) suggest guidelines in their respective ethical standards. These ethical codes are principles that serve as guidelines for behavior. As such, they do not negate the use of clinical judgment and interpretation. Regarding confidentiality, the *Ethical Principles of Psychologists* (APA, 1981) and the *Ethical Standards* (APGA, 1981) do not suggest age restrictions. This implies that the privilege of confidentiality extends to all clients, regardless of age.

Children's rights are also based on their needs system. For example, Erickson (1963) suggests eight stages of ego development. Each stage involves the resolution of stage-relevant tasks. Each task requires the individual to balance individual needs with societal expectations. During the elementary school years (grades K-8) children are coping with the stages of initiative versus guilt, industry versus inferiority, and identity versus role diffusion.

Children in the stage labeled initiative versus guilt are characterized by a lively imagination (e.g., imaginary friends, fear of monsters), vigorous reality testing (e.g., testing of the reality of

Santa Claus, parental rules), and imitation of adults. The successful resolution of the industry versus inferiority stage involves greater self-reliance, autonomy, and mastery of certain interpersonal and physical skills. Identity versus role diffusion reflects the challenge of learning about self-individuality and working toward actualizing potential.

Musser, Conger, and Kagan (1974) describe the social environment of "the psychologically favored child" (p. 452) as an environment that values the child as an individual. This implies, among other things, that the child is not viewed as a mere extension of parents or siblings. The basic needs of autonomy, self-reliance, and mastery are provided for within this social milieu, as well as opportunities for development of the child's potential.

As mental health professionals in the schools, aware of the developmental needs of children and concerned with educating parents, teachers, and adminstrators about these needs, we must also be aware that some of our own behaviors may be counterproductive to our best efforts. Specifically, a breach of confidentiality may reflect a belief that children neither need nor deserve the individuality and autonomy that we are trying to help them achieve.

For example, a child may ask to talk with you about a problem, such as how to get along with a new stepparent. After discussing the child's concern, you arrange a time to meet at a later date. The following day one of the child's parents calls you to ask about the content of your counseling session. It seems obvious from the questions that the parent is aware of some of the issues that you discussed with the child. Would you disclose information that you received from the child to the parent? What would be the effects on the child, parents, and you if you comply with the parent's request? If the child's self-referral is viewed as a step toward autonomy and independence in solving his or her problems, have you handicapped the child's efforts? Would these questions be answered differently if the parent had asked you to speak with his or her child and then asked about the content of your counseling session?

This article suggests principles that elementary school counselors and child psychologists may use when circumstances involve the question of disclosing to parents or guardians of child clients information received within the privacy of the counselor's office while doing individual or group counseling. The questions that were suggested by the above example will be answered based on the recommendations at the end of this article.

Ethical Considerations

Confidentiality is a term that implies exclusivity. Information exchanged between people becomes theirs, not to be shared with the larger community. Van Hoose and Kottler (1978) suggest that a confidential communication between two parties must meet the following criteria:

1. The communications must originate with the understanding that they will not be disclosed.
2. Confidentiality must be essential to the maintenance of the relationship.
3. The relationship must be fostered because the community desires it.
4. Injury inflicted on the relationship as a result of disclosure or communication must be greater than the benefit gained from proper disposal of litigation. (p. 86)

Stude and McKelvey (1979) and Goldman (1969) stated that the privilege of confidentiality belongs to the client, not the counselor. In most instances the client can freely discuss issues with the counselor with the assurance that the content of those issues will be kept from society. Under certain circumstances society's need to know supersedes the individual's right to privacy. These circumstances include, but are not limited to, occasions when the client has told the counselor of harm to be directed to himself or herself or to someone else or of participation in an illegal activity and plans to continue with such activity.

In a survey of elementary, middle, and high school counselors, Wagner (1981) found that a general pattern emerged. Counselors who perceived no detrimental effects to children tended to honor parents' requests for information even though the youthful client asked that the information not be released. The counselors also tended to form greater allegiance to the parents of younger clients.

The results of Wagner's survey (1981) are disturbing for several reasons. First, rather than using ethical guidelines for the dissemination of confidential information to the parents or guardians of child-clients, some counselors rely on their general perceptions of the harmful effects that release of information will have for the client. Such calculated risk-taking needs to be discouraged because the risk is for the child who discloses the information, not the counselor who releases it. Rather than the counselor experiencing the consequences of a misperception, the client will feel the consequences to a degree that cannot be predicted by the counselor.

A counselor using his or her perceptions of probable effects of disclosure takes about as much risk as one who places bets with someone else's money.

A second disturbing result of Wagner's survey is that the younger the client, the greater the allegiance of the counselor to the parents of the client. This may create a no-win situation for the child. Based on the author's experiences, parents request information regarding their child's conversations with a counselor for three reasons: curiosity, to have a better understanding of their child, and/or to protect (defend) themselves. When parents are merely curious or request information with the intention of understanding their child and the counselor grants their request, this action reinforces the mistaken idea that children do not need or deserve privacy. This issue involves the negotiation of the parents' right to know about their child and the child's rights of freedom of speech and thought. When parents request information to protect or defend themselves, that is, to neutralize the child's information given to the counselor or suggest that the child has been less than honest with the counselor, a hidden motive may be involved that cannot be adequately assessed because the counselor usually does not know in advance why the parent is requesting the information. This is not to suggest that most parents have something to hide but that some counselors may be losing sight of the rationale for confidentiality, that is, the client's right to confidentiality regardless of age.

It might be that counseling clients who are less than 10 years old does not meet the first requirement of a confidential communication, as suggested by Van Hoose and Kottler (1978), namely that client and counselor understand that information from a counseling session will not be shared with anyone else. Counselors may not include, as a part of their counseling behavior, a discussion or explanation of confidentiality to their 6-year-old clients. It is the author's hunch that counselors do one of the following: (a) early in the counseling session, regardless of the age of the client, explain the issue of confidentiality, including when the counselor will and will not keep information confidential; (b) choose not to discuss confidentiality until the client brings up the issue; (c) have the intention of keeping the child's information confidential, but, when pressed (by parents, teachers, principals), sometimes reveal the information communicated by the child. It is apparent that the first approach is congruent with Van Hoose and Kottler's first requirement of a confidential communication. The second approach may meet the requirement of mutual understanding of confidentiality but depends on the client's initiative. Finally, counselors who intend to keep confidences, but may, in fact, disclose information (for the good of the child, because the parent has a right to know— "If I were the parent I would like this information," to ensure the teacher's or principal's cooperation) do not meet Van Hoose and Kottler's first criterion for a confidential communication.

Is confidentiality essential to the maintenance of the child-counselor relationship? Would giving parents and teachers confidential information shared by the child do any harm if these adults promise not to tell the child or to hold the content of the confidence against the child or promise to use the information for the child's benefit? Would the release of information in fact harm the relationship the counselor has established with the client? Unfortunately, the answers are unknown, and again the counselor seems to be placing a bet with the client's money.

There are occasions when a counselor must reveal a confidence. They include: (a) when the client requests it, (b) when not to do so would result in clear danger to the client or others, and (c) when the courts request it. Some children will request the counselor to speak to parents, teachers, or other children. Given that confidentiality is a privilege of clients, such a request is well within their rights. When the counselor suspects that to reveal confidential information will protect the child from harm (in cases of child abuse or neglect, for example), the counselor is legally and ethically bound to report such information. In some instances child-clients do reveal information about someone else (peer or parent) that poses a dilemma for the counselor. For example, a child may report that another child is being abused (even if they do not use the term *abused*, their description of the activity sounds like abuse). The counselor must now make two decisions: first, are the child's reported observations accurate; and second, if they seem accurate, should the counselor take steps to investigate and report the abuse if it has occurred.

The courts may also ask a counselor to disclose confidential information. This is most likely to occur as a follow-up to a reported case of child abuse or when the child is a foster child and placement decisions need to be made. Van Hoose and Kottler (1978) and Stude and McKelvey (1979) state that unless a state statute specifically deals with privileged communication between a counselor and client, one cannot assume the courts will hold such communication legally privileged.

Recommendations

The issue of confidentiality is involved in every counseling interaction. The following suggestions are offered as guidelines for legal and ethical behavior on the part of the counselor who works with children.

1. Whether the topic of confidentiality is discussed or not, all communications between the child-client and counselor are, in fact, confidential (APA, 1981; APGA, 1981). Therefore, the counseling session itself, and not explicit agreements between the counselor and client, determines the validity of confidentiality for the child.

2. Informal discussion of case material, as opposed to a consultation, with persons not directly involved is a breach of confidentiality. Case material may be discussed with another professional when the focus of the discussion is on helping the client. Counselors who feel the need to "vent their feelings" should center the discussion on themselves, keeping the identity of the client private.

3. "Written or oral reports present only data germane to the purposes on an . . . evaluation and every effort is made to avoid undue invasion of privacy" (APA, 1981, p. 5). If you are asked to report on a child's behavior in the classroom, do not include your opinions of the parents' social standing or siblings' extracurricular activities.

4. When a client has revealed information that indicates involvement in an activity that is likely to bring harm to himself or herself or to someone else, the counselor should: (a) try to persuade the client to discontinue the activity and (b) explain the counselor's responsibility to inform appropriate authorities about the "condition" without revealing the client's identity. If steps (a) and (b) do not deter the client, the counselor is ethically bound to (c) "take reasonable personal action or inform responsible authorities" (APGA, 1981, p. 1). The authorities (parents, school, legal) will be determined by the context of the situation and the counselor's judgment of which authority will best serve the needs of the client.

5. If the counselor is subpoenaed to testify in a legal proceeding but does not wish to reveal information to protect the client's best interests, the counselor may: (a) become an agent of the client's attorney (that is, by revealing the

child's case, the counselor may invoke the attorney-client—
the counselor in this case—privilege. The attorney must
raise the privilege in court for the counselor to be protected
by it.) and (b) request that the information be received in
the judge's chamber rather than in open court. Neither of
these options guarantees the counselor's privilege not to
reveal information. "Ethical codes do not supersede the
law" (Stude & McKelvey, 1979, p. 456).

6. In instances in which the counselor is not sure of actions'
to be taken, "consultations with other professionals must
be used where possible" (APGA, 1981, p. 1). Other professionals include, but are not limited to, members of the
pupil personnel team, school administrators, community
mental health agencies, the school solicitor, university professors, and various experts in the field (errors of omission
or commission may be more expensive than a long-distance
phone call).

7. When parents or school personnel request information about
the client, the counselor should first consider the client's
right to privacy. If, in the counselor's judgment, significant
others have a need to know and revealing information would
be in the child's best interest, the counselor should respond
by telling these adults what they can do or refrain from
doing to help the child. In this way the child's communications are still privileged. In the author's experience this
suggestion has been well received by parents and teachers.
Adults who request information because they are curious
or truly interested in their child's welfare seem satisfied
with this approach.

The Parent's Request Revisited

Based on the above recommendations the answers to the questions posed in the example cited above are as follows:

1. The child may have spoken to a parent about the counseling
session. Confidentiality is the child-client's privilege, and
disclosing information is well within his or her rights. Even
if the child has spoken with a parent, however, the counselor is ethically bound to refrain from disclosing information without the permission of the child-client unless
the counselor has reason to believe that the child may

become involved in self-destructive behavior or may harm someone else.

2. The specific effects on the child, parent, or counselor are unknown. It would seem logical to assume that, to some degree, the child may trust you, as well as other adults, less than before. The parent may believe that the counselor is like a big brother or sister watching their child and willing to report back whenever the parent requests it. The counselor may begin to believe that if no harm came to the child this time, there will be no risk the next time. This belief may be hazardous to the child's psychological health.

3. In the author's experience, many children who referred themselves were trying to solve interpersonal as well as intrapersonal problems and were asking for guidance. These children used the counselor as a reference and not as a referee. They were taking steps toward greater self-reliance and personal control. Revealing the confidences of these children would discourage their efforts to develop their own repertoire of problem-solving behaviors.

4. Regardless of the referral source, when parents or teachers request information about the content of counseling sessions with a child-client, it is suggested that the counselor offer suggestions about what the interested adult can do to help the child rather than disclosing specific information.

Conclusion

Counselors and psychologists who work with children quickly learn that the size of the problems do not always correspond to the size of the client. These professionals need to take special care to protect their client's best interests. They are frequently involved in the task of deciding how to negotiate the rights and privileges of their clients with the rights of adult caregivers. It is the author's hope that the suggestions above will aid counselors and psychologists in their efforts to deal with the issue of confidentiality with children.

References

American Personnel and Guidance Association. *Ethical standards*. Falls Church, Va.: Author, 1981.

American Psychological Association. *Ethical principles of psychologists*. Washington, D.C.: Author, 1981.

Erikson, E.H. *Childhood and society* (2nd. ed.). New York: W.W. Norton, 1963.

Goldman, L. Privilege or privacy I. *Personnel and Guidance Journal*, 1969, *48*, 88.

Musser, P.H., Conger, J.J., & Kagan, J. *Child development and personality* (4th ed.). New York: Harper & Row, 1974.

Stude, E.W., & McKelvey, J. Ethics and the law: Friend or foe? *Personnel and Guidance Journal*, 1979, *57*, 453–456.

Van Hoose, W.H., & Kottler, J.A. *Ethical and legal issues in counseling and psychotherapy*. San Francisco: Jossey-Bass, 1978.

Wagner, C.A. Confidentiality and the school counselor. *Personnel and Guidance Journal*, 1981, *59*, 305–310.

Ethics and School Records

Margaret M. Walker and *Marva J. Larrabee*

Maintaining the confidentiality of school records was a problem for many educational institutions in the 1970s. Federal legislation brought public attention to the problem of maintaining and gaining access to those records. Counselors who are concerned with safeguarding the rights of students are often asked to manage some aspects of school record keeping. Without specific guidelines for interpreting school district policy regarding records, personnel who have little or no training in the legal and ethical aspects of record keeping can harm the public image of the school system and may precipitate court cases with long-range, damaging effects to students and to schools.

Detailed guidelines for implementing school board policy concerning school records are especially necessary for schools in which a certified counselor is not available or for schools in which a counselor is employed on a part-time basis. Of course, it is important for all school counselors to examine the ethical issues regarding school records, but counselors must also be knowledgeable of the state and local legislation related to handicapped students.

To assist counselors in safeguarding the rights of students and parents, this article summarizes relevant literature that defines school records, clarifies content and access terminology, and provides a basis for developing specific guidelines that local school personnel may use daily to cope with conflicting opinions on record keeping procedures and with the complications introduced by computer use.

School Records and Legislation

The Family Educational Rights and Privacy Act of 1974, or the Buckley Amendment, became law in November 1974, and the final rules for its implementation were published in June 1976 (reprinted in Callis, Pope, & DePauw, 1982). Perhaps the most important segment of the law stated that any school district may be denied federal funds if parents are not permitted to inspect the school records of their children or if other relatives who are not guardians have access to these records without parental consent (Department of Health, Education, and Welfare, 1976, reprinted in Callis et al., 1982).

In an early study of counselors' opinions, Rezny and Dorow (1961) commented that counselors believed the "common yardstick for measuring who should have access to confidential information is based on personal opinion rather than a prevailing attitude among all teachers" (p. 250). The apparent differences between the attitudes of counselors and teachers regarding confidentiality continue because teachers are generally unaware of the ethical standards that counselors must follow and the relevance of those standards to school records. Since the Buckley Amendment was passed, the American Association for Counseling and Development (AACD) and state and local boards of education have attempted to define the rights of students regarding their school records (Getson & Schweid, 1976; Kazalunas, 1977).

Although policy statements have been issued by boards of education, as required by federal law, specific guidelines for daily use by counselors and other school personnel may not exist. In the absence of these guidelines counselors and other school personnel are left with little more than personal conviction about what constitutes legal or ethical standards for record keeping. The professional ethical standards of teachers, administrators, and counselors may aid decision making, but these documents do not address specific situations involving school records and their access.

Contents of Records

The term *school records*, as used in this article, includes those individual records for each student, including academic progress, test scores, and other data, that are generally kept in a cumulative folder in the main office of many schools. The clarification of the contents of school records offered by Bernard and Fullmer (1977) and Schrier (1980) is specifically related to student records as described in the Buckley Amendment. Bernard and Fullmer identified the contents of student records as identification data, home background, health information, educational history, anecdotal remarks, case summaries, and recommendations. The first four terms are understood readily, but the headings that are not self-explanatory are defined as follows:

- *Anecdotal remarks*—observation of interest, prominent abilities (art, athletics, leadership), relationships with peers and school personnel, disciplinary incidents.
- *Case summary*—usually employed only for pupils with a personal or social dilemma that impedes growth. The purpose is to draw from the data obtained in the anecdotal remarks those elements that seem significant in understanding the student, planning counseling sessions, and choosing methods for working with the student.
- *Recommendations*—remarks of previous counselors and teachers or the result of staff conferences. These should be dated, and, of course, brief (Bernard & Fullmer, 1977, p. 83).

In one example of school district guidelines referring to the contents of student records, Shannon (undated) stated that these records should include:

any and all official records, files and data directly related to. . .children, including all material that is incorporated into each student's cumulative folder, and intended for school use or to be available to parties outside the school or system, and especially including, but not necessarily limited to, identifying data, academic work completed, level of achievement (grades, standardized achievement test scores), attendance data, scores on standardized intelligence, aptitude and psychological tests, interest inventory results, health data, family background information, teacher or counselor ratings and observations, and verified reports of serious or recurrent behavior patterns. (p.5)

Perhaps all of the contents described above should be contained in students' cumulative files. In that case the use of and access to these files must be controlled and carefully monitored according to the law.

Access to Records

Some counselors and administrators need to be more familiar with the law regulating access to school records, especially access by nonschool personnel. When individual privacy is violated by the actions of local school personnel, the results usually are damaging to the school in which the mishandling of records occurred. Three critical obligations that ensure compliance with the Buckley Amendment are: (a) to establish policies regarding record keeping, (b) to establish guidelines for inspecting records, and (c) to provide an opportunity for parents to challenge the accuracy of the school records (Kazalunas, 1977; Shannon, undated). These obligations are the responsibilities of the school system, the counselors, and the administrators. The law specifies that policies must be written to determine who has access to records and student information without the written permission of parents. Any ambiguities that develop outside the scope of the specific information already discussed must be resolved in local school district regulations which guide school counselors and other school personnel.

In school districts where there are no regulations, where regulations are not publicized regularly, or where there are minimal general guidelines available, decisions regarding use of records are usually left to local school personnel. Because of the diversity of personnel making these decisions (e.g., administrators, counselors, teachers, nurses, psychologists, social workers, attendance officers, or other support staff), the decisions invariably reflect personal views, standards, and values (George, 1972). George contended that the legal status of various kinds of school records is of primary concern. He clearly delineated the records classified as "public records," even though confusion continues about which school records are truly public.

Public Versus Quasi-Public Records

It is not usually clear whether student records are public or private (George, 1972). For school counselors this confusion raises at least two ethical issues:

(a) How should information be released to parents, other schools, and interested parties? (b) How should counselors resolve conflicts between district guidelines for handling student records, local school implementation of policy, and the counselor's own interpretation of the applicable ethical standards and law regarding which records are public or quasi-public? George explained the distinction between public and quasi-public records by asserting:

> Public records are generally defined as those being open to all with "lawful, proper, and legitimate interests,"

such as police, researchers, journalists, employers, etc. Quasi-public records are usually defined as those open only to "real parties of interest," e.g., the public, parent legal counsel, or physician. (p. 45)

The Buckley Amendment specifies the scope of student records as "including all material that is incorporated into each student's cumulative record folder and intended for school use or to be available to parties outside the school or school system" (Gibson & Mitchell, 1981, p. 367).

Considering these descriptions and definitions, counselors should probably view school records as quasi-public. This view, advocated long ago by Burt (1964), seems to afford the most protection for students and to be in accord with the legal regulations that must be translated into actual daily practices in local schools.

Although student records may be considered actual property of students and their parents, they are also state property in the custody of school districts (George, 1972). George cited the American Bar Association Section of Individual Rights and Responsibilities to explain that improper disclosure can be avoided by separating academic records from disciplinary records and by formulating an explicit policy statement regarding content of and access to records. Of course, the Buckley Amendment addressed these issues and gave legislative credence to earlier recommendations that information "from disciplinary or counseling files should not be available to unauthorized persons within the institution or to any person outside the institution without the express consent of the student involved except under legal compulsion or in cases where the safety of persons or property is involved" (George 1972, p. 47). Compliance with the law requires permission from the parents of minors. This position on counseling records seems generally compatible with the ethical standards of counselors; however, to comply with the Buckley Amendment a counselor should not share his or her notes or make them accessible to any other school personnel if they are to be considered separate from school records.

Gibson, Mitchell, and Higgins (1983) stated conditions under which the establishment of ethical standards is appropriate: "In any activity where one human being is professionally concerned with the well-being of another, consideration must be given to providing ethical guidelines for the guidance and protection of both the professionals' membership and the clients they serve" (pp. 168–169). School record keeping and related counselor duties certainly fit these conditions although AACD and American School Counselor Association ethical standards do not address specifically the daily concerns resulting from the Buckley Amendment.

Ethical Dilemmas for Counselors

Many changes have occurred in schools since the Buckley Amendment was passed. Because of changing social patterns in our culture and new legislation or interpretations of various aspects of the law, school policies need continuous review to remain fair and reasonable (Ball, 1973). It is often impossible for school personnel to foresee situations involving content and access to student records that are not covered by existing policies of the local school district. Atypical situations pose ethical dilemmas for most school counselors and for other school personnel. For example, when computers were first used in school record keeping, new problems compounded record-keeping procedures that were not yet delineated clearly. Through computer use information is stored and retrieved easily and quickly. The nature of the storage-retrieval action sometimes forces school personnel to make rapid decisions regarding use and access to student data.

To answer the legal and ethical questions raised by computer use, professionals must reconsider such issues as security of record-keeping, inspection and release of records, and the rights of parents and children to privacy. These student record dilemmas are aligned closely with the ethical standards of confidentiality for school counselors. Wagner (1978) specified six areas in which information may or may not be shared and he clearly stated that such decisions require knowledge of the American Personnel and Guidance Association (now AACD) *Ethical Standards* (1981) as well as:

> state statutes on privileged communication . . ., the state education department's position on the counselor and confidentiality in the schools, the state laws of child abuse, parental attitudes in the local community, the school board's position on the counselor and confidentiality, the details of the Buckley Amendment, and their own values towards children, parental authority, and school authority. (p. 247)

Guidelines for Record Keeping

Although Burt (1964) was emphatic two decades ago about establishing relevant procedures for record keeping, policies developed by school districts to comply with the Buckley Amendment may be too vague to be practical for the daily dilemmas encountered by counselors and other school personnel. Elementary and middle school counselors are guided by legislation and school district policies, but additional guidelines may be essential for the protection of students and staff. Considering the technological advances in school record keeping procedures, many school district guidelines may need revision. In addition, school personnel have 10 years of experience implementing the Buckley Amendment, and counselors in particular may have first-hand knowledge of school record-keeping procedures that may be questionable or illegal. It is reasonable that counselors and other school personnel may need more specific guidance on daily operational procedures than legislation or school district policies provide. The pressures of daily operations may be reduced when highly specific local school procedures are developed by school staff and made available to all personnel in each local school.

Before the Buckley Amendment, McMahan (1970) indicated that state and local authorities hesitated or sometimes neglected to provide specific guidelines and policies regarding the issues associated with school records, their contents, and the persons granted access to those records. Although the Buckley Amendment requires school districts to develop written policy on these matters, there may be little consistency in the actual handling of records on a daily basis in local schools. As a result of the limits usually stated in district policies, school counselors may be pressured by nonschool sources or by school personnel to overlook policy or ethical considerations. Practical local school guidelines developed in accordance with district policy and with the ethical standards of counselors would be beneficial in coping with these pressures.

Although administrators and teachers are bound by the ethical standards of various national education groups, some individuals actually pressure elementary and middle school counselors to violate confidentiality (Patterson, 1971). Marsh and Kinnick (1970) cautioned counselors not to assume that other school personnel will maintain all confidences. They concluded that counselors should participate in the formulation of policies related to students' rights to confidentiality. Of course, such a recommendation is also applicable to establishing specific local school guidelines related to student records. Once local schools establish specific guidelines for using the law and the record-keeping policies of the school district, all school personnel can be expected to abide by them if they are regularly discussed by elementary and middle school staff. Other steps must also be taken. It is important to teach the legal responsibilities related to the counselor's role in counselor education programs and to include similar instruction in the educational training programs of other school personnel.

In-service training related to the legal and ethical aspects of record keeping is possible on a regular basis for professional school personnel, but such matters may be neglected for other school staff. Wagner (1981) reported that approximately 50% of elementary, middle, and secondary counselors agreed that they were concerned about secretarial handling of confidential material. In some districts this worry may be expanded to include teachers aides, student workers, or other school personnel who have access to any particular student's record or to school records in general. Counselors may need to address these issues by participating in the review and development of specific record-keeping procedures in their local schools. In addition counselors may find that initiating in-service training regarding these matters or conducting the training themselves may be well within the consultative role of the counselor in the school.

As indicated above in our review of selected school district policies on record keeping, development of specific guidelines requires knowledge of the law, periodic review of changes in the law, development of a policy that is specific for guiding the use of records (Allendale County School Board, 1983), specification of who has access to particular records, and procedures for release of information contained in the records. Certainly, a periodic review of district policies is essential, but actual examination of local school implementation procedures is needed to ensure that school district policy complies with the law in daily practice.

The existence of problems with maintenance and confidentiality of school records requires counselors to work in a professional manner to safeguard the rights of students. Elementary and middle school counselors who accept the challenge of protecting student rights can be instrumental in initiating district policy review and revision and in developing local school procedures for implementing policy. Specific guidelines for the use of school records can be formulated to enable school personnel to protect student rights, to maintain confidentiality, to monitor and govern access to records, and to promote reasonable amounts of procedural uniformity throughout each school system. Elementary and middle school counselors have the skills to facilitate an exchange of ideas among school personnel that may result in establishing or correcting record-keeping procedures to ensure the best possible implementation of legal and ethical standards for school records in daily practice.

References

American Personnel and Guidance Association. (1981). *Ethical standards*. Falls Church, VA: Author.

Allendale County School Board. (1983, July). *Proposed school board policy* (revised). Allendale, SC: Author.

Ball, M.A. (1973). Do counselors need to know about due process? *School Counselor, 21*, 130–135.

Bernard, H.W., & Fullmer, D.W. (1977). *Principles of guidance* (2nd ed.). New York: Crowell.

Burt, L.A. (1964). Inspection and release of records to parents. In M.L. Ware (Ed.), *Law of guidance and counseling* (pp. 37–49). Cincinnati: W.H. Anderson.

Callis, R., Pope, S.K., & DePauw, M. (1982). *Ethical standards casebook* (3rd ed.). Falls Church, VA: American Personnel and Guidance Association.

George, T.W. (1972). The law and pupil school records. *NASSP Bulletin, 56*, 132–141.

Getson, R., & Schweid, R. (1976). School counselors and the Buckley Amendment—Ethical standards squeeze. *School Counselor, 24*, 56–58.

Gibson, R.L., & Mitchell, M.H. (1981). *Introduction to guidance*. New York: Macmillan.

Gibson, R.L., Mitchell, M.H., & Higgins, R.E. (1983). *Development and management of counseling programs and guidance services*. New York: Macmillan.

Kazalunas, J.R. (1977). Conscience, the law, and practical requirements of the Buckley Amendment. *School Counselor, 24*, 243–247.

McMahan, I. (1970, September). School records: Invasion of privacy? *Parents' Magazine*, pp. 64–99.

Marsh, J.J., & Kinnick, B.G. (1970). Let's close the confidentiality gap. *Personnel and Guidance Journal, 48*, 362–365.

Patterson, C.H. (1971). Are ethics different in different settings? *Personnel and Guidance Journal, 50*, 251–259.

Rezny, A.A., & Dorow, E. (1961). Confidential information and the guidance program. *Journal of Educational Research, 54*, 243–250.

Schrier, C.J. (1980, November). Guidelines for record-keeping under privacy and open-access laws. *Social Work*, 452–457.

Shannon, T. (undated). *Privacy and the right to know as applied to schools receiving federal funds*. San Diego: Deputy Superintendent, San Diego Schools.

Wagner, C.A. (1978). Elementary school counselors' perceptions of confidentiality with children. *School Counselor, 25*, 240–248.

Privileged Communication in School Counseling: Status Update

Vernon Lee Sheeley and *Barbara Herlihy*

In this article we report the findings of research conducted in 1985 to update the status of privileged communication statutes pertaining to school counselors and pupils they counsel. Privileged communication is a legal right that exists by state statute and protects pupil clients from having their confidential communications disclosed in court without their permission.

Rationale

It has been suggested that clients will be more likely to seek counseling help and to share concerns if their counselors can guarantee that their confidences will be protected from disclosure (Deblaissie, 1976; Gade, 1972; Litwack, Rochester, Oates, & Addison, 1969; Norton, 1970; Nugent, 1981; Peters, 1970). Such assurances are important in the school setting.

Children and youth in modern society act out major events and transitions of their lives with organizations, including educational institutions, as attentive partners. Among the educators are school counselors involved in face-to-face encounters with pupils to help them develop positive self-concepts. The extent of pupil client disclosures to school counselors depends on how much personal information the situations warrant; however, confidential treatment of specific pupil self-revelations is often necessary to maintain communication relationships.

Ethical standards of professional associations, including the American School Counselor Association (ASCA), support the legitimate expectation of confidentiality—to withhold information (either voluntarily or in response to a demand when the counselor does not have authorization from clients) except under certain conditions. Therefore, school counselors have a professional obligation to honor the pupils' rights to have private conversations with them. Privileged communication statutes further advance societal concerns for student rights.

School counselors who want to know whether their communications with pupils are privileged by statutes and exactly what these statutes mean for them in practice may find it difficult to obtain answers to these questions. One source of confusion has been that the terms *ethical confidentiality* and *privileged communication*, although they are not synonymous, have sometimes been used interchangeably in the literature (Litwack et al., 1969). Also, sources to whom school counselors might turn for information have not always been clear in their understanding of privileged communication law. For example, Peer (1985) surveyed state guidance directors late in 1982 and found that only 627 were certain whether pupil clients of secondary school counselors under their supervision were protected by privileged communication statutes. Our study, conducted about 2 years later, revealed that 78% were certain.

Method

Contacts with the legislative research commission council, state librarians, and Department of Education officials in the 50 states, the District of Columbia, and the six U.S. trust territories yielded relevant privileged communication statutes. Statutes pertaining solely to privacy of student records were excluded.

Results and Discussion

We found that 20 states have currently existing privileged communication statutes that provide full or partial protection of communications between school counselors and their pupil clients. School counselors in one state (Ohio) are extended privileged communication rights under the professional counselor licensure law.

The following are questions school counselors might ask about privileged communication. Responses are based on data obtained in this study and a review of the literature.

What is the background of school counselor efforts to obtain privileged communication rights?

Because professional codes of ethics are based on the belief that confidentiality is essential to successful counseling, privileged communication legislation would logically seem to have accompanied the development of ethical and professional standards. Yet, although the American Personnel and Guidance Association (APGA) (now American Association for Counseling and Development [AACD]), has stressed the importance of confidentiality in its ethical standards first published in 1961 (AACD, 1981), privileged communication legislation has been a more recent phenomenon.

At the end of the 1960s, only three states (Michigan, 1963; Indiana, 1965; North Dakota, 1969) had legislated privileged communication rights for pupil clients with school counselors. Early in the next decade, there was much more legislative activity. In 1974, the Privileged Communication Committee of ASCA conducted a national survey and found that 16 states provided full or partial protection to school counselors (Shafer, 1974). In addition to Indiana, Michigan, and North Dakota, the 14 states we found and the years in which their privileged communication statutes took effect are: Idaho, Maryland, Montana, North Carolina, Oklahoma, Oregon, South Carolina, South Dakota, and Washington, 1971; Pennsylvania, 1972; Maine and Nevada, 1973; Iowa and Kentucky, 1974.

By 1974, however, the momentum had begun to stall. In 1973 alone, school counselors in 13 states failed in their attempts to acquire privileged communication rights (Shafer, 1974). In some cases, legislation was introduced but failed to gain committee approval; in others, the bill was forwarded out of committee but not approved by the legislature. In New York, the bill was vetoed by the governor, who feared that it would inhibit counselors from reporting pupil drug usage. Despite continuing legislative efforts since 1974, only three more states (Connecticut, 1978; Wisconsin, 1979; and Ohio, 1984) have established privileged communication statutes specifically for pupil clients of school counselors.

To which school professional personnel is privilege extended?

State statutes vary considerably with respect to which professional relationships are granted privileged communication rights. Statutes in six states (Kentucky, Maine, North Carolina, North Dakota, South Carolina, and Washington) extend privilege specifically and exclusively to the pupil client–school counselor relationship.

The statutes in the remaining states include other school professional personnel in addition to counselors. Five states (Connecticut, Maryland, Michigan, Oklahoma, and Oregon) extend privileged communication to all professional employees in the school. The nine remaining states extend privileged communication to school counselors and in various combinations to other specified professionals including psychology teachers (Montana and Ohio), psychologists (Idaho, Iowa, Montana, Nevada, Ohio, Pennsylvania, South Dakota, and Wisconsin), school nurses (Indiana, Iowa, Montana, Pennsylvania, and Wisconsin), home and school visitors (Pennsylvania), and social workers (Indiana, Iowa, Ohio, and Wisconsin).

What limitations and exceptions do the statutes impose?
In five states (Connecticut, Maryland, South Carolina, Washington, and Wisconsin), the only communications between school counselors and their pupil clients that are privileged are those related to student alcohol and drug problems. At the other extreme, some states specify no limitations. For example, the Indiana statute reads in its entirety, "A school counselor is immune from disclosing privileged or confidential communication made to him as a counselor by a student. The matters communicated are privileged and protected against disclosure" (N. Thoms, personal communication, March 7, 1983). Other states vary in their degree and scope of protection. Some statutes apply to criminal and civil cases, while others apply only to civil cases.

A number of states specify circumstances under which the counselor must provide information. These should be viewed as exceptions, however, rather than as limitations, because they describe circumstances in which school counselors are legally or ethically obligated to disclose information for the safety and well-being of the pupil client and others. Exceptions to privileged communication laws and states that require each include (a) reporting crime or likelihood of crime (Connecticut); (b) reporting child abuse or neglect (North Carolina, Ohio, Pennsylvania, and Washington); (c) when there is clear and imminent danger to the client or others (Maine, Ohio, Oregon, and South Dakota); (d) when presiding judge compels disclosure (North Carolina and Ohio); and (e) when client's condition requires others to assume responsibility for him or her (Maine). States other than Indiana with statutes that do not specify major limitations or exceptions to privileged communication include Idaho, Kentucky, Michigan, Montana, North Dakota, and Oklahoma. Nevada has an exception only for communications relating to criminal offense.

Who may waive counselor privilege?

Several writers have noted that it is important for counselors to remember that privileged communication is the client's right (Corey, Corey, & Callanan, 1984; Eberlein, 1977; Locke, 1984; Nugent, 1981). Thus, if the pupil chooses to waive privilege, the counselor has no grounds for withholding information. Four state statutes include provisions for involving parents in the decision whether to waive counselor privilege when the pupil is a minor child. Two of these states (Michigan and Pennsylvania) require parent consent for disclosure and the two others (Kentucky and Montana) require student and parent consent when the pupil is a minor.

Implications for Practice

As Remley (1985) has noted, ethical and legal standards sometimes disagree in such areas as confidentiality and privileged communication, presenting conflicting approaches to the same situation. Thus, school counselors in the 30 states without privileged communication protection may find themselves faced with an ethical dilemma when called on to testify in court. They are not completely without recourse, however. They may explain their codes of ethics to the presiding judge and ask that privilege be extended to them. Or, as Stude and McKelvey (1979) have suggested, the counselor might reveal the client's confided information to the attorney handling the client's case, thus making the counselor an agent of the attorney and perhaps entitling the counselor to invoke the attorney-client privilege. Finally, counselors may request that their testimony be heard *in camera* (in the judge's chambers or in open court without spectators). Some attorneys advise that judges may be sympathetic to such requests.

On the other hand, school counselors need to remember that privileged communication laws run counter to the common law tradition that the public has a right and the court has a need to hear every person's evidence. Thus, school counselors should not automatically assume that an existing statute will exempt them from testifying in court, because "privileged communication laws are an exception under the rules of evidence, and the courts may require that every detail of the law be met before allowing a privilege to stand" (Knapp & VandeCreek, 1983, p. 95).

Conclusion

Questions of confidentiality and privileged communication defy simple answers. School counselors need to exercise their professional judgment and weigh their obligations to confidentiality and nondisclosure against their obligations to others. Professional codes of ethics state that the counselor must reveal information under certain circumstances, such as when there is a clear and imminent danger to the client or to others. In working with clients who are minors, school counselors must frequently involve adults for counseling to be effective. As a result, the pupil's right to confidentiality is sometimes outweighed by the need to inform parents, guardians, teachers, or other adults. In such cases, the counselor should secure the pupil's consent to disclose whenever possible (Remley, 1985). Corey et al. (1984) have pointed out that counseling is a risky venture.

School counselors need to be knowledgeable about privileged communication laws and their applications, and at the same time they must remain sensitive to the broader implications of their decisions in practice.

References

American Association for Counseling and Development (AACD) (1981). *Ethical standards*. Alexandria, VA: Author.

Corey, G., Corey, M.S., & Callanan, P. (1984). *Issues and ethics in the helping professions* (2nd ed.). Monterey, CA: Brooks/Cole.

Deblaissie, R.R. (1976). The counselor, privileged communication, and the law. *Educational Leadership*, 33, 522–524.

Eberlein, L. (1977) Counselors beware! Clients have rights! *Personnel and Guidance Journal*, 56, 219–223.

Gade, E.E. (1972). Implications of privileged communication laws for counselors. *School Counselor*, 19, 150–152.

Knapp, S., & VandeCreek, L. (1983). Privileged communications and the counselor. *Personnel and Guidance Journal*, 62, 83–85.

Litwack, L., Rochester, B., Oates, R., & Addison, W. (1969). Testimonial privileged communication and the school counselor. *School Counselor*, 17, 108–111.

Locke, D.C. (1984). Counselor registration in North Carolina. *Journal of Counseling and Development*, 63, 45–46.

Norton, J. (1970). Privilege or privacy: Different issues. *Personnel and Guidance Journal*, 48, 523–524.

Nugent, F.A. (1981). *Professional counseling: An overview.* Monterey, CA: Brooks/ Cole.

Peer, G.G. (1985). The status of secondary school guidance: A national survey. *School Counselor, 32,* 181–189.

Peters, D. (1970). Feedback—Confidentiality and colleges. *Personnel and Guidance Journal, 48,* 522–523.

Remley, T.P., Jr. (1985). The law and ethical practices in elementary and middle schools. *Elementary School Guidance & Counseling, 19,* 181–189.

Shafer, J.D. (1974). *Committee report: Privileged communication.* Washington, DC: American School Counselor Association (ERIC Document Reproduction Service No. ED 092 845).

Stude, E.W., & McKelvey, J. (1979). Ethics and the law: *Friend or foe? Personnel and Guidance Journal, 57,* 453–456.

3

LEGAL ISSUES

Legal standards of practice are different from ethical standards. Remley (1985) explores the differences and comments on the legal implications of confidentiality, court testimony, and counseling malpractice. He provides specific recommendations for school counselors who seek to practice in an ethical manner within the law.

Many schools have policies that differentiate between the rights of custodial and noncustodial parents, and school counselors often are required to implement such policies. The law is clear that, barring a specific court order to the contrary, noncustodial parents have all rights regarding their children except the right to have custody of the children permanently in their homes. Aiello and Humes (1987) explore the background and reasoning behind this legal concept in relation to access to children's school records.

When federal legislation known as the 1978 Hatch Amendment was passed and revised regulations were issued in 1984, a great deal of misinterpretation occurred that inhibited the offering of school counseling services. Eventually it was realized that the amendment's requirement of written parental consent for children to participate in certain school programs covered only a narrow range of activities that were federally funded, were experimental in nature, and involved psychological tests or treatment. Kaplan and Geoffroy (1987) clarify the areas of school activity affected by the Hatch Amendment, and recommend actions for school districts and school counselors in order to comply with this federal mandate.

School counselors often play a major role in administering the school's testing program. Rather than simply giving tests that are selected and scheduled by administrators and then posting the scores in students' records, school counselors also should provide expert advice to school policymakers regarding the appropriate use of tests. Counselors should assist in evaluating each test to determine whether it discriminates in any way against any segment of the school population; whether the test is valid and reliable; whether it is appropriate for the purposes for which it is being used; and whether the test is necessary to achieve the school's objectives. Moreover, the counselor is responsible for helping students to understand the nature and purposes of tests and to interpret test results for students in a clear and understandable manner. Talbutt (1983, in "The Counselor and Testing . . .") summarizes some of the case law and the ethical standards regarding school testing programs.

Because school counselors have access to confidential information about children, there is always a danger that a counselor might disclose some details that might cause embarrassment to students or their families. If a school counselor were to disclose confidential information inappropriately and a student were harmed in some way as a result, the student could bring legal action against the counselor for defamation of character. Talbutt (1983, in "Libel and Slander . . .") sets forth the basis for the law of libel and slander and warns school counselors to avoid common violations.

Even as this book is being printed, the laws regarding abortions for minors are changing. Talbutt (1983, in "Current Legal Trends . . .") gives a background of the laws in effect prior to publication of her article, and discusses implications for school counselors. Generally, school counselors may discuss a student's decision of whether to seek an abortion with the student, but they should also encourage parental involvement when possible. Each case must be decided individually based on the facts as presented.

Herlihy and Sheeley (1988) review relevant court cases and statutes pertaining to "the duty to warn," and they offer advice regarding clients who could be contemplating violence against others. Although the authors suggest guidelines and a decision-making model, school counselors must realize that ultimately they will be required to exercise their own professional judgment as to whether a client poses a real threat to another person.

The Law and Ethical Practices in Elementary and Middle Schools

Theodore P. Remley, Jr.

Although *law* and *ethics* are often mentioned in the same breath, they are separate concepts that need differentiation to be fully understood. Elementary and middle school counselors must understand basic ethical and legal issues to function effectively in their school settings.

Ethical standards are the rules of practice set forth by a profession. Such standards tend to be general and idealistic, seldom answering specific questions for the practitioner. Elementary and middle school counselors seek guidance from the *Ethical Standards* of the American Association for Counseling and Development (AACD, formerly American Personnel and Guidance Association [APGA]) (APGA, 1981) and the *Ethical Standards for School Counselors* (1984) of the American School Counselor Association (ASCA). The AACD and ASCA standards do not address every foreseeable professional dilemma, but they do provide professional counselors with a general framework for making sound ethical decisions regarding their behavior.

Laws, on the other hand, are the standards of behavior a society demands of its members. Laws set forth the rights of citizens and usually define minimal acceptable behavior rather than idealized expectations. There are three basic sources of law: constitutions, statutes, and common law. Constitutions and statutes are passed by state and federal legislative bodies, and common law is inherited from our English ancestors and accepted as the traditional standard of behavior in the United States. The judiciary interprets constitutions, statutes, and the common law and, as a result, often changes the practical application of laws through its decisions.

To practice counseling in a professional manner, elementary and middle school counselors must know and abide by the AACD and ASCA ethical standards. To ensure that they are not abridging the rights of others and that they are abiding by the rules society has set forth, counselors must also have some knowledge of the law.

Unfortunately, ethical and legal standards sometimes disagree in areas such as confidentiality, thus presenting conflicting approaches to the same issue. If a counselor is aware of ethical and legal standards, however, sensitive and potentially explosive situations usually can be resolved in everyone's best interest.

It is impossible to cover comprehensively all the legal issues related to elementary and middle school counseling. As a result, three important topics that involve legal and ethical issues have been chosen for analysis: (a) confidentiality and privileged communication, (b) the counselor as a witness in court proceedings, and (c) counselor malpractice.

Confidentiality and Privileged Communication

Counselors have an ethical responsibility to keep confidential their communication with clients. This simple statement is not so easy, however, for elementary and middle school counselors to put into practice.

Legal Status of Children

Children occupy an unusual position in our legal structure. Although they are guaranteed some of the same protections adults are guaranteed, in many respects the protection of their individual rights depends on the interpretations of those rights by their adult parents or guardians. Before the 19th century children were treated under the law as property of their parents and owed their parents total subservience (Pappas, 1981). A 1979 U.S. Supreme Court decision declared:

> We have recognized three reasons justifying the conclusion that the constitutional rights of children cannot be equated with those of adults: the peculiar vulnerability of children; their inability to make critical decisions in an informed, mature manner; and the importance of the parental role in child rearing. (*Bellotti v. Baird*, 1979)

Some legal experts have argued that each child's capacity to make sound decisions should be evaluated before the right to make decisions is given to the parents (Batey, 1982; Eglit, 1981). Despite this proposition, the prevailing view in our soceiety is that children under the age of majority do not have the capacity or right to make decisions for themselves.

Because of the special status of minors in our society, professionals who work with children feel obligated to involve significant adults in the therapeutic or counseling process. For example, elementary and middle school children may lack the maturity or capacity to solve problems on their own; therefore, counseling these children often involves additional consultation with adults who are important in the child's life. Parents, guardians, siblings, other relatives, teachers, and friends may become clients, consultees, or consultants of the elementary or middle school counselor as a result of a child's presenting problem.

Guidelines for Confidentiality

To whom do counselors owe the ethical obligation of confidentiality? Even the youngest child who becomes a client in the elementary or middle school is entitled to some privacy in a counseling relationship. Cooper and Wanerman (1977) suggested that exact comments of children should not be disclosed to adults and the counselor's impressions should be conveyed with discretion. To be sure that they are fulfilling their confidentiality responsibilities to children who are clients, counselors can take the following steps:

1. Always inform the child before another person is consulted regarding the child's problem. The child's consent is desirable but not always necessary.
2. Try to involve the child in the decision-making process once adults are contacted. Avoid taking actions that may create for the child a feeling of betrayal by the counselor or other involved adults.
3. Keep the child informed of decisions as they are made.

Parents and guardians of children often assume the status of clients when they are contacted by the elementary or middle school counselor regarding a child's problem. Seldom does the counselor simply inform the parents or guardians of a problem and then withdraw from the process. School counselors may even find themselves involved with the family in a counseling relationship. Certainly, parents and guardians expect privacy when they discuss their family problems with an elementary or middle school counselor.

With only one obvious exception, counselors should never
voluntarily disclose information gained in a counseling session with
a family unless the family has consented to such disclosure. The
exception is a situation in which the counselor feels someone is in
"clear and imminent danger" (See Ethical Standard B4, APGA,
1981).

The elementary or middle school counselor must decide whether
the child who is the client or someone associated with the child is
in danger (Ferris and Linville also discuss this counselor decision
in *Elementary School Guidance and Counseling, 19,* 1985). If danger exists, the counselor is obligated, according to the Ethical
Standards (APGA, 1981), to disclose the danger to appropriate
authorities. If a counselor is not sure whether a clear danger exists,
he or she should consult colleagues in a professional manner before
making any disclosures. Many states have statutes requiring counselors to disclose *suspected child abuse,* but fail to define the term.
Thus, counselors must use their professional judgment. Because
of their training, professional counselors are competent to determine whether a party is in danger or whether a child might be the
victim of abuse. Before disclosures of confidential information are
made, however, counselors must be clear about their reasons for
disclosure so they can defend their decisions if necessary at a later
time.

The obligation to keep confidential the information about a
child's problem that is gained in interactions with other adults
seems to vary according to the circumstances. Teachers and principals probably would not expect their conversations regarding a
child's problem to be confidential if they are involved in the child's
problem only as consultants. Relatives of the child or others who
have been identified as closely involved with the problem a child
is experiencing, however, probably would expect the counselor to
keep their communications confidential.

Privileged Communication

If an interaction is designated as privileged communication
under the law, a judge may not force the professional involved to
disclose what was said by a client in an interview. Many counselors
are hesitant to assure clients that their interactions are confidential
because they realize that in most states communications between

elementary or middle school counselors and clients are not legally privileged. Under common law only attorney-client interations were privileged. By statute the legal privilege has been extended to communications with physicians, clergymen, psychologists, social workers, and other mental health professionals. The statutes vary from state to state regarding which relationships are privileged. As reported in a recent survey of ASCA state presidents, only 14 states (California, Idaho, Indiana, Kentucky, Maine, Michigan, Montana, Nevada, North Carolina, North Dakota, Oklahoma, Oregon, Pennsylvania, and South Dakota) have enacted statutes making the interactions between school counselors and clients privileged (Cummings, 1983).

The lack of a statute making confidential the communication between elementary or middle school counselors and their clients in no way affects the counselor's ethical responsibility to keep confidential almost all communications with clients (Corey, Corey, & Callanan, 1979). It is appropriate to assure clients that their interactions with school counselors are confidential, even though there are some exceptions. Only in rare situations must the counselor either take action because clients may be dangerous to themselves or others or disclose the content of communications in a court of law.

Middle school counselors often wonder what their legal responsibilities are to parents when they work with minors regarding issues such as birth control and abortion. The U.S. Supreme Court has held that minors may receive birth control and abortions without parental consent (*Belloti v. Baird*, 1979; *Carey v. Population Services International*, 1977; *Planned Parenthood v. Danforth*, 1976). Although parental consent is not necessary under the law, school counselors must help their clients who are minors decide whether parents or guardians should be involved in birth control or abortion decisions. In such situations, counselors must keep in mind their responsibility to disclose potential dangers to their clients or others if they determine that such dangers exist. Counselors have no legal obligation to inform parents when their clients who are minors indicate their use of birth control, disclose a pregnancy, or discuss an abortion decision. If they do not disclose these situations to parents or guardians, however, these counselors must be ready to defend their decisions that their clients were mature enough to make such decisions without parental involvement and that no clear danger existed for the minors.

Counselors in elementary and middle schools often must involve adults in the problems of their clients who are minors. As a result, the child's expectation of privacy sometimes is outweighed by the need to inform parents, guardians, or other adults. On the other hand, school counselors should keep as confidential as possible details of interactions with their clients who are minors. They also should recognize that some adults involved in a child's problem have expectations of privacy identical to those of the client. Although the child's rights are the primary concern, it is important for counselors to make sure that no person's right to confidentiality is totally disregarded. In fact, because situations requiring disclosure of confidential information are rare, it is essential that the child's consent to disclose be secured whenever possible.

Court Testimony

Elementary and middle school counselors occasionally find themselves involved in the legal system as witnesses. There are a number of situations in which a counselor may appear in court. In a child custody case, elementary or middle school counselors can be subpoenaed by one of a student's parents to provide informational testimony regarding that parent's interaction with school authorities (Ruback, 1982). Also, counselors may have to testify in the prosecution of a parent or guardian accused of child abuse or in a civil challenge of the denial of a petition for a child to be placed in a costly special education program. These situations have been known to involve elementary and middle school counselors; there are numerous other possibilities.

Guidelines for Court Testimony

Elementary and middle school counselors who agree to testify at the request of a party in a case or who are forced through a subpoena to testify against their wishes should follow these guidelines:

1. Avoid discussing the case in casual conversations. Do not offer opinions regarding the merits of the case. Words spoken informally without careful consideration can be used against counselors during cross-examination.
2. Before the court date, attempt to speak either with the attorney representing the side that will be helped by your testimony or to the prosecutor who will be conducting the direct examination. Ask the attorney to review anticipated

questions in advance and to predict questions that might be asked during cross-examination by the opposing attorney.

3. When testifying, be as objective as possible. Relate facts without personal interpretations. If asked an opinion, you should state it freely but be prepared to give the reasoning behind the opinion. Try to relax. All the counselor must do in these situations is tell the truth in an objective manner.

4. If asked to disclose information that you consider confidential, turn to the presiding judge and request that you not be ordered to answer the question. Clearly state that the reason for your request is the importance of confidentiality in counseling relationships and the expectation of privacy the client had at the time the interaction took place. If ordered by the judge to answer the question posed, you should do so; otherwise you can be held in contempt of court and fined or jailed. If you believe that answering such a question would breach an ethical obligation to a client, ask the judge for an opportunity to consult with an attorney.

Expert Witness Issues

In rare cases an elementary or middle school counselor may be asked to appear in a case as an expert witness. An attorney might be interested in such areas of expertise as general child growth and development, effective parenting, emotional needs of children, or standardized testing. Unless counselors are very secure in their knowledge of these areas, they probably should decline requests to appear as expert witnesses. There are many professionals with outstanding educational and experiential expertise in these areas. School counselors should be aware that any expert testimony they give can be challenged by someone with the same or more credibility as an expert.

The credentials of an expert witness are often questioned very closely. Questions may be asked regarding the number of courses taken in the field, whether other professionals know more about the topic, and the witness's specific experiences related to the case. In addition, extensive knowledge of specific subject matter is expected of an expert witness. In most cases the opposing attorney will call an equally or better qualified expert witness to refute testimony given by the first expert witness. Unless elementary and middle school counselors are unusually knowledgeable about a given topic, they will have a difficult time during cross-examination attempting to answer detailed questions that are designed to destroy the counselor's credibility as an expert.

Malpractice

Malpracftice occurs when a professional is guilty of negligent practice (Beis, 1984). Although some professionals are plagued by malpractice suits, school counselors and other mental health professionals and educators are seldom sued (Halleck, 1979). There are few appellate court cases involving school counselors (Burgum & Anderson, 1975). This lack of litigation, however, should not lead elementary and middle school counselors to assume they are immune from such suits.

Elements of Malpractice

For a plaintiff to bring a successful malpractice suit against a professional, the individual must be harmed either physically or emotionally, and the harm must be the direct result of a negligent action or an omission by the professional. For example, elementary or middle school counselors may be sued for malpractice if they fail to notify parents of self-destructive actions being taken by a child, if they compromise someone's reputation in the community by breaching the ethical standard requiring confidentiality, or if they fail to refer a child with deep emotional problems to a psychiatrist or psychologist. These three examples illustrate how varied the allegations may be in malpractice litigation.

To be successful in malpractice suits, plaintiffs must prove through evidence (a) that someone (the plaintiff or perhaps the child of the plaintiff) was harmed, (b) that this harm was the direct result of a counselor's negligent action or omission, and (c) that other counselors practicing in a similar community would not have handled the situation in the same manner.

Preventive Measures

Malpractice suits should not be a major concern for elementary and middle school counselors, but counselors should take preventive measures that are congruent with the current ethical standards (APGA, 1981). Such measures include:

1. Knowing their job descriptions and not deviating significantly from them in their daily work; revising a job de-

scription if it does not reflect current responsibilities or practices.
2. Knowing the AACD and ASCA ethical standards and practicing according to those standards.
3. Consulting with other professionals before acting when difficult legal or ethical situations arise.
4. Attending workshops and conferences to stay informed of current developments in the counseling field.

Most elementary and middle school counselors are either immune from malpractice suits because they are employed by a governmental agency or are covered for malpractice damages by insurance purchased by their schools (Schutz, 1982). Counselors should know whether their schools have such insurance policies and should find out the exact language in the document. As a safety measure, in case the school counselor is exempt from coverage for some reason or in the event the limits of the school policy are exceeded, school counselors should purchase individual professional liability insurance. AACD offers its members the opportunity to participate in a relatively inexpensive group professional liability policy. Counselors who are supervising counselor trainees should insist that these students also purchase liability insurance before beginning their practicum or internship. If these supervisory activities are not a part of a counselor's actual job description, individual professional liability insurance for both parties is essential.

Conclusion

Professional elementary and middle school counselors must be committed to ethical and legal practices. Because ethical standards are much more idealistic than legal standards, the counselor who knows and abides by the rules of practice established by the profession will have little difficulty staying within the law.

Elementary and middle school counselors should keep all client interactions confidential except in a few specific instances. If the counselor relationship is to be effective, clients must be assured of confidentiality so they can feel free to talk openly.

If it is necessary for a school counselor to testify in court, he or she should be as honest and objective as possible. As a witness, the counselor's only obligation is to tell the truth. Elementary and middle school counselors should carefully consider requests to serve as expert witnesses, declining such offers if they do not feel exceptionally well qualified.

Although malpractice is not a major threat to elementary school counselors, they still should take a number of steps to avoid situations in which malpractice suits might be successful. Practicing within their job descriptions, adhering to ethical standards, and keeping informed of current developments in the professional field can help counselors avoid malpractice litigation.

Counseling children necessarily involves adults. Elementary and middle school counselors must be careful to balance the interest of all people involved. There are no specific ethical standards and few laws that tell a counselor when to disclose to an adult information given by a child, how to work with adults with different interests (such as divorcing parents), or how to determine when an adult should be consulted without a child's consent. The recently adopted ASCA *Ethical Standards for School Counselors* (1984) are very helpful, however, and should be reviewed. Because many issues raise questions of judgment, consultation with more experienced counselors or with other peers may be beneficial in resolving dilemmas. Fortunately, most elementary and middle school counselors can face difficult issues successfully and make positive, informed decisions without guidelines that tell them exactly what to do in all possible situations.

References

American Personnel and Guidance Association. (1981). *Ethical standards*. Falls Church, VA: Author.

American School Counselor Association. (1984). *Ethical standards for school counselors*. Alexandria, VA: Author.

Batey, R. (1982). The rights of adolescents. *William and Mary Law Review, 23*, 363–384.

Beis, E.B. (1984). *Mental health and the law*. Rockville, MD: Aspen Systems.

Bellotti v. Baird, 443 U.S. 622 (1979).

Burgum, T., & Anderson, S. (1975). *The counselor and the law*. Washington, DC: American Personnel and Guidance Association Press.

Carey v. Population Services International, 431 U.S. 678 (1977).

Cooper, S., & Wanerman, L. (1977). *Children in treatment*. New York: Brunner/Mazel.

Corey, G., Corey, M.S., & Callanan, P. (1979). *Professional and ethical issues in counseling and psychotherapy*. Monterey, CA: Brooks/Cole.

Cummings, K.E. (1983). *Survey of the status of school counselor privileged communication statutes*. Unpublished report, American School Counselor Association, Alexandria, VA.

Eglit, H. (1981). Of age and constitution. *Chicago Kent Law Review, 57,* 859–914.

Halleck, S.L. (1979). Malpractice in psychiatry. In S.L. Halleck (Ed.), *New directions for mental health services no. 4* (pp. 111–161). San Francisco: Jossey-Bass.

Pappas, A.M. (1981). Introduction. *Columbia Human Rights Law Review, 13,* xxvii-lv.

Planned Parenthood v. Danforth, 428 U.S. 52 (1976).

Ruback, R.B. (1982). Issues in family law: Implications for therapists. In J.C. Hansen & L.L. L'Abate (Eds.), *Values, ethics, legalities and the family therapist* (pp. 100-120). Rockville, MD: Aspen Systems.

Schutz, B.M. (1982). *Legal liability in psychotherapy.* San Francisco: Jossey-Bass.

Counselor Contact of the Noncustodial Parent: A Point of Law

Helen Aiello and *Charles W. Humes*

A persistent issue confronting elementary school counselors is clarification of the noncustodial parent's status regarding access to a child's educational records in the absence of a specific court order or other restraint. The issue becomes a real concern with the passage of the 1974 Family Rights and Privacy Act (FERPA), commonly known as the Buckley Amendment. This federal legislation, part of the sweeping due process reforms of the 1970s, brought public attention to the problem of maintaining and gaining access to records (Gibson, Mitchell, & Higgins, 1983; Hummel & Humes, 1984). The law and regulations do define important terms such as *parent, custody,* and *court order* ("Privacy Rights," 1980), but there is room for interpretation, particularly regarding the ethics of confidentiality (Remley, 1985).

During the past decade much has been written about the law and its regulations, with an entire issue of *Elementary School Guidance & Counseling* (Larrabee & Terres, 1985) devoted to the topic. The law and regulations, however, do not address the issue of whether a school counselor, with good reason, may contact a non-custodial parent to share information without notifying the custodial parent. Obviously, this is a highly charged emotional issue and can engender both rancor and litigation. The answer to the dilemma may be found in case law. These points interpret the law and regulations through judicial decisions. An actual case is presented below, including the question posed, a statement of facts, the issues, and a conclusion.

Question

Should a counselor contact a noncustodial parent when the records are devoid of a court order or other document prohibiting such contact and when the counselor's best professional judgment indicates such contact be made?

A divorced mother has custody of twin daughters enrolled in an elementary school. The father has visitation rights. There is a history of conflict between the mother and the twins, conflict centered around the mother's restrictive notion of discipline and a preoccupation with grades. A recent incident was the basis of the twins seeking counseling intervention. Thereafter, they sought frequent counseling and guidance. Their academic records revealed that grades and behavior were suffering.

A referral from a teacher and the counselor's observation of their depressed states prompted a referral to a social worker. The counselor suggested a call to their mother. The twins begged the counselor not to do so. Instead, they asked that their father be called because it was his weekend to have the girls. A careful examination of their file indicated no court order or other paper prohibiting such contact. The father's name and work and home telephone numbers were included on the emergency care card. The counselor consulted with the supervisor, the school's guidance director, and the social worker, and they all agreed that a call to the father was in the children's best interest. Thereafter, the social worker called the father to suggest a conference with both parents.

The counselor called the mother, who became enraged when she learned the father had been contacted. In her view the school acted improperly by contacting the father before contacting her and by not seeking her permission to contact the father. She refused to allow the school representative to meet with the father with or without her.

Issues

The issues in this point of law are:

1. Do both parents have equal access to school records?
2. Does the noncustodial parent have access to school records and the right to be included in conferences?
3. When it seems to be in the child's best interest to contact the noncustodial parent, is the school obligated to notify the custodial parent before doing so?
4. When information gleaned during the counseling relationship indicates the noncustodial parent should be contacted, what is the obligation of the counselor?

Issue No. 1: Equal Access to School Records

Access to school records in school districts that are receiving federal funds is governed by the regulations that implement Public Law 93-380, the FERPA (1974). This act states, in general, that each parent has equal access to the child's educational records. The federal regulation that implements FERPA is quite clear:

> An educational agency or institution may presume that either parent of the student has authority to inspect and review the educational records of the student unless the agency or institution has been provided with evidence that there is a legally binding instrument or a state law or court order governing such matters as divorce, separation or custody, which provides to the contrary. ("Privacy Rights," 1980, p. 30913)

In *Mattie T. v. Johnston* (1976), the Court pointed out that the FERPA does not prevent release of records to parents, but is aimed at preventing release of records to unauthorized individuals or organizations without the consent of the student or the parent. Thus, it is clear that either parent of a student has access to the records of that student, in the absence of a court order or other official instrument prohibiting that access.

Issue No. 2: Access for the Noncustodial Parent

In only a few cases have the federal statute and regulations been interpreted. These cases involve the noncustodial parent seeking the records of the child. In *Page v. Rotterdam-Mohonasen Central School District* (1981), the Court held that when the natural father and mother were living apart under terms of a separation agreement providing custody of the child to the mother and rights of visitation to the father, the father was entitled to inspect and review the educational records of the child even though the natural mother had signed a statement, prepared by school officials, indicating that she did not authorize the school district to transmit such records to the natural father. The Court reasoned that the presence of the signed statement did not constitute the kind of barring document specified in the statute and regulations as would prohibit the school district from permitting the noncustodial parent to review the records or attend conferences with designated school employees.

A recent issue of *A Legal Memorandum* (Punger, 1984) issued by the National Association of Secondary School Principals, carried a reprint article on the topic and stated that some educators incorrectly believe that the custodial parent can legally control access to their child's educational records and can prevent the noncustodial parent from seeing them.

The Court pointed out in *Page v. Rotterdam-Mohonassen Central School District* (1981) that a noncustodial parent has not abandoned the child simply by reason of noncustody. And, although legal custody may be given to one or both of the parents, the fact that it is given to one does not necessarily terminate the role of the other as a psychological guardian and preceptor (*Weiss v. Weiss,* 1981).

Another reason for protecting this relationship is that the noncustodial parent is presumably entitled to custody after the death of the custodial parent. In *People ex rel Moffet v. Cooper* (1970), the Court in this case explored the concept of the welfare of the child, which is the foundation on which the question of access turns. The Court held that it is important for the noncustodial parent to be informed so as not to be be ill-prepared in the event that he or she were suddenly cast into a custodial role after the death of the custodial parent. Even if the noncustodial parent has been denied visitation rights (which is not the case here), the parent probably would not lose access to school records. As a practical matter, visitation rights and access to records are separate rights and privileges.

Obtaining access to school records need not involve direct contact with the child, and it may be the only means available for the noncustodial parent to follow the child's growth and development. In the absence of a specific statement in the court order denying the noncustodial parent the right of access to school records, the general rule should remain in effect (Punger, 1984).

Issue No. 3: Contacting Custodial or Noncustodial Parents

Although it is held that custody carries the right and obligation to make decisions regarding a child's education, noncustodial parents can obtain information about the child's development as a student, as seen in *Page v. Rotterdam-Mohonasen Central School District* (1981). The FERPA specifically states that funds shall not be available to educational agencies that deny to parents the right to inspect and review the educational records of their children. The regulation implementing the FERPA allows inspection by either parent regardless of custody, unless access is barred by state law, court order, or legally binding instrument ("Privacy Rights," 1980).

In *Page v. Rotterdam-Mohonasen Central School District* (1981), the Court pointed out that educators and school districts are charged with the duty to act in the best educational interests of the children committed in their care. Those interests dictate that educational' information be made available to both parents of every school child who has two parents interested in the child's welfare. In *Weiss v. Weiss* (1981), the Court regarded the welfare and best interests of the child as being predominant in any contest involving the rights of the parents.

> Where the physical and emotional well-being of a child is involved, it is, at best, anomalous that its protection should be dependent on the vindication of the "rights" of the parents. Again, this view does not lose sight of the fact that while legal custody may be in one or both of the parents, the rights of the custodial parent are subservient to the primary right of the child to have the other as a psychological guardian and preceptor. (*Weiss v. Weiss*, 1981, p. 214)

It seems clear that case and statutory law allow the noncustodial parent access to the records of the child, and the welfare of the child is the predominant consideration by those charged with its care (including the school); therefore, when the professional judgment of the school representative so indicates, it is not only permissible but the duty of that representative to contact the noncustodial parent. Under these circumstances there can be no requirement to notify first the custodial parent.

Issue No. 4: Counselors' Obligation of Notification

Section B.4 of the *Ethical Standards* of the American Association for Counseling and Development (AACD) states:

> When the client's condition indicates that there is a clear and imminent danger to the client or others, the member must take reasonable personal action or inform the responsible authorities." (AACD, 1981, p. 1)

The California Supreme Court in *Tarasoff v. Regents of the University of California* (1974) held that a counselor, or a person in such a relationship has a duty to warn a person who is in danger. The Court stated that privileged communication between a psychotherapist and client must yeild to disclosure when someone is in danger. Consultation with other professionals must be used when possible.

School counselors do not have privileged communication in most states (Hummel & Humes, 1984). Although counselors generally do not have this burden, they do have the ethical responsibility not to disclose confidential information obtained in counseling sessions. This responsibility must give way to the greater responsibility, noted above, to take reasonable personal action and to inform responsible authorities after careful deliberation.

In the case used here as an example, the clients—the children—were informed and consented to the revelation of the school-related information to the social worker and noncustodial parent. The counselor has a responsibility to act in the best interests of clients in the school setting, including making the appropriate referrals and contacting responsible authorities (AACD, 1981). In this case, the appropriate referral was to the social worker, and the responsible authority was the noncustodial parent.

Conclusion

Because public schools in all states accept federal funds, the FERPA applies. Hence, schools cannot deny to parents the right to inspect and review the educational records of their children. The applicable regulation ("Privacy Rights of Students," Federal Register, 1980) allows inspection by either parent without regard to custody, unless that parent is barred by one of the mechanisms mentioned in the regulation.

Case law indicates that the noncustodial parent has a right to review the child's record and attend conferences even when the custodial parent has attempted to forbid such interaction. Furthermore, the cases have held that the welfare of the child is of predominant concern over any rights of the parents.

Finally, it is clear that a counselor has an ethical obligation to contact responsible authorities, which could include the noncustodial parent, when the failure to do so might bring harm to another.

Counselors, educators, and school district officials are charged with the duty to act in the best educational interests of the children committed to their care. It is incumbent on them, when the best interests of the child clearly indicate such, to contact either the custodial or noncustodial parent as the judgment of school representatives indicates. It would be detrimental to the welfare of the child if access to the noncustodial parent were denied in such cases.

References

American Association for Counseling and Development. (1981). *Ethical standards*. Alexandria, VA: Author.

Family Rights and Privacy Act of 1974, §512, 20 U.S.C. §1232g (1974).

Gibson, R.L., Mitchell, M.H., & Higgins, R.E. (1983). *Development and mangement of counseling programs and guidance services*. New York: Macmillan.

Hummel, D.L., & Humes, C.W. (1984). *Pupil services: Development, coordination, administration*. New York: Macmillan.

Larrabee, M.L., & Terres, C.K. (Eds.) (1985). Special focus on ethical and legal issues [Special issue]. *Elementary School Guidance & Counseling, 19*(3).

Mattie v. Johnson, 74 F.R.D. N.D. (MS 1976).

Page v. Rotterdam-Homonasen Central School District, 441 N.Y.S. 2d 323, 109 Misc. 2d 1049 (NY 1981).

People ex rel Moffett v. Cooper, 63 Misc. 2d 1005, 314 N.Y. 52nd, 248 (NY 1970).

Privacy rights of parents and students. (1980, May 9). *Federal Register, 45*, 30913–30918.

Punger, D.S. (1984, September). The nontraditional family: Legal problems for schools. A *Legal Memorandum*, pp. 1–8.

Remley, T.P. (1985) The law and ethical practices in elementary and middle schools. *Elementary School Guidance & Counseling, 19*, 181–189.

Tarasoff v. Regents of University of California, 529 P 2d 533 (CA 1974).

Weiss v. Weiss, 52 N.Y. 2d 170, 418 N.E. 2d 377 (NY 1981).

The Hatch Amendment: A Primer for Counselors

Part II: Protective Legislation and Recommendations for Action

Leslie S. Kaplan and *Kevin Geoffroy*

In Part I of "The Hatch Amendment: A Primer for Counselors" (Kaplan & Geoffroy, 1987) we examined the historical antecedents of parental consent for students' education. In this part we explore the legislative decisions concerning parental versus state control of education and suggestions for counselors and educators.

Relationship of Current Litigation to the Hatch Amendment

The Hatch Amendment regulations have yet to be challenged by litigation, but a look at relevant precedents may provide a context for how such a challenge might be received by the courts.

Parental Rights

The U.S. Constitution protects parents' rights to raise their children. In 1923 the U.S. Supreme Court recognized that parents have a constitutional right to "establish a home and bring up children" (Dittersdorf, 1983–84, p. 592). Although the constitutional source of this right is unclear, the modern court has consistently reaffirmed the constitutional right of child rearing, citing as support the 14th Amendment's guarantee of due process (*Meyer v. Nebraska*, 1923; *Pierce v. Society of the Sisters of the Holy Names of*

113

Jesus and Mary, 1925) and the Bill of Rights (*Roe v. Wade*, 1973) or generally citing the right of privacy derived from these sources (Runyon v. McCrary, 1976).

Plaintiffs must be able to identify and articulate the parental interests burdened by the activity or curriculum in question if courts are to uphold their claims (Dittersdorf, 1983–84). In *Moody v. Cronin* (1979) parents successfully defended their right to have children excused from coeducational physical education classes, which the court ruled interfered with the Pentecostal Christian parents' rights to teach their children the value of modesty. In *State of Wisconsin v. Yoder* (1972), the Supreme Court recognized a "cardinal consitutional right" of parenthood, which included control over a child's values (p. 234). Here the Supreme Court declared that teaching moral standards was an important American tradition that is constitutionally protected.

First Amendment Rights

The purpose of education in this country is to provide citizens with information and skills so they can draw conclusions from that information and make informed, intelligent judgments. Politically and economically, educated individuals act productively in their own as well as in the national interest. Gordon (1984) identified two basic methods of teaching values. The directive or prescriptive method involves transmitting information and accepted truths to passive students. The discursive or analytical method provides an active examination of data by both teacher and student, who present, discuss, and analyze the moral, logical, and practical consequences of those values. The directive method is coercive indoctrination; the discursive method minimizes coercion and indoctrination.

In a diverse, complex society such as the United States it is difficult to identify a common set of values and beliefs that should be transmitted through the socialization process of schooling. Almost every value is objectionable to someone. Teaching religious values violates the Establishment Clause of the First Amendment. If there are essential, basic values in American society as a whole, they must be found in the Constitution: justice, promotion of general welfare, liberty, majority rule, individual autonomy, privacy, due process, and others (Gordon, 1984). The discursive method of teaching is compatible with First Amendment principles of minimal intrusiveness or coercion because it does not require students to believe in the values taught. It does not restrict access to information, reward desired beliefs, or punish undesired ones.

All teaching involves choices of what and what not to teach. Curriculum choices reflect the values of local and state decision makers. The First Amendment protects access to information and ideas in the pursuit of a better understanding of reality and prohibits the government from requiring an individual to hold a particular understanding of reality or from controlling the general content of that understanding (Gordon, 1984). The ruling in *Board of Education v. Pico* (1982) demonstrates that the First Amendment prohibits a school board from removing books from the school library for the purpose of restricting access to the political ideas or social perspectives discussed in them. The government cannot restrict student access to information and ideas already available to them solely because it disagrees with the content of the information and ideas.

Proponents of a wider interpretation of Hatch regulations might attempt similar First Amendment challenges to present curricula and activities. Challenges against sex education on similar grounds have all been unsuccessful (Gordon, 1984). Implicit in the Establishment Clause is the value of secularism and the guarantee of free expression (Gordon, 1984). Courts have also rejected Establishment Clause challenges on the grounds that secularism is not a religion, as in *Citizens for Parental Rights v. San Mateo County Board of Education* (1975). Courts cannot impose a narrow, sectarian view of reality without violating free expression.

Furthermore, according to some views, the application of the First Amendment to public schools includes development as well as expression of ideas, beliefs, opinions, and world views (Gordon, 1984). In addition, *Mozert v. Hawkins County Public Schools* (1984) held that the First Amendment does not guarantee that nothing offensive to any religion will be taught in schools. The First Amendment does guarantee that state schools will be neutral on the subject of religion, neither advocating a particular religious belief nor expressing hostility toward any or all religions.

In the *Witters v. State Commission for the Blind* (1984) decision, the court determined that persons who claim violation of free exercise of religion must show the coercive effect of enactment as it operates against them in the practice of their religion. The challenged state action must somehow compel or exert pressure on the individual to violate a tenet of his religious belief.

In *Aguillard v. Edwards* (1985), it was held that the Establishment Clause does not require the public sector to be insulated from all that may have religious origin or significance. In *Epperson v. Arkansas* (1969), a case that overturned an Arkansas law prohibiting the teaching of Darwinism in public school science classes, the Supreme Court declared that secular subjects that directly challenge certain religious views are permissible. The court could not permit certain religious sects to advance or prohibit information to reinforce their own beliefs in violation of the Establishment Clause. Finally, a New Jersey court held in *Smith v. Ricci* (1982) that a family life education program focusing on human sexuality in public elementary and secondary schools did not violate the Establishment Clause because it did not enhance any particular religious viewpoint nor did it favor a "secular" over a "religious" one.

In short, the First Amendment protects students' rights to receive information at school. Parents challenging "objectionable" curricula such as sex education or possible affective-psychological education, would not find judicial relief if they sought to restrict a child's access to information and ideas.

State Versus Parents' Rights

Even courses designed primarily to transmit information also transmit values. Simple openness about certain personal issues conflicts with the traditional values of privacy, intimacy, and modesty that many parents hold.

In addition, nonjudgmental discussions imply freedom of choice that is free of the moral restrictions to which parents still subscribe. Moreover, courses that support a pragmatic morality based on rational consideration of consequences conflict with the traditional stress on absolute moral and religious ethics. Thus, by teaching contrary values, schools interfere with parents' control over their children's moral development. Nevertheless, although school authorities may not attempt rigid indoctrination, they are charged with teaching values (Dittersdorf, 1983–84).

Freedom of choice for students, the opposite of indoctrination, allows a range of choices regarding attitudes and behaviors and permits consideration of the consequences of one's actions. Children can still consider the consequences of violating or conforming to their parents' beliefs and life-styles. It is the state's educational mandate to foster societal values of freedom of choice, and the state needs significant freedom to fulfill this task.

Although parents have the right to direct their children's upbringing and education, the parental right is not absolute. The state has a substantial interest in the welfare of children, which may take priority over the rights of parents. In the area of education, the state serves as the primary protector of the child's best interests.

In *Prince v. Massachusetts* (1943) the court ruled that although the guardian had the right to teach her child values, these interests were outweighed by those of the state. In *Cornwell v. State Board of Education* (1969) the public health issue of teenage pregnancies predominated over the parents' wish to remove their children from a sex education class. In *Citizens v. San Mateo* (1975), *Hopkins v. Hamden Board of Education* (1971), and *Medeiros v. Kiyosaki* (1970), privacy claims have been unsuccessful in overcoming what courts have viewed as compelling state interests in public health. Parental rights have also given way to state interests in using audiovisual equipment. In *Davis v. Page* (1974) Apostolic Lutherans unsuccessfully sought to have their children excused from class during audiovisual presentations, claiming the equipment was immoral. Although parents' interests were recognized, the court ruled that the state's interest was primary. Parents' rights have also given way in the face of countervailing interests of the child (*Planned Parenthood v. Danforth*, 1976). It is apparent that parent, state, and child sometimes have competing interests in the child's welfare.

Questions of substantive due process are involved in deciding whether activities such as clarification of values or decision making are essential to fulfilling the educational goals of the state. In substantive due process cases, the courts have been willing to relinquish the premise that parents invariably act in their children's best interests. The courts continually evaualte the validity of contemporary values (Dittersdorf, 1983–84). For example, the court may override a parent's refusal to consent to an immature minor's request for an abortion if it determines that the surgery is in the child's best interests (*Bellotti v. Baird*, 1978).

Families who, unlike the Amish in *Wisconsin v. Yoder* (1972), do not wish to totally isolate their children from the American mainstream and who do not remove their children from public schools altogether, may find it difficult to press for heightened protection of family rights in the classroom. In any case, parents may argue that education about values invades their prerogative over family life-style by attempting to standardize instruction about value choices that are critical to the child's moral development. Such teaching may undermine American pluralism by countering parents' attempts to instruct their children (Dittersdorf, 1983–84).

The "captive audience" doctrine, by prohibiting the government from forcing an unwilling person to listen, protects the listener's privacy. It prevents a speaker from imposing his or her particular ideas and information about reality on the listener. This doctrine holds true for public school students who are compelled by attendance laws to be in school. Schools cannot force students to hear ideas that impose conformity, encourage intolerance, or present a factually skewed view of the world (Gordon, 1984). If school policies permit parents to limit or prevent their child's participation in a particular program, the court finds no interference with parental control (*Medeiros v. Kiyosaki*, 1970).

Although exemption from participation is an attractive alternative because it protects minority interests without burdening the majority, it does not completely satisfy state, child, or parent interests. Removed children are denied the benefits of the educational experience, thwarting the state's interest. A child removed from class by parents then risks unpleasant teasing by classmates. The Constitution requires the interests of all parties to be sensitively balanced. Nothing in the Constitution guarantees that the state will attain all its goals or that parents will have complete control over their children's education (Dittersdorf, 1983–84).

Finally, ultimate responsibility for management and control of programs in public schools rests with the state board of education (*Mills v. Buell*, 1985). States have the right to prescribe academic curricula for their public school systems. Therefore, the court of appeals exercises great care and restraint when called on to interefere in the operation of public schools (*Aguillard v. Edwards*, 1985). The Sweezy decision (*Sweezy v. New Hampshire*, 1957) calls into question state or federal laws prohibiting grants to school districts in which teachers teach courses that emphasize "secular humanism." The intensive scrutiny required to identify and rid the schools of secular humanism may result in an invasion of academic freedom or a "pall of orthodoxy" over the classroom, which courts will probably reject.

The Hatch Amendment Applied to Schools

Conclusions and Recommendations

Congress passed the Hatch Amendment in 1978, and the Department of Education issued formal regulations in 1984 ("Student Rights in Research," 1984, Parts III and IV). If broadly interpreted and applied, these regulations could significantly hinder classroom teaching, education about values and affective education programs, teacher-student advisory programs, and counseling services available in public schools. Although active groups of conservative parents were influential in enacting their agenda in the initial legislation and the issuing of formal regulations, the educational profession was caught unaware and off guard. Now, as the conservative lobby agitates for a more restrictive interpretation and application of the Hatch regulations and seeks to intimidate school administrators by misrepresenting the scope and intent of the Hatch Amendment, professional educators are playing "catch-up" with their own occasional overstatement, public relations, and lobbying.

As written, the Hatch Amendment regulations are applicable in a limited number of cases. First, applicable programs must be fully supported by federal funds. Second, they must be experimental, used for demonstration activities or programs. Third, their primary purpose of testing or treatment must be to reveal personal information about students. All three conditions must be met before a program is covered by the amendment. If the educational lobby is to be effective, it will help keep the applicability to the present scope and work to contain the broadness of interpretation and application of the Hatch regulations.

At present, both sides are guilty of overstatement and "worst case scenarios." Educators are trying to stem the damage, to limit the definitions of "psychiatric and psychological testing, examination, and treatment," and to prevent additional restrictions on their abilities to educate youngsters. Conservative parents are working to widen the scope of the amendment's application according to what they view as Senator Hatch's real intent as evidenced by his *Congressional Record* remarks (1978) and their own goals. Senator Hatch, himself, is less than candid when he expresses his "amazement" at the uproar arising in both quarters in reaction to his amendment's regulations (*Congressional Record*, 1985). He was correct, however, when he commented, "Let the rule of common sense prevail" (p. S. 1390).

The Hatch regulations constitute unfinished business. The regulations require more appropriate definitions and scope. Educators and the public at large can still affect the final wording of definitions. The regulations can clarify what is meant by "experimental" or "unproven." The definitions will markedly affect how broadly the regulations will be applied.

Next, the appeals process needs clarification. Do complainants need to exhaust or simply "touch base" with local and state officials about their concerns regarding curriculum, programs, or activities in their schools before filing with the U.S. Department of Education?

In addition, school districts need to develop systemwide procedures for determining when written parental consent is required by Hatch Amendment regulations. Most schools already require such consent for assessment instruments (cognitive ability tests, personality and interest inventories, situation tests, and certain educational achievement tests) except for those routinely administered by local and state school districts. The Hatch regulations do not change these practices. When in doubt, it may be wise for schools to require written parental consent.

School divisions need to review the entire school curricula to see which programs or activities are fully supported by federal funds. If no federal monies are involved, the Hatch regulations do not apply.

School divisions should also determine which federally funded education programs and activities, if any, involve psychological or psychiatric examination, testing, or treatment in which the primary purpose is to obtain personal information in one or more of the seven areas designated. Furthermore, until the U.S. Department of Education becomes more specific in its own definitions, school divisions should develop a policy regarding what constitutes "psychological or psychiatric test, examination, or treatment" and decide who will determine this in case of confusion.

It is also advisable that school divisions develop, adopt, and publish a comprehensive policy to be used in setting criteria for selection of instructional materials and establishing procedures for handling parental complaints. The policy should apply to textbooks, library books, periodicals, and audiovisual materials. It should include a statement of the basic principles governing educational goals, curricular objectives, and responsibility and procedures for selection and reconsideration of materials. This statement of policy should spell out the role of guidance counselors and the state mandates under which they operate. Moreover, the policy should state the school division's commitment to academic freedom and include guidelines for treating controversial subjects in the classroom and for selecting outside speakers. It should also include appropriate forms to implement these policies and procedures. School personnel and parents should be informed of these policies and procedures.

Legally, although several complaints have been filed with the U.S. Department of Education, all have been judged invalid. Parents' groups are trying to intimidate school officials into curtailing or dropping controversial programs by making oblique references to Hatch regulations in situations where they do not apply. The issue has not yet been litigated, but prior court decisions seem to support education that broadens alternatives and expands information available to pupils rather than restricting them. First Amendment and substantive due process issues support present curricular activities, education about values, affective education, teacher advisory programs, and other activities that involve personal issues and decision making. Parents' rights in their children's education and upbringing are legitimate, but states' interests in fully educating their young people override parental interests when necessary.

Going beyond the Hatch Amendment itself, the education profession has its own lesson to learn in contemporary political action. Educators must learn how to handle antagonistic pressure groups and how to activate and mobilize their own colleagues when political opportunities to enhance or protect their profession arise. Conservative groups have gathered supporters and have focused their attention on influencing legislation that affected education and subsequent regulations, which went completely unnoticed by professional educators. Educators also need better public relations, especially emphasizing the need for education "beyond basics." This need must be sensitively yet vigorously addressed as the social and personal purpose of education. Educators must also face and resolve the issues of misguided, misinformed, or just plain inept teachers and counselors who misuse their responsibility and act dogmatically or in ways that invade students' privacy.

The Hatch Amendment and regulations have awakened educators from their political naïveté. The regulations have alarmed educators who believed in their unquestioned right to teach what and how they pleased without any challenge from lay persons. Much has changed inside and outside the classroom. Challenges to educational practices from parents and organized groups will be a reality in the future. The Hatch Amendment has opened the eyes of educators to this phenomenon, and they must be aware of developing challenges that are certain to come in ensuing years.

References

Aguillard v. Edwards, 765 F.2d 1251 (C.A. 5. La. 1985).
Belloti v. Baird, 443 U.S. 622 (1978).

Board of Education v. Pico, 457 U.S. 853 (1982).

Citzens for Parental Rights v. San Mateo County Board of Education, 51 Cal. App.3d 12. 124 Cal. Rptr. 68 (1975).

Congressional Record. 95th Cong. 2d. Sess. 1978. Vol. 124, pt. 134.

Congressional Record. 99th Cong. 1st Sess. 1985. vol. 131, pt.15.

Cornwell v. State Board of Education, 314 F. Supp. 340 (U.S. Dist. Md. 1969).

Davis v. Page, 385 F. Supp. 395 (D. N.H. 1974).

Dittersdorf, N. (1983–1984). Public school sex education: Does it violate parental rights? *New York University Review of Law and Social Change, 12,* 591–616.

Epperson v. Arkansas, 393 U.S. 97, 89 S.Ct. 266 (1968).

Student rights in research, experimental activities, and testing: Proposed rule-making. (1984). *Federal Register,* Part III, Department of Education, 34 CFR, Pts. 75, 76, and 98, *49,* 6645–6650.

Student rights in research, experimental activities, and testing: Final rules with invitation to comment (1984). *Federal Register,* Part IV, Department of Education, 34 CRF, Pts. 75, 76, and 98, *49,* 35317–35322.

Gordon, Robert M. (1984). Freedom of expression and values inculcation in the public school curriculum. *Journal of Law and Education, 13,* 523-579.

Hopkins v. Hamden Board of Education, 29 Conn. Supp. 397, 289 A.2d (1971).

Kaplan, L.S., & Geoffroy, K. (1987). The Hatch Amendment: A primer for counselors. Part I. Development and implementation of the amendment by conservative parent groups. *School Counselor, 35,* 9–16.

Medeiros v. Kiyosaki, 52 Hawaii 436, 478 P.2d 314 (1970).

Meyer v. Nebraska, 262 U.S. 390, 43 S.Ct. 625 (1923).

Mills v. Buell, 685 S.W.2d. 561 (App. Ky. 1985).

Moody v. Cronin, 484 F. Supp. 270 (C.D. Ill. 1979).

Mozert v. Hawkins County Public Schools, 582 F. Supp. 201 (D.C. Tenn. 1984).

Pierce v. Society of the Sisters of the Holy Names of Jesus and Mary, 268 U.S. 510, 45 S.Ct. 571 (1925).

Planned Parenthood v. Danforth, 428 U.S. 52 (1975).

Prince v. Massachusetts, 321 U.S. 158 (1943).

Roe v. Wade, 410 U.S. 113 (1973).

Runyon v. McCrary, 427 U.S. 160, 177, 178 (1976).

Smith v. Ricci, 89 N.J. 514, 446 A.R.2d.501 (1982).

State of Wisconsin v. Yoder, 406 U.S. 205. 92 S.Ct. 1526 (1972).

Sweezy v. New Hampshire, 354 U.S. 234, 77 S.Ct. 1203 (1957).

Witters v. State Commission for the Blind, 689 P.2d 53 (Wash. 1984).

The Counselor and Testing: Some Legal Concerns

Lou Culler Talbutt

Standarized tests have been misused in education. First, educators have often misinterpreted test results, which has resulted in discrimination against certain groups of students. Second, testing instruments themselves, standardized on samples of white middle class students, have discriminated against the emotionally disadvantaged, the handicapped, and racial minorities. Both misuses will be discussed throughout this article. Because school counselors are involved in testing, they should be familiar with some legal implications related to misinterpretation of test scores. This article summarizes significant laws and court cases pertaining to discrimination in educational testing, discusses their implications for counselors, and concludes with specific recommendations for counselors.

Legal Review

Public laws, as well as the courts, have addressed issues of discrimination in education. Public Law 93-380, the Elementary and Secondary Education Amendments of 1974, declared that all children have equal educational opportunities. Title IX of Public Law 92-318 denies federal funds to institutions engaged in sexual discrimination. Public Law 94-142 or the "Education for All Handicapped Children Act of 1975", was created to assure that all handicapped children have an appropriate public education. In *Brown v. Board of Education* (347 U.S. 483, 1954), the United States Supreme Court determined that when a state makes a public education available, "it is a right which must be made available to all on equal terms" (p. 493). McCarthy and Thomas (1977) identified

Pennsylvania Ass'n for Retarded Children (P.A.R.C.) v. Common-wealth (Pa., 343 F. Supp. 279, 1972) as the "first notable case involving the rights of handicapped children" (p. 77).

That court determined that no mentally handicapped student could be denied a public education or procedural due process of law. Then, in *Mills v. Board of Education* (D.C., 348 F. Supp. 866, 1972), that right to an education was expanded to those other than the mentally retarded. *Mills* (Supra) held: "Children who have been labeled as behavioral problems, mentally retarded, emotionally disturbed or hyperactive could not be denied a public education" (p. 866).

Historically, standardized test scores have been used in educational settings to place students and to identify them for special programs. Unfortunately, discrimination because of sex, race, and handicaps has resulted. The problem lies in the difficulty of classifying students correctly.

Test results have often been misinterpreted by educators. McCarthy and Thomas (1977) identified special education assignments as a crucial area because incorrect classification of a student could have harmful psychological effects (p. 82). In *Hoffman v. Board of Education* (410 N.Y.S. 2d 99, 1978), charges were brought against the Board of Education for placing a student of normal intelligence in a class for retarded students and permitting him to continue there for 11 years. The student was just below the cutoff point according to an intelligence test; thus, the school psychologists had recommended reevaluation within 2 years. The school board had failed to follow the recommendation. Although the lower court found the school board liable for damages, the court of appeals determined that the court should not interfere with the professional judgment of those involved in educational settings unless gross violations have occurred (424 N.Y.S. 2d 376). Even though many individuals would personally view the *Hoffman* case as an example of gross violation, the court upheld the traditional view that the courts should not interfere in academic decisions in educational settings unless absolutely necessary. The case, nevertheless, illustrates the harmful results of classifying a student with borderline test scores according to a single testing without the recommended follow-up tests. Hoffman also is a reminder to educators that legal charges for damages may be brought against school boards when students are misclassified.

Another form of test discrimination is racial. The courts have held that students may not be assigned to classrooms according to standardized tests when this method perpetuates segregated classrooms in recently desegregated schools. To use tests in this way is a violation of the 14th Amendment rights of Black students according to *Moses v. Washington-Parish School Board* (456 F.2d 1285; 409 U.S. 1013, 1972).

Testing instruments, themselves, lead to discrimination. In *Hobson v. Hansen* (D.C. 269 F.Supp. 401, 1967) the court rules that ability tracking in the District of Columbia "unconstitutionally deprived Negro and poor public school children of their right to equal educational opportunities" (p. 401).

The test produced inaccurate and misleading scores. Judge Wright in Hobson concluded that the aptitude tests used in tracking students have been "standardized primarily on and (were) relevant to a white middle class group of students" (p. 514). Students were actually being classified according to their socioeconomic and environmental influences, not their innate ability. In other words, unless a minority group has been represented in the norm group for the standardization of a test, bias against that minority group may exist. Kamin (1975) wrote: "Since its introduction to America, the intelligence test has been used more or less consciously as an instrument of oppression against the underprivileged—the poor, the foreign-born, and racial minorities" (p. 317).

Because tests may discriminate, students should not be classified or grouped solely on standardized and intelligence test scores. McCarthy and Thomas (1977) suggested that student placement be based on a substantial variety of data, not merely test scores. They wrote, "Anecdotal, historical records, direct observation, testing, and pupil-parent conferences" should be utilized (p. 51).

In a 1981 case, a federal appeals court emphasized the importance of test validity in competency testing. In *Debra P. v. Turlington* (644 F.2d 397, 1981) the court determined that a state could not "constitutionally so deprive its students (of their high school diplomas) unless it has submitted proof of the curricular validity of the test" (p. 400).

Also, the court determined that the failures of Blacks on the test may have been caused by the "unequal education they received" during the time of segregated schools (p. 407). Although competency testing is another whole category of testing and may be more of a legal concern for administrators, school boards, and test specialists than for counselors, it clearly illustrates the court's view that schools are expected to prove a test's validity when charged with discrimination.

Testing instruments also reflect sex discrimination. Donlon, Ekstrom, and Lockheed (1979) reported: "Bias in test is not only demonstrated by statistical differences in test scores, but by the relative incidence of references to males and females" (p. 216).

In interpreting Title IX of Public Law 92-318, PEER (1975), the Project on Equal Education Rights, explained that counselors should use the same tests in evaluating students of different sexes. In a similar explanation, Virginia's Assistant Attorney General Ryland (1975) wrote: "If your placement procedures are getting most of the girls in home economics and most of the boys in shop, you have to make sure that your placement procedures are not inherently discriminatory" (p. 49).

Thus, Ryland recommended that boys and girls be given the same aptitude test. Ryland further explained that when aptitude tests show that all girls should seek traditional women's occupations, counselors should determine whether the tests are valid.

Counselors should also be aware that sex discrimination may occur in the counseling process itself or through other counseling materials. The *University of Pennsylvania Law Review* (1976) stated that discouraging a young girl from a certain career illustrates sex bias. In a study regarding career selection, Donahue and Costar (1977) found that high school counselors tended to view women in terms of occupations with less pay, less education, and more supervision than men. In another study involving 40 college freshmen women, Sauter, Seidl, and Karbon (1980) found that guidance counseling had influenced only those women who had selected traditional careers. They concluded, "Counseling experiences may propagate sex-typed career selection" (p. 247). Harway (1977) wrote that sex bias existed in college admission manuals, textbooks, occupational handbooks, and college catalogs. In a more recent study, Birk, Tanny, and Cooper (1979) examined over 2,000 illustrations from occupational information and detected sterotyping of women. Thus, counselors should note that discrimination occurs not only through testing instruments and the interpretation of tests but may occur through the counseling process and other materials as well.

This section has reviewed some of the laws and court cases that have dealt with discrimination in testing. Because counselors are involved in testing, it is important that they not misuse test results. The next section offers some practical recommendations for school counselors.

Recommendations

1. Counselors should be knowledgeable of their individual job responsibilities in testing; likewise, they should understand the

testing duties of psychologists, medical personnel, and administrators. In one study, for example, Talbutt (1979) indicated that school psychologists, not school counselors, were responsible for tests given in the evaluation of students for special education. A counselor, rather, might serve as a team member in classifying students. Counseling duties vary among states; Talbutt found that counselors could be responsible for interpreting test results for students, self-appraisal, conducting individual and group interpretation sessions for career development, using test results as a partial means of identifying students with special needs, and conducting individual and group interpretation sessions with parents.

2. Counselors should follow all regulations and guidelines from their state and local boards of education. Talbutt (1979) illustrated the type of information counselors might receive from these sources.

(a) Administrators and teachers should especially be aware of the limitations of tests in terms of their validity, reliability, or predictability for minority students.
(b) Test results alone should not be used to determine the program for a student or group of students.
(c) Test results should not be used in a way that results in racial or socioeconomic violation of students.
(d) Test results should not be used to exclude a student's participation in school-sponsored activities with the exception of honor societies. (p. 113)

3. Counselors should be familiar with and should follow their own professional guidelines. Both APGA *Ethical Standards* (1981) and *Ethical Standards of Psychologists* (American Psychological Association, 1973) address testing. The Ethical Standards (1981) recommends that counselors refer to the *Standards for Educational and Psychological Tests and Manuals*, revised edition, 1974, published by the American Psychological Association, the American Research Association, and the National Council on Measurement in Education regarding the preparation, publication, and distribution of tests.

4. Counselors should keep abreast of current testing information in professional journals and through professional meetings. The *Ethical Guidelines* (1981) recommends two articles: "The Responsible Use of Tests: A Position Paper of AMEG, APGA, and NCME" in *Measurement and Evaluation in Guidance*, 1972, 5, 385–388, and "Responsibilities of Users of Standardized Tests", APGA, *Guidepost*, October 5, 1978, 5–8.

5. Counselors should note that Section C of APGA *Ethical Standards* deals with the topic of measurement and evaluation. Section C:2 relates to test usage and Section C:10 relates to testing and minority students:

> C:2 In selecting tests for use in a given situation or with a particular client, the member must consider carefully the specific validity, reliability, and appropriateness of the test(s). General validity, reliability and the like may be questioned legally as well as ethically when tests are used for vocational and educational selection, placement, or counseling.
>
> C:10 The member must proceed with caution when attempting to evaluate and interpret the performance of minority group members or other persons who are not represented in the norm group on which the instrument was standardized.

In Section C:2, validity refers to the extent to which a particular test measures what it purports to measure, whereas reliability refers to a test's stability. In administering tests, counselors should carefully review all test manuals and follow all instructions. Even though much information about a particular test can be found in the publisher's test manual, counselors should check the latest edition of Buro's *Mental Measurements Yearbook* (1978) for a complete evaluation. The yearbook discusses such things as the grade level for which the test was designed, the cost of the test, whether machine scoring is available, the reliability and validity of the test, and the construction and standardization of the test. In addition, the reviews often discuss interpretative and other problems related to a particular test.

Section C:10 of the APGA Ethical Standards is consistent with the *Hobson* case discussed earlier. Both serve as a reminder that testing instruments may discriminate against minority groups unless such groups are represented in the norm group for standardization of a particular test. Otherwise, minority groups are compared to white, middle Americans who have different socioeconomic backgrounds and, in some cases, different language.

Conclusion

Court rulings and laws have indicated that tests should not result in the discrimination of students because of sex, race, or handicaps. The courts have ruled that test scores should not be misused by educators and that the instruments, themselves, should not discriminate. Because school counselors have a major role in testing, they should keep up with the laws and court cases pertaining to testing. Unfortunately, legal journals, court cases, and laws are difficult for counselors to access. Consequently, this article has summarized some legal issues related to testing and discussed their implications for school counselors.

References

American Personnel and Guidance Association, *Ethical Standards*, 1981.

Birk, J.M.; Tanney, M.F.; & Cooper, J.F. A case of blurred vision: Stereotyping in career information illustrations. *Journal of Vocational Behavior*, 1979, *15*, 247–257.

Brown v. Board of Education, 347 U.S. 483 (1954).

Buros, O.K. (Ed.). *Mental Measurements Yearbook* (8th ed.). Highland Park, N.J.: Gryphon Press, 1978.

Debra P. v. Turlington, 644 F.2d 397 (1981).

Donahue, T.J., & Costar, J.W. Counselor discrimination against young women in career selection. *Journal of Counseling Psychology*, 1977, *24*, 481–486.

Donlon, T.F.; Ekstrom, R.B.; & Lockheed, M.E. The consequences of sex bias in the content of major achievement test batteries. *Measurement and Evaluation in Guidance*, 1979, *11*, 202–216.

Harway, M. Sex bias in counseling materials. *Journal of College Student Personnel*, 1977, *18*, 57–63.

Hobson v. Hansen, 269 F. Supp. 401 (D.C., 1969).

Hoffman v. Board of Education, 410 N.Y.S. 2d 99 (New York, 1978) and 424 N.Y.S. 2d 376, 1976.

Implementing Title IX: The HEW regulations. *University of Pennsylvania Law Review*. 1976. *3*, 806–830.

Kamin L. Social and legal consequences of I.Q. tests as classification instruments: Some warnings from our past. *Journal of School Psychology*. 1975. *13*, 317–323.

McCarthy, M.M., & Thomas, S.B. The rights to an education: New trends emerging from special education litigation. *NOLPE School Law Journal*. 1977, 78–87.

Mills v. Board of Education, 348 F. Supp. 866 (D.C., 1972).

Moses v. Washington Parish School Board, 456 F. 2d 1285 (Fifth Circuit, 1972; 409 U.S. 1013, 1972).

PEER (Project on Equal Education Rights). Summary of the regulation for Title IX education amendments of 1972. Washington, D.C.: Office for Civil Rights, U.S. Department of Health, Education, and Welfare, 1975.

Pennsylvania Association for Retarded Children (P.A.R.C.) v. Commonwealth,
    343 F. Supp. 279 (Pa. 1972).
Ryland, W.H. Title IX Regulations. In *Attorneys General's Conference on School
    Law, Transcript of Proceedings.* Conference presented in Va., July 26, 1975.
Sauter, D.; Seidl, A.; & Karbon, J. The effects of high school counseling expe-
    rience and attitudes toward women's role on traditional or nontraditional
    career choice. *The Vocational Guidance Quarterly,* 1980, *28,* 241–249.
86 Stat. 373.
88 Stat. 514.
89 Stat. 775.
Talbutt, L. *Law and Virginia Public School Counselors.* Unpublished dissertation,
    Virginia Polytechnic Institute and State University, 1979.

Libel and Slander: A Potential Problem for the 1980s

Lou Culler Talbutt

In today's legal climate, counselors face the potential for litigation in a number of areas. One such area is libel and slander. Yet, few current professional articles deal with this topic. In order to guard against such litigation, counselors should be familiar with issues regarding this area and should follow professional guidelines for avoiding legal pitfalls. The APGA *Ethical Standards* (1981) and ASCA Position Statements (1976) provide such guidelines. This article addresses some key issues related to libel and slander and offers practical recommendations for counselors.

Both libel and slander refer to the defamation of a person's character or reputation. Historically, libel has meant defamation expressed in written form, whereas slander is expressed by word of mouth. Alexander, Corns, and McCann (1969) offered the following definition and explanation:

> Slander and libel consist of false and intentionally published or communicated statements . . . If the statement is communicated by word of mouth or gestures, it is known as slander. If it is communicated in writing, printing, or pictures, it is libel. Simply stated, libel is written defamation and slander is oral defamation. (p. 325)

The necessary elements for a tort of libel and slander are:

> (1) a false statement concerning another was published or communicated: (2) the statement brought hatred, disgrace, ridicule or contempt on another person; (3) damages resulted from the statement. (p. 325)

Educators, including counselors would be likely to face litigations for libel and slander if these three factors were present.

Outlook for the 80s

Burgum and Anderson (1975) wrote that there are few court cases involving libel and slander in education; however, they reminded school counselors that they have "no more right to defame a student than any member of society has a right to defame any other member" (p. 71). Are libel and slander, then, likely areas of litigation for counselors in the 80s? Hummel and Talbutt (1980) wrote, "There are several clues which strongly suggest that counselors may face more litigation in the future" (p. 2). Even though the authors were referring to all types of litigation, libel and slander would certainly be included. Counselors should be aware of the possibilities of lawsuits for defamation arising from their work. Killian (1970) identified three examples that illustrate such risks today:

> (a) talking on the telephone about a child's mental test score; (b) telling a bystander in the office about a boy's failing grade; and (c) relaying information about a student to a third party when it is clearly not a professional obligation. (p. 423)

The fact that there has been little such litigation in the past is no assurance for the future. Hummel and Talbutt worte, "More than at any time in the history of counseling, counselors must know their legal boundaries and responsibilities" (p. 2). Counselors, because of the nature of their work, have many opportunities for defamation that could result in litigation. First, counselors are privy to conversations, records, and personal information. Second, their jobs require that they communicate with a range of individuals who may pressure them to reveal confidential information. The misuse of personal information, whether intentional or unintentional, could result in libel and slander charges.

Historical Court Cases and Their Implications

Even though case law for school counselors regarding libel and slander is limited, several historical court cases dealing with educators have established certain implications significant for counselors today. In *Baskett v. Crossfield* (228 S.W. 673, 1921), a college president was charged with libel because of two letters he wrote to the father of a student. The letters explained that Baskett had been asked to withdraw from college for indecently exposing himself from the window of his dormitory room. In ruling in favor of the president, the court concluded that the letters were written in good faith. Also, the court pointed out that the burden was on the plaintiff to show malice. The president, acting in an official capacity, had qualified privileged communication and in the absence of malice was found not guilty of defamation.

In a similar libel suit, *Kenny v. Gurley* (Alabama, 95 So. 34, 1923), action was brought on behalf of a student against the school principal, medical director, and dean of women for libelous letters written to the parents. Action was based on statements pertaining to the student's having a venereal disease and "not living right." The Alabama Supreme Court concluded that no malice existed, and reversed the lower court ruling that had awarded the plaintiff damages.

In another case concerning the official report of a psychologist, *Iverson v. Frandsen* (Tenth Circuit, 237 F. 2d. 898, 1956), libel charges were placed against a psychologist for language used in a psychological report. The report stated that the plaintiff's "intelligence quotient . . . classified her as 'feeble-minded,' at the high grade moron level . . ." (pp. 899–900). The court reasoned that the report "though qualifiedly privileged, was positively free from any actionable malice whatsoever" (p. 900). The court pointed out that the psychologist had followed standard procedures and concluded: "It was a professional report made by a public servant in good faith, representing his best judgment, and therefore could not be maliciously false" (p. 900).

These court cases suggest recommended behavior for counselors. First, counselors should always act in good faith and keep their communications free from malice. Second, counselors should report student behavior objectively and factually and should avoid psychological jargon that can be misinterpreted. Butler, Moran, and Vanderpool (1974) warned counselors that "anecdotal reports should be stripped to the bare facts and devoid of value judgments" (p. 42). Third, communications should be made in answer to a request and made only when such a duty exists. Fourth, counselors should believe the communication to be true and should not go beyond the necessary facts. Also, counselors are reminded against communicating in the presence of uninvolved parties.

Along with understanding the danger for legal problems regarding libel and slander, counselors must also understand the two common defenses for defamation. The historical court decision in *Basektt v. Crossfield* (228 S.W. 673, 1921) identified these two defenses, truth and privileged communication. Truth is a defense unless the statements are malicious. Counselors should obviously act in good faith and be truthful. Ware (1971) concluded that counselors who follow ethical standards would probably meet the legal standards of good faith.

A second defense for defamation is privileged communication. Marsh and Kinnick (1970) defined absolute privileged communication as "unconditional" and wrote that it applied to "official proceedings of legislative and judicial agencies" (p. 363). They maintained, however, that conditional privilege, the type that counselors may possess, must meet certain conditions, such as "absence of malice, fair comment, and official status," (p. 363). The court in *Baskett v. Crossfield* also suggested that the communication should not go beyond the facts requested and that the party should believe the communications to be true. Ware (1971) offered the following explanation for privileged communication:

> Communications made to third persons in good faith
> on any subject matter in which the person communicating
> has an interest, or in reference to which he has a duty,
> is qualifiedly privileged if the communications are made
> to a person having a corresponding interest or duty whether
> the duty is legal or only social or moral. (p. 308)

Ware also explained two limitations of the privileged relationship rule. First, communications should not be made in front of others who do not possess a similar interest or duty. And, second, the privilege is stronger if the communication is made at the request of another. For example, a school counselor could report to a school principal or other school officials and be covered by the privileged communication rule, but the counselor could not slander a student in front of other students, the public, or other professionals not involved with the student (Ware, 1971).

Conclusions

This article has identified a number of problems related to the counselor's role regarding libel and slander. Counselors should remember their professional guidelines as well as keep in mind the implications of the above court cases. In addition to APGA *Ethical Standards* (1981), which address confidentiality, the American School Counselor Association (1976) presented a position statement on student records that addressed many of the issues identified in this article. These guidelines, if followed, should help counselors avoid legal problems related to libel and slander.

1. Counselors should maintain confidentiality unless there is danger to the client or others, or unless the counselor has a legal obligation to testify in a court of law. Section B-2 of *Ethical Standards* (1981) stated that;

> The counseling relationship and information resulting therefrom be kept confidential, consistent with the obligations of the member as a professional person.
> Section B-4 Counseling Relationship.
> When the client's condition indicates that there is clear and imminent danger to the client or others, the member must take reasonable personal action or inform responsible authorities. (American Personnel and Guidance Association, 1981)

2. Counselors should not reveal confidential information over the telephone. Guideline 9 of the ASCA Position Statements (1979) explained: "Counselors must not discuss matters over the telephone. A counselor should insist that a request for information be made in writing on official stationery" (p. 287).

3. Counselors should allow only appropriate individuals access to confidential information. Guideline 5 of the ASCA Position Statement (1976) stated: "Counselors must be concerned about individuals who have access to confidential information. Counselors must adhere to PL 93-380."

4. Counselors should assume responsibility for educating other staff members in the school about the privacy rights of students. Guideline 6 of the ASCA Position Statement (1976) stated: "All faculty and administrative personnel should receive inservice training concerning the privacy rights of students. Counselors should assume the primary responsibility for educating school personnel in this area" (p. 287).

5. Counselors should act in good faith at all times regarding confidential information about students. Such information should not be reported to uninvolved parties or revealed in front of those not professionally involved. Counselors who act out of malice or display improper behavior may be subject to libel or slander damages. Pertaining to privileged communication as a defense against libel or slander, Guideline 11 of the ASCA statement (1976) sated:

Communications made in good faith concerning a student may be classified as privileged by the courts, and the communicating parties will be protected by law against legal actions seeking damages for libel or slander. Generally, it may be said that an occasion of this particular privilege arises when one acts in the bona fide discharge of a public or private duty. This privilege may be abused or lost by malice, improper or unjustifiable motive, bad faith, or excessive publication. (p. 288)

References

Alexander, K., Corns, R., & McCann. W. *Public school law*. St. Paul, Minn.: West Publishing Co. 1969.

American Personnel and Guidance Association. *Ethical Standards*. 1981.

ASCA Position Statements. *School Counselor*, 1976, *23*, 281–288.

Baskett v. Grossfield, 228 S.W. 673 (Ky., 1921).

Burgum, T., & Anderson, S. *The counselor and the law*. Washington, D.C.: APGA Press, 1975.

Butler, H.E., Jr., Morgan, K.D., & Vanderpool, F.A. Legal aspects of student records. *School Psychology Digest*, 1974, *3*, 31–43.

Iverson v. Frandsen, 237 F. 2d 898 (Tenth Circuit, 1956).

Kenny v. Gurley, 95 So. 34 (Ala., 1923).

Killian, J.D. The law, the counselor, and student records. *Personnel and Guidance Journal*, 1970, *48*, 423–432.

Marsh, J.J., & Kinnick, B.C. Let's close the confidentiality gap. *Personnel and Guidance Journal*, 1970, *48*, 362–365.

Hummel, D., & Talbutt, L. Message from the guest editors. *Virginia Personnel and Guidance Journal*, 1980, *8*, 2.

Ware, M. The law and counselor ethics. *Personnel and Guidance Journal*, 1971, *50*, 305–310.

Current Legal Trends Regarding Abortions for Minors: A Dilemma for Counselors

Lou Culler Talbutt

In the middle and late 1970s, professional journals addressed the counselor's role in abortion counseling in light of U.S. Supreme Court rulings granting minors the right to abortions. Several court cases determined that statutes requiring parental permission for minors to obtain abortions were unconstitutional.

Although there have always been certain unclear areas regarding the counselor's role in abortion counseling, the legal rights of minors seem clear. Two U.S. Supreme Court cases, *Bellotti v. Baird* (1979) and *H. L. Etc. Appellant v. Scott M. Matheson* (1981), indicated that parents may be legally notified about abortions of minors in some situations.

More recently, in June 1983, the U.S. Supreme Court restated its position on abortion in three court decisions—*City of Akron v. Center for Reproductive Health, Planned Parenthood Assn. of Kansas City, Mo., Inc. v. Ashcroft*, and *Chris Simopoulos, Appellant v. Virginia*. States may not require that all second-trimester abortions be performed in a hospital, may not impose a 24-hour waiting period, may not require that physicians discuss the fetus as "a human life," and may not impose absolute parent consent for minors (51 LW 4767—4791). Clearly, the U.S. Supreme Court reaffirmed that abortions are constitutional for both adults and minors.

What then should be the counselor's legal responsibility to the parents of minors? Is the client the only concern of the counselor? Can parents of minors sue counselors for not informing them about the decisions of minors? This article discusses pertinent court cases dealing with abortion and the counselor's role in abortion. It concludes with some practical recommendations for counselors on abortion counseling for minors.

In a study on the medical rights of minors, Talbutt (1980) wrote, "There are still unresolved issues on which counselors need direction" (p. 406). At the same time, Talbutt called for guidelines from professional organizations to help counselors in abortion counseling for minors. Since that study, the previously mentioned court cases have clouded the issue even more.

Court Cases

A number of court cases, including U.S. Supreme Court decisions, have involved abortions. In *Roe v. Wade* (1973), the U.S. Supreme Court ruled that a Texas law restricting legal abortions to those who are needed for saving a mother's life was in violation of the Due Process Clause of the Fourteenth Amendment. With this historical case, the legal right to abortions was expanded. The court determined that women had a legal right to terminate a pregnancy for reasons other than saving their own life.

In *Doe v. Bolton* (1973), the U.S. Supreme Court declared that a Georgia statute requiring certain hospital requirements for abortions was unconstitutional. The Gerogia statute required a review committee, consent by two physicians, and residency in the state before a woman could obtain an abortion. The *Doe* decision expanded the abortion rights of women because hospitals and clinics became more accessible for obtaining abortions.

A number of cases have dealt with minors and abortions. The Supreme Court of Washington, in *State of Washington v. Koome* (1975), determined that a statute requiring unmarried minors to have parental consent prior to abortion was an invasion of privacy rights and that it discriminated between types of women.

> We hold that this statute too broadly encumbers the right of unmarried minor women to choose to terminate pregnancy, and unjustifiably discriminates between similarly situated groups of women in terms of their right to obtain a legal abortion. (p. 262)

In *Planned Parenthood v. Danforth* (1976), the U.S. Supreme Court ruled that a Missouri law requiring consent by a parent in the case of an unmarried minor prior to an abortion was unconstitutional. Citing *Roe v. Wade* (1973), the court concluded:

> The state may not constitutionally impose a blanket parental consent requirement . . . as a condition for an

unmarried minor's abortion during the first 12 weeks of her pregnancy for substantially the same reasons as in the case of the spousal consent provision, there being no significant state interests . . . (p. 53)

More recently. *Bellotti v. Baird* (1979) struck down a Massachusetts statute that required minors to obtain parental consent prior to an abortion. The U.S. Supreme Court concluded:

> We therefore conclude that if the State decides to require a pregnant minor to obtain one or both parents' consent to an abortion, it also must provide an alternative procedure whereby authorization for the abortion can be obtained.
>
> A pregnant minor is entitled in such a proceeding to show either: (1) that she is mature enough and well enough informed to make her abortion decision, in consultation with her physician, independently of her parent's wishes; or (2) that even if she is not able to make this decision independently, the desired abortion would be in her best interests. In sum, the procedure must ensure that the provision requiring parental consent does not in fact amount to the "absolute, and possible arbitrary, veto" that was found impermissible in *Danforth*.

The *Bellotti* decision opened the door for statutes to legally require the notification of parents of minors about abortions *if* an alternative is provided. The court's conclusion recognizes that there are times when a minor may be mature enough to make a decision about abortion without parental consent, and in such situations, statutes requiring parental permission must provide an alternative procedure wherein minors can obtain permission from an officer of the court or other appropriate person.

In *H. L. Etc. Appellant v. Scott M. Matheson* (1981), the U.S. Supreme Court seemed to shift its direction by upholding a state law requiring physicians to notify parents of minors about abortions under certain conditions. The court decided that a state may make the notification requirement if the girl depends on her parents, when she is not emancipated, and when she had made no claim that she is mature enough to make the decision alone or that her relationship with the parents might be seriously affected by such notification. This decision certainly indicates that physicians and possibly other professionals have responsibilities for notifying par-

ents of minors about abortions in the four situations stated by the
court.

Clearly, minors have the right to abortions according to several
U.S. Supreme Court decisions. Yet conflits created by the court
case discussed in the previous paragraph cause some uncertainty
for counselors and other professionals working with minors.

Counselor's Role in Abortions

In defining the role of the school counselor with respect to
abortion, Duncan and Moffett (1974) explained that counselors should
establish a setting for clients to examine feelings and evaluate alternatives. They warned counselors against imposing their views
and attitudes on clients.

Walleat (1975) summarized the counselor's responsibilities into
four areas. First, counselors should view abortion in relation to the
student's total development rather than a crisis situation. Second,
counselors should work in conjunction with other community and
school programs. Third, counselors should help students "process"
information. Finally, counselors should help students use information about abortion, even when schools fail to supply that information.

Walleat also emphasized that there were possible legal and
ethical issues regarding schools providing abortion information.
The extent to which schools can or should provide abortion information to minors is unclear. For example, do schools display information on abortion clinics openly? Is the information held
discreetly for students requesting it? Can parents of minors legally
object to schools' disseminating information about abortion? Can
the dissemination of information be interpreted as encouraging
abortions? These questions should be addressed by the professional
associations to clarify the school counselor's role in disseminating
abortion information.

Burgum and Anderson (1975) made some recommendations
to help counselors avoid lawsuits regarding abortions. They suggested that counselors give advice only in those areas in which
they are competent according to their education and work experience. The authors concluded, "Referring a counselee to a clinic's
care is the wise, commonsense course for a counselor to follow"
(p. 52). They also wrote that counselors who too "vociferously encourage abortion" (p. 193) or those who "negligently interfere with

the parents' right to advise a minor" (p. 193–194) may face legal difficulties.

In view of the proposed legislation and legal shift toward parental notification about abortions of minors, counselors of minors should strongly encourage their clients to discuss their situations with parents. The major questions remaining are: How far must counselors go in providing information to parents of minors? Is the legal responsibility strong enough to require counselors to break confidentiality under certain conditions? Unfortunately, until a major court case or legislation addresses these questions, the school counselor's role is undefined. Because parental notification about abortion for minors is unclear, professional guidelines are urgently needed to aid counselors.

Professional counseling groups should address the unresolved issues in a position paper or other materials. Until such time, the concluding recommendations should be of value to counselors.

Concluding Recommendations

Counselors should note that they can face litigation if they go beyond their professional training and skill in abortion counseling. For example, counseling regarding medical or serious psychological problems related to abortions should be left to medical and psychiatric personnel. This is consistent with the *Ethical Standards* (APGA, 1981). According to Section B:10 on the counseling relationship:

> If the member determines an inability to be of professional assistance to the client, the member must either avoid initiating the counseling relationship or immediately terminate that relationship. In either event, the member must suggest appropriate alternatives. . . (APGA, 1981)

Counselors should urge minors to discuss abortion plans with parents and involve families in the counseling process, if possible. Counselors should be familiar with laws and current court rulings that have implications for abortion counseling. Professional awareness through journals, conferences, and workshops is necessary for counselors to be well informed.

Counselors should consider the social mores of the local community. Not only do laws change, but attitudes change. Regardless of counselors' personal views, they must be objective and aware of and accepting of attitudes that are different from their own. Counselors should be aware that they can face legal problems if they impose their views and attitudes on minors regarding abortions. The final decision on abortion is for the client, not the counselor. The counselor's role is to provide the setting for clients to explore feelings and alternatives and to examine information.

Counselors should work through their national, state, and local professional organizations for directions and guidelines on abortion counseling and dissemination of abortion information for minors. Counselors working with supervisors and department chairpersons should establish general procedures for dealing with abortion counseling. Such procedures would enable counselors to deal more effectively with abortions and prevent a "crisis" type approach. Procedures could include steps for involving appropriate family members, local referral agencies, and school resources.

Finally, counselors should be knowledgeable about appropriate referral agencies dealing with abortions. This recommendation is also consistent with the *Ethical Standards* (APGA, 1981). According to Section B:10 on the counseling relationship, "The member must be knowledgeable about referral resources so that a satisfactory referral can be initiated . . ." (APGA, 1981).

References

APGA. (1981). *Ethical standards.* Falls Church, VA: American Personnel and Guidance Association.

Bellotti v. Baird, 47 LW 4969 (July 2, 1979).

Burgum, T., & Anderson, S. (1975). *The counselor and the law.* Washington, DC: APGA Press.

City of Akron v. Center for Reproductive Health, Planned Parenthood Assn. of Kasnas City, Mo., Inc. v. Ashcroft, Chris Simopoulos, Appellant v. Virginia, 51 LW 4767–4791 (June 1983).

Doe v. Bolton, 410 U.S. 179 (1973).

Duncan, J., & Moffett, C. (1974). Abortion counseling and the school counselor. *The School Counselor. 21,* 188, 195.

H. L. etc. Appellant v. Scott M. Matheson, 101 S.Ct, 1161 (1981).

Planned Parenthood v. Danforth, 428 U.S. 52 (1976).

Roe v. Wade, 410 U.S. 113 (1973).

State of Washington v. Koome, 530 P.2d 260 (1975).

Talbutt, L.C. (1980). The medical rights of minors: Some answered and unanswered questions. *The School Counselor, 27,* 403–406.

Walleat, P.L. (1975). Abortion information: A guidance viewpoint. *The School Counselor, 22,* 338–341.

Counselor Liability and the Duty To Warn: Selected Cases, Statutory Trends, and Implications for Practice

Barbara Herlihy and *Vernon Lee Sheeley*

The authors review selected case law and recently enacted state statutes pertinent to "the duty to warn." Guidelines for practice in dealing with dangerous clients are offered.

Since the California court ruling in the *Tarasoff* appeal (*Tarasoff v. Regents of University of California*, 1976) 12 years ago, mental health professionals have been seriously concerned about (a) the implications of that and subsequent judicial rulings for the "duty to warn and protect," and (b) their potential liability in court actions (Denkowski & Denkowski, 1982; Knapp & VandeCreek, 1982; Mabe & Rollin, 1986; Mappes, Robb, & Engels, 1985; Snider, 1985; Stude & McKelvey, 1979; VandeCreek & Knapp, 1984; Wise, 1978). In our increasingly litigious society, the legal notion of civil liability for personal injury has been expanding and now exceeds the traditional risk limits of a generation ago. The emerging attitude that "someone is injured, therefore someone must pay" suggests that loss need not lie with the victim. Legislators, judges, and juries have aligned themselves with this social impulse by pushing out the frontiers of responsibility.

The California Supreme Court, concluding that a psychotherapist who treats a potentially violent or dangerous client "bears a duty to use reasonable care to give threatened persons such warnings as are essential to avert foreseeable dangers" (*Tarasoff II*, p. 559), enmeshed mental health professionals in this emerging trend. The American Psychological Association (APA) Committee on Legal Issues listed outcomes of 50 malpractice lawsuits brought from 1947 to 1984 against mental health care providers as defendants for violent acts to clients. The final disposition of 18 cases decided before *Tarasoff I* (1974) indicated that plaintiffs prevailed in 5 cases

143

(28%), and defendants were awarded in 13 (72%). The 32 cases decided since *Tarasoff I* reflect the emerging trend: Plaintiffs were successful in 20 cases (62.5%), whereas defendants prevailed in only 12 (37.5%) (Committee on Legal Issues, 1985).

Counselors, as a relatively new and still maturing professional group, may not have extensive experience with involvement in lawsuits. Nonetheless, they have shared psychologists' concerns about the lack of clear guidelines for determining whether, when, and how to exercise the duty to warn and protect. They have experienced anxiety and confusion regarding whether this duty, if it exists, is an ethical obligation, a legal obligation, or both.

Codes of ethics are unclear on this issue. The *Ethical Standards* of the American Association for Counseling and Development (AACD) state that: "When the client's condition indicates that there is a clear and imminent danger to the client or others, the member must take reasonable personal action or inform responsible authorities" (AACD *Ethical Standards*, 1981, Section B.4, p. 1). This standard has been variously interpreted as (a) a statement that counselors are obligated to pursue threats to others reported by clients (DePauw, 1986), and (b) silent on the issue of the duty to warn (Mabe & Rollin, 1986). Future revisions of ethical codes may include specific criteria for warning intended victims of clients, as has been recommended by Mappes, Robb, and Engels (1985). Although such a clarification would be helpful, counselors cannot rely solely on ethical standards. Rulings made by legal forums also have implications for the duty to warn and for potential liability. This article first reviews legal rulings, statutes, and analyses, and then suggests guidelines for counseling practice that may be drawn from this review.

Legal rulings relevant to the counseling profession may arise from two major sources: case law and statutory law. Case law pertains to rulings in individual court cases; its importance lies in its potential to set precedents for future cases and in the possibility that, cumulatively, it may form a rationale for future statutory enactments. Statutory law is enacted by the legislative branch of government. Statutory laws relating to therapist liability have been enacted in some states, and statutes granting privileged communication between therapists and clients may also have implications for the duty to warn or protect.

Review of Selected Cases

The first *Tarasoff* opinion (1974) was vacated after a rehearing and was replaced by *Tarasoff II* in 1976. In the wake of this well-publicized ruling, considerable case law was established regarding clients who pose a danger to others. In this review of selected cases, no attempt is made to delineate differences in the "duty to warn" among the various helping professionals (this generic term includes psychiatrists, psychologists, community mental health counselors, child, marriage and family therapists, and social workers). The *Tarasoff II* ruling applied to "psycho-therapists," a designation that has left these boundaries unclear in jurisdictions outside California. In this article, cases are discussed according to Kelleher's (1984) suggestion that courts rely upon a certain criterion to determine therapist liability: The potential victim's identifiability. Kelleher distinguished among three types of situations: the presence or absence of a readily identifiable victim, the existence of a specific foreseeable victim, and foreseeable danger in general.

Identifiable Victims

In both *Tarasoff II* and the case that followed it in New Jersey, *McIntosh v. Milano* (1979), the courts required that there be an identifiable potential victim before liability for failure to warn could be imposed. As has been noted by Knapp and VandeCreek (1982), the controlling facts in *McIntosh* were similar to those in *Tarasoff*. Dr. Milano's patient had a background of hostile feelings toward his former girlfriend and had revealed to the therapist that he had previously shot at her car with a BB gun and wanted to see her suffer. The patient, while still in therapy, obtained a pistol and killed the ex-girlfriend. The court imposed liability, therefore implying that a therapist may have a duty to take reasonable steps to protect an intended or potential victim.

A court of appeals in Michigan used similar reasoning in upholding a lower court's judgment against a psychiatrist in *Davis v. Lhim* (1983). In this case, the psychiatrist released a patient, who had a history of psychological disorders, into the care of the patient's mother. The patient later fired a shotgun and killed his mother while she was attempting to restrain him. The siblings of the mother sued the psychiatrist for negligent discharge of the patient, and the court upheld the principle that the psychiatrist owed a duty of reasonable care to persons who are readily identifiable as foreseeably endangered by a patient. The jury award of $500,000 seemed to support mental health providers' concern that they may be viewed as "deep pocket" defendants for victims of violent crime.

Applying the same principle of identifiability, courts have in at least four cases refused to impose liability in the absence of a readily identifiable victim. In *Thompson v. County of Alameda* (1980), a California court ruled against the parents of a young murder victim. A juvenile, while in custody in a county facility, made a threat to take the life of a young child (although he did not specify a particular child) in a certain neighborhood. After the juvenile was released, he killed a young boy in that neighborhood. The child's parents were denied a cause of action against the facility that had released the murderer because threats had not been directed at any specific person. Although a warning to the limited group of parents in the neighborhood who had young children might possibly have averted the killing and been an effective warning, the court denied liability. The significance of *Thompson* is its clarification of the requirement that the victim be "readily identifiable" in order for the *Tarasoff* duty to apply.

A federal district court used similar reasoning in refusing to impose liability in *Leedy v. Hartnett* (1981). In this situation, a patient who had been in and out of psychiatric hospitals for 20 years went to live with his friends, the Leedys, after he had been released from the hospital. The patient was known to be violent when intoxicated. He later became intoxicated while drinking with the Leedys and assaulted them. The court held that the patient posed no greater threat to the Leedys than to anyone else who might have been present when he became violent, and refused to impose liability because the Leedys were not readily identifiable victims.

In *Brady v. Hopper* (1983), suit was brought against the therapist of John Hinckley, Jr., who injured Brady while attempting to assassinate President Reagan in 1981. The court dismissed the case because Hinckley had not made specific threats toward anyone in particular, and thus harm to the plaintiff was not foreseeable.

Finally, a California court refused to impose liability in *Mavroudis v. Superior Court of San Mateo County* (1980) when the identity of the intended victim was unknown. In this case, a hospital released a boy into the custody of his parents, whom he later assaulted with a hammer. The court, although acknowledging that the hospital's therapist might have been able to determine on reflection that the parents were potential victims, recognized that the therapist was not obligated to take extreme measures to learn the intended victims' identities.

These rulings indicate that therapists must have adequate information about a client's potential to harm *certain* victims before they have the duty to warn those victims.

Specific Foreseeable Victims

Courts in some jurisdictions have extended the duty to warn to "foreseeable" victims who may not be readily identifiable by the therapists, but who would be likely targets if the client became violent.

In *Jablonski v. United States* (1983), the Ninth Circuit Court allowed a cause of action to a victim who was foreseeable, although not identifiable. This case involved a client who had a history of violence toward women and whose psychological profile indicated that he would direct his violence against women who were close to him. He lived with a woman who became the victim of his assault. The court, although acknowledging that no threats had been made to any specific individual, reasoned that the victim was a likely recipient of his violence.

In *Hedlund v. Superior Court of Orange County* (1983), the California Supreme Court allowed a cause of action to the son of a woman whom a client had threatened with harm and had later killed in the son's presence. Although no threats had been made against the son, he suffered emotional trauma in witnessing the murder, and was found to be a foreseeable victim. In this case, failure to warn even a third party victim was ruled to be professional negligence.

Foreseeable Danger in General

Confounding the criterion of identifiability or foreseeability, several courts have imposed liability when the danger was to the general public rather than to a particular individual. In *Lipari v. Sears, Roebuck, & Co.* (1980), a former psychiatric patient of a VA hospital purchased a shotgun and then resumed outpatient care. He terminated therapy shortly thereafter against the therapist's advice. Six weeks later he went into a nightclub and began firing a shotgun, killing Dennis Lipari and injuring Lipari's wife. In this case, there was no clear danger of harm to a particular person, nor was there any basis for the therapist to identify a potential victim. Nevertheless, the court broadened the circumstances of therapist liability by ruling against the therapist. The court stated that there were ways other than alerting the victim to act on the duty to warn, such as attempting to detain the patient.

In *Peterson v. State* (1983), the court followed the logic of *Lipari* by imposing on a therapist a duty to control a potentially dangerous patient. The therapist had released a patient who had drug-related mental problems; later a woman was injured when this patient, under the influence of drugs, negligently collided with her car. The court held that the therapist had a duty to protect anyone who might be a foreseeable victim of his patient's drug-related problems. Because the therapist knew of the patient's tendencies toward drug abuse, yet released him, the therapist could be liable for the injury caused by that patient. Both *Lipari* and *Peterson* imply that the therapist has a duty to keep a patient committed or to secure the commitment of a patient who poses a risk of harm to others.

The findings in a recent case, *Division of Corrections v. Neakok* (1986), suggest that the courts are continuing to refine the guidelines established by earlier cases. In this case, a supervised parolee, who had been mandatorily released from prison 6 months previously, had become intoxicated and shot and killed his teenaged stepdaughter and her boyfriend and raped, assaulted, and strangled to death another woman. The relatives of the three victims brought suit against the State of Alaska, the Division of Corrections, and the parole board, claiming negligence in part for failure to warn the victims. The Alaska Supreme Court, hearing the case on appeal, refused to overturn the lower court's verdict of negligence. The Supreme Court noted that in both *Lipari* and *Peterson* the specific identity of the victim had been wholly unforeseeable. In this case, however, the victims were foreseeable as more than simply members of the general public. The murderer had been released into an isolated community of fewer than 100 residents, one of the victims was the murderer's stepdaughter, and the others were her boyfriend and her aunt. The court stated that because the stepdaughter was foreseeably endangered, her close friends and relatives may also have been within a zone of especially foreseeable victims. Thus the court, although disclaiming any intention that potentially dangerous individuals "be emblazoned with scarlet letters" (p. 1131), ruled that the releasing agency may be held liable for failure to warn a foreseeable group of victims.

Other courts continue to grapple with complex issues in attempting to clarify the duty to warn. A number of precedent-setting cases, as discussed above, hinged upon psychotherapists' decisions to release clients from inpatient treatment. A recent case, *Currie v. United States of America* (1986), has particular implications for psychotherapists who treat clients on an outpatient basis. This case involved a Vietnam veteran suffering from post-traumatic stress disorder who entered his former place of employment after being fired, killed one of his coworkers, and wounded several others. The client had been sporadically attending outpatient group therapy at a VA clinic. In telephone conversations with his therapist, he had threatened harm to his employer and to the therapist. The psychotherapist warned law enforcement authorities and the employer, but concluded in consultation with other clinic staff members that involuntarily committing the client was not feasible under state law.

Suit was brought against the psychotherapy staff for negligence in failing to petition to involuntarily commit the client; this led the court to address the distinction between the duty to commit and the duty to warn. The court, recognizing that there is an inherent conflict between protecting society by confining dangerous persons and protecting the individual patient by giving him the least restrictive environment, acknowledged that both goals probably can never be met in practice. The court sought a compromise by suggesting that a "psychotherapist judgment rule" be applied, in which the court would examine the good faith, consultation sought, and thoroughness of the therapist's decision not to commit a client. Applying this standard, the court ruled that because the therapists' decision not to seek commitment involved serious personal risk to themselves, the therapists had acted in good faith. The claim was then dismissed.

Clarifications and Conflicts in Statutory Laws

The Committee on Legal Issues of the American Psychological Association (APA) has been concerned that the gradual accumulation of case law extending the *Tarasoff* duty, along with reforms in civil commitment laws, has led to a redefinition of the psychotherapist as a predictor of violent behavior, a protector of potential victims, and a "deep pocket" defendant for the victims of violent crime. In response to this concern, the committee has developed a White Paper on the duty to protect (APA, 1985). It contains a model bill to limit psychotherapists' civil liability for the violent acts of mental patients. Bills based on this model, if enacted into law by state legislatures, would override the precedents set by courts and would clarify therapists' legal responsibilities.

Despite this recommendation, legislatures in only four states have enacted statutes that limit therapist liability. Because *Tarasoff* and a number of subsequent cases occurred in California jurisdictions, it is not surprising that California in 1985 was the first state to add to its Evidence Code a section limiting therapist liability. This section states:

> There shall be no monetary liability on the part of, and no cause of action shall arise against . . . a psychotherapist . . . in failing to warn of and protect from a patient's threatened violent behavior or failing to predict and warn of and protect from a patient's violent behavior except when the patient has communicated to the psychotherapist a serious threat of physical violence against a reasonably identifiable victim or victims.
>
> If there is a duty to warn and protect under the limited circumstances specified above, the duty shall be discharged by the psychotherapist making reasonable efforts to communicate the threat to the victim or victims and to a law enforcement agency. (California Evidence Code, Civil Code, Section 43.92)

A similar enactment protecting mental health care providers was passed in Colorado in 1986. The language is quite similar to that of the California statute, except that the serious threat of physical violence must be "imminent" and directed against "a specific person or persons," and the duty may also be exercised by "taking other appropriate action including, but not limited to, hospitalizing the patient." In addition to immunity from civil liability, mental health care providers cannot be subject to professional discipline for issuing warnings or making predictions of dangerousness.

A Kentucky statute, also enacted in 1986, imposes more specific conditions for liability. The patient must have communicated to a mental health professional "an actual threat of some specific act." The duty to warn is discharged when the professional makes reasonable efforts to communicate to the victim and to notify police. The Kentucky statute provides for instances when no particular victim is identifiable; in these cases, the professional must attempt to communicate the threat to law enforcement authorities.

A New Hampshire statute, effective January 1, 1987, is unique in that it requires psychologists to warn or protect when there is "a serious threat of substantial damage to real property" as well as to persons. Although the majority of suits have involved injury to persons rather than to property, a recent appeal case opinion in Vermont illustrated that provider liability may extend beyond personal injury. In *Peck v. Counseling Service* (1985), the court ruled negligence against a health care provider who failed to warn patients that their son (a client) had threatened to burn their barn. The court declared arson a violent act that represented a lethal threat to humans who may have been near. The parents, the plaintiffs, were also found to be 50% comparatively negligent in causing their barn and its contents to be destroyed because they were aware of their son's proclivity to violent behavior.

The New Hampshire statute, although unique in including damage to property, resembles other statutes in that the duty may be exercised by attempting to communicate the threat to the victim, notifying the police, or obtaining civil commitment of the client. Similar bills have been drafted in Florida, Kansas, Louisiana, Massachusetts, and Washington, but have not been enacted into law.

In summary, statutory laws in California, Colorado, Kentucky, and New Hampshire provide therapists covered under those statutes with clear guidelines for dealing with potentially dangerous clients. In some states, however, other statutes, specifically those regarding privileged communication, can create serious dilemmas for conscientious therapists. Therapists breach confidentiality when they exercise the duty to warn third parties who may be endangered by a client. Whereas confidentiality is an ethical standard, its legal counterpart is privileged communication that prohibits therapist disclosure of clients' confidential communications except under certain specified circumstances. Thus, these "exceptions to privilege" should provide guidance regarding the duty to warn.

A Maryland case, *Shaw v. Glickman* (1980), illustrates the dilemma that can be created when statutory law conflicts with precedents established by case law. In this case, a psychotherapy team was leading a group that included a man, his wife, and the wife's lover. The husband subsequently discovered the affair and shot and severely wounded the lover who sued, claiming that the psychotherapy team should have warned him of the danger. The court, stating that there was no basis on which the team could have foreseen the assault, exonerated the psychotherapists. The court's reasoning was similar to that of the courts in *Thompson, Leedy, Brady,* and *Mavroudis,* but is remarkable for the further comments it made regarding privileged communication. The court noted that because Maryland's privileged communication statute does not allow for breaches of confidentiality when the lives of others are threatened, the psychotherapists could not have warned the victim even if they had known about the threat (Knapp & VandeCreek, 1982). Thus, it seems that a literal interpretation of statutes that extend privileged communication without including an exception for cases of clear and imminent danger to others might actually prevent therapists from warning potential victims.

Licensed professional counselors in some states may be particularly vulnerable to such a dilemma. Of the 18 states that had enacted counselor licensure laws through the summer of 1986, 12 (Alabama, Arkansas, Idaho, Mississippi, Missouri, Montana, Nebraska, North Carolina, Ohio, Oklahoma, Virginia, West Virginia) were found to contain privileged communication provisions (Herlihy & Sheeley, 1987). In Alabama and Arkansas, the statutes guarantee that privileged communication between licensed professional counselors and their clients is the same under law as that between an attorney and client; no exceptions are specified. Because attorney-client privilege statutes typically contain a "future crime exception," however, licensed counselors in those two states are advised to study their respective attorney-client privilege statutes for guidance regarding their duty to warn.

The statutes in three other states make exceptions relevant to the duty to warn. The Mississippi statute makes an exception to privilege "when a communication reveals the contemplation of a crime or harmful act, or intent to commit suicide." The Montana statute stipulates that the counselor "need not treat as confidential a communication otherwise confidential that reveals the contemplation of a crime by the client or any other person or that in his professional opinion reveals a threat of imminent harm to the client or others." In Ohio, one of the conditions under which otherwise confidential communications may be revealed is when "the communication or advice indicated clear and present danger to the client or to others." It should be noted that these provisions do not *require* a licensed professional counselor to breach confidentiality and exercise the duty to warn or protect; they only *allow* the counselor to do so. By contrast, in the states of Idaho, Missouri, Nebraska, North Carolina, Oklahoma, Virginia, and West Virginia, a literal reading of the privileged communication statutes might actually prevent a licensed counselor from warning a potential victim.

Guidelines for Practice

With respect to the duty to warn and protect, both case law and statutory law, with the exception of the four recently enacted state statutes that limit therapist liability, are confusing and unclear, leaving counselors in a quandary. It seems clear that a duty to warn does exist if, in the counselor's professional judgment, the client is likely to commit a violent act against a third party. Counselors need to exercise care against the tendency to overpredict violence as a means of self-protection; not only are such practices ethically questionable, they provide no real safety. If counselors do overreact and mistakenly deliver a warning to a third party, it is possible that they may be sued by the client for invasion of privacy or defamation. On the other hand, an overcautious approach leading to a failure to warn could in some jurisdictions and in certain circumstances lead to a lawsuit in which the counselor would be held liable. In addition to the legal ramifications, personal and ethical consequences need to be considered. No counselor wishes to be faced with a situation in which a warning was not given and the client's violence resulted in an injury or death to a third party. Counselors might be tempted, given the complexity of the quandary and the seriousness of the consequences of a mistaken judgment, to avoid dangerous clients. It would be a breach of ethics, however, to close the doors of the profession to a segment of the population that clearly needs help (Snider, 1986).

Although no absolute answers can be formulated at this time, it does seem clear that counselors, when they determine that a client poses a danger to others, have a duty to take affirmative steps. Kelleher (1984) suggested that therapists should consider three factors in deciding what steps are reasonable: (a) whether the client is still in treatment or in contact with the therapist, (b) whether the danger is imminent, and (c) whether the client poses a danger to a foreseeable or identifiable victim or to the general public. Kelleher further suggested six possible affirmative duties that have emerged from case precedents. Actions that focus on the client include:

(A) intensifying treatment,

(B) attempting to persuade the client to accept voluntary treatment, and

(C) attempting to secure involuntary commitment.

Alternatives that involve third parties include:

(D) warning the potential victim,

(E) warning family or friends who might apprise the victim of the danger, and

(F) notifying the police.

The factors to consider can be related to the possible affirmative actions to produce a suggested decision-making model, illustrated in Figure 1.

Figure 1

THE DUTY TO WARN AND PROTECT: A SUGGESTED DECISION MAKING MODEL

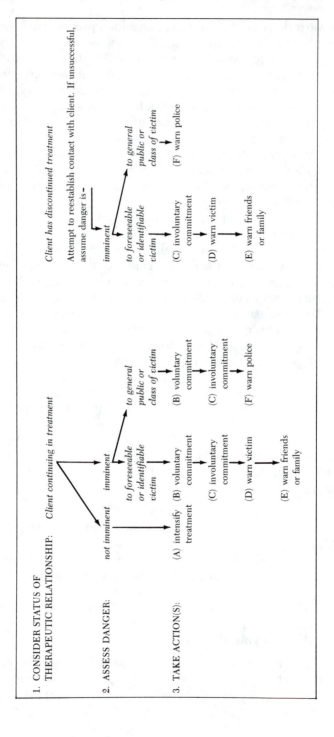

The actions included in the model are not intended to be an all-inclusive list. Depending on the specific circumstances of the situation, ethically conscientious therapists may select to take additional steps. Several writers (Denkowski & Denkowski, 1982; Halleck, 1980; Roth & Meisel, 1977; VandeCreek & Knapp, 1984) have suggested further guidelines for therapists who deal with dangerous clients:

1. Keeping in mind that the primary objective should be to keep the client in therapy, deal with the aggression as part of the treatment.
2. To avoid overreacting, remember that clients without a history of violence rarely implement their threats; to be prudent, pursue other options before breaching confidentiality.
3. Take an informed consent approach by securing the client's permission for disclosure and inviting the client to participate in the process, or by contacting the third party in the presence of the client.
4. Attempt environmental manipulations such as having the client get rid of lethal weapons.
5. Be prepared by formulating contingency plans that are derived in consultation with an informed attorney, a local psychiatric hospital, and area law enforcement personnel.
6. Consult with professional colleagues and attorneys who have expertise and experience in dealing with dangerous clients.
7. Keep careful records and document all actions taken.
8. Issue warnings to third parties only as a last resort after actions directly involving the client have been ineffective.
9. If warning a third party is unavoidable, disclose only the minimum amount necessary to protect the victim or the public, stating the specific threat but reserving any opinion or prediction.
10. If consideration is given to seeking involuntary commitment of an outpatient client, act in good faith, consult with colleagues, and thoroughly research applicable laws and standards.
11. Finally, do not practice without professional liability insurance.

VandeCreek and Knapp (1984) have noted that although counselors value both the sanctity of human life and the privacy of the counseling relationship, these values can conflict in situations involving clients who pose a danger to others. Conflicts in accumulated case law and variations in statutory law regarding privileged communication place counselors in a legal, as well as an ethical, quandary. Perhaps the most effective means that counselors can employ to clear this confusion is to lobby for the passage of state statutes that define the limits of counselor liability. In the interim, for counselors in states that lack such statutes, the decision-making model described here may provide a basis for taking responsible action. At this point in the development of the counseling profession, however, there are no absolute answers. In the last analysis, there is no substitute for the counselor's professional clinical judgment in dealing with the conflicting demands of confidentiality versus disclosure.

References

American Association for Counseling and Development. (1981). *Ethical standards*. Alexandria, VA: Author. (Originally published by American Personnel and Guidance Association).

Brady v. Hopper, 570 F. Supp. 1333 (D. Colo. 1983).

Civil Evidence Code, California. §§ 43.92 (1986).

Committee on Legal Issues of the American Psychological Association. (1985, November). *White paper on duty to protect*. Washington, DC: Author.

Currie v. United States of America, Memorandum Opinion, Civil No. C-85-0629-D. United States District Court for the Middle District of North Carolina, Durham Division. (North Carolina, 1986).

Davis v. Lhim, 335 N.W. 2d. 481 (Mich. App. 1983).

Denkowski, K.M., & Denkowski, G.C. (1982). Client-counselor confidentiality: An update of rationale, legal status, and implications. *Personnel and Guidance Journal, 60*, 371–375.

DePauw, M.E. (1986). Avoiding ethical violations: A timeline perspective for individual counseling. *Journal of Counseling and Development, 64*, 303–305.

Division of Corrections v. Neakok, 721 P.2d. 1121 (Alaska, 1986).

Halleck, S. (1980). *Law in the practice of psychiatry*. New York: Plenum Medical Book Company.

Hedlund v. Superior Court of Orange County, 34 Cal. 3d 695, 669 P.2d. 41, 194 Cal. Rptr. 805 (1983).

Herlihy, B., & Sheeley, V.L. (1987). Privileged communication in selected helping professions: A comparison among statutes. *Journal of Counseling and Development, 65*, 479–483.

Jablonski v. United States, 712 F.2d. 391 (9th Cir. 1983).

Kelleher, M. (1984). Psychotherapists and the duty to warn: An attempt at clarification. *New England Law Review, 19*, 597–617.

Knapp, S., & VandeCreek, L. (1982). Tarasoff: Five years later. *Professional Psychology, 13*, 511–516.

Leedy v. Hartnett, 510 F. Supp. 1125 (M.D. Pa. 1981).

Lipari v. Sears, Roebuck & Co., 497 F. Supp. 195D (Neb. 1980).

Mabe, A.R., & Rollin, S.A. (1986). The role of a code of ethical standards in counseling. *Journal of Counseling and Development, 64*, 294–297.

Mappes, D.C., Robb, G.P., & Engels, D.W. (1985). Conflicts between ethics and law in counseling and psychotherapy. *Journal of Counseling and Development, 64*, 246–252.

Mavroudis v. Superior Court of San Mateo County, 102 Cal. App. 3d. 594, 162 Cal. Rptr. 724 (1980).

McIntosh v. Milano, 403 A.2d. 500 (1979).

Peck v. Counseling Service, 146 Vt. 61, 499 A.2d. 422 (1985).

Peterson v. State, 671 P.2d. 230 (Wash. 1983).

Roth, L.H., & Meisel, A. (1977). Dangerousness, confidentiality, and the duty to warn. *American Journal of Psychiatry, 134*, 508–511.

Shaw v. Glickman, 415 A.2d. 625 (Md. App. 1980).

Snider, P.D. (1985). The duty to warn: A potential issue of litigation for the counseling supervisor. *Counselor Education and Supervision, 25*, 66–73.

Stude, E.W., & McKelvey, J. (1979). Ethics and the law: Friend or foe? *Personnel and Guidance Journal, 57*, 453–456.

Tarasoff v. Regents of the University of California, 118 Cal. Rptr. 129, 529 P.2d. 533 (Cal. 1974).

Tarasoff v. Regents of the University of California, 113 Cal. Rptr. 14, 551 P.2d. 334 (Cal. 1976).

Thompson v. County of Alameda, 614 P.2d. 728 (Cal. 1980).

VandeCreek, L., & Knapp, S. (1984). Counselors, confidentiality, and life-endangering clients, *Counselor Education and Supervision, 24*, 51–57.

Wise, T. (1978). Where the public peril begins: A survey of psychotherapists to determine the effects of Tarasoff. *Stanford Law Review, 31*, 165–190.

4

THE SCHOOL COUNSELOR AND CHILD ABUSE

In most states, school counselors are obligated to report suspected cases of child abuse. Camblin and Prout (1983) discuss the legal and ethical issues surrounding such reports, provide a summary listing of the basic provisions of each state law, and make recommendations for counselors. The article by Sandberg, Crabbs, and Crabbs (1988) addresses many of the specific legal questions that school counselors have asked regarding the reporting of suspected child abuse. Spiegel (1988) provides the perspective of a parent who has been accused of child abuse. He cautions against the loss of objectivity and provides specific recommendations for counselors. In responding to Spiegel's article, Krugman (1988) delineates possible reasons for unfounded reports and questions the data as presented. Ferris (1988) reasserts the need for a balanced perspective and Howell-Nigrelli (1988) suggests a team approach to issues of child abuse reporting and prevention. Finally, Gerler (1988) concisely summarizes recent research findings pertaining to child abuse.

School Counselors and the Reporting of Child Abuse: A Survey of State Laws and Practices

Lanthan D. Camblin, Jr. and *H. Thompson Prout*

A distraught 13-year-old girl sought out a school counselor and asked for help. She told the counselor that she had been raped several times by her stepfather. It was his habit to awaken her each morning, she explained, but two weeks ago he suddenly got into bed with her and sexually assaulted her. It had happened twice more, most recently that morning and she was frightened. The counselor called the welfare department at once, but was met with indifference. . . . The counselor pressed for action, and reluctantly the agency agreed to make a home visit "to see whether (the child) is enjoying this." (Broadhurst, 1978, p. 22)

Alan was pummeled for perhaps four hours before he died, at times with fists, at times with a wooden club wrapped with gauze and labeled "The Big Stick." He was five years old. Police found his frail body on the living room floor, his blond hair red with blood, his hand bruised from trying to deflect the blows. . . . On the day of the kindergarten class photograph, Alan came to school with his face so bruised he couldn't be in the picture. . . . (He was described as) "a sweet kid" who got lost in the bureaucracy, falling victim to a tragic series of reports never forwarded, questions never asked, evidence never given. (Cincinnati Enquirer, 1981, p. A-3)

These case profiles are not dissimilar to those stories reported daily by the media and to those situations that counselors will encounter on an all-too-frequent basis in their schools. In recent years, the problem of child abuse and neglect has received considerable attention, resulting in a general expectation of greater vigilance and in more exacting laws pertaining to this social issue.

Child abuse may include varying aspects of physical abuse, sexual abuse, verbal abuse, general neglect, emotional neglect, abandonment, and failure to thrive because of inadequate supervision. The problem could be considered epidemic, with estimates of suspected abuse ranging from half a million (Antler, 1978; Gelles, 1975; Light, 1974) to a million (Solomon, 1979) cases annually. The American Humane Society has indicated that up to two-thirds of the cases of abuse/neglect involved school-age children (Broadhurst, 1978).

All states and the District of Columbia have enacted laws that deal with child abuse. These laws establish regulations for reporting and following up on suspected cases of child abuse (Moore & McKee, 1979). School personnel, specifically counselors, are among those required by many states to report suspected cases. The laws mandate that certain individuals must report suspected cases to a public agency—usually county or state welfare. Many states have "hotline" numbers where the information is relayed to the appropriate local agency.

A number of authors have written specifically on the role of the counselor in dealing with child abuse. Griggs and Gale (1977) have written on the need for counselors to be aware of legal definitions of child abuse, to be reporting laws within their particular jurisdiction, to be knowledgeable in procedures of recognizing and identifying abuse, and to be developing skills in dealing with the consequences of child abuse. The counselor may be the first professional helper to come in contact with the abused child. Moore and McKee (1979) offer specific suggestions for counselors who are faced with possible child abuse. Miller and Miller (1979) offer guidelines for identifying potential child abuse.

It is inevitable that front-line pupil personnel specialists will have to deal with child abuse in their work. Those professionals must be aware of identification and intervention strategies, as well as the legal issues involved in child abuse. Swoba, Elwork, Sales, and Levine (1978), in a survey of mental health practitioners (non-school), found that a significant number were unaware of their right to privileged communication under child abuse laws as well as the legal mandate to report suspected cases. While there are no similar data for pupil personnel workers, it is not unlikely that a similar situation may exist among school-based professionals.

The purpose of this survey was to collect state-by-state information on reporting laws as they relate to school personnel, to obtain data on reporting practices by school personnel, and to analyze school-oriented programs of state child abuse offices.

Method

The study involved two phases. Initially, a questionnaire was mailed to the office or department in each state and the District of Columbia that is responsible for enforcement, development, and management of child abuse programs. The questionnaire asked informants to indicate:

1. whether the state required mandatory reporting by certain individuals/professionals who have reason to believe a child has been abused;
2. whether the mandatory reporting laws applied to physical abuse, emotional neglect/mental injury, general maltreatment/failure to provide, sexual abuse, abandonment and/or any other specified types of abuse;
3. which school personnel were required to report cases of suspected child abuse, choosing from school administrators, teachers, school counselors, consulting psychologists, nursery school personnel, school psychologists, speech therapists, school social workers, visiting/itinerant/homebound teachers, state-operated hospital/institution/facility personnel and/or any other designated personnel;
4. whether reporting requirements applied to both public and private school personnel;
5. whether the required reporters, when making reports of suspected child abuse, were immune from any civil or criminal liability provided that such persons acted in good faith;
6. what percentage (official statistics or estimate) of the total reports of child abuse originate with school personnel; and
7. a rating of school personnel's compliance with the child abuse mandatory reporting laws by estimating the extent to which school personnel tend to report "most appropriate cases," or to "not report cases in almost all circumstances."

In the second phase of the study, states were rank ordered on the basis of the percentage of reports originating from school personnel. Child abuse officials in five states with a relatively high percentage of school-originated reports and four with a relatively low percentage of school-originated reports were contacted by telephone and interviewed with regard to specific programs or materials directed toward school personnel. Questions were structured to obtain information about (a) any special materials on child abuse routinely sent to school personnel, (b) any specific programs, conferences, workshops or inservice training on child abuse for school personnel, and (c) whether any office of child abuse personnel had specific duties to work with schools.

Results

Responses from all 50 states and the District of Columbia were received. An analysis of responses indicated consensus among states in three areas: (1) all 51 respondents indicated they have a mandatory reporting law; (2) all but 2 of the respondents indicated that their laws applied to both public and private schools (Louisiana's law does not specify, while Vermont's law specifies public schools only, but a proposed law will specify both); and (3) all the respondents indicated that the law provides immunity from civil or criminal liability for those reporting in good faith.

Table I presents state-by-state information with regard to types of abuse reportable by law, school personnel required to report, percentage of school-originated reports, and the estimated degree of compliance with the law.

A further analysis found that 39 of the respondents (76%) require the reporting of all types of child abuse, while 12 (24%) limit their definition by excluding one or more of the types of abuse. There are 9 states that do not require the reporting of emotional neglect; 4 exclude abandonment and 3 exclude general maltreatment. All states require reporting on physical abuse and sexual abuse. There are 4 states that add "exploitation"; 1 state adds "mental suffering" and another adds "at risk for abuse."

All states require reporting by school personnel, and 34 respondents indicated that all school personnel are required to report suspected cases of child abuse. The counselor is a mandatory reporter in 46 of the respondents. In the 5 states not specifically including the counselor as a mandatory reporter, 2 have statutes that are somewhat ambiguous and might include the counselor. Among the various disciplines, the speech therapist is most often not identified as a mandatory reporter, with 24% ($N = 12$) of the states excluding them.

Table 1

STATE REPORTING REQUIREMENTS, PERCENTAGE OF SCHOOL ORIGINATED REPORTS, AND RATED REPORTING COMPLIANCE BY SCHOOL PERSONNEL

Reporting state	Types of abuse law requires reported	School personnel required to report	% of reports originating with school personnel	Rated degree of compliance with reporting abuse of school personnel
Alabama	All but abandonment	All but speech therapists	5-15 (est.)	Report only obvious
Alaska	All but emotional neglect	Only teachers, school nurses, and hospital personnel	None indicated	Not to report
Arizona	Physical abuse and sexual abuse	All but nursery, itinerant, and hospital personnel	12 (of substantiated) 15 (with preschool) 20 and 27 (with unsubstantiated)	Report only obvious
Arkansas	All	All	5-15 (est.)	Report only obvious
California	Physical abuse, mental suffering, sexual abuse	All but speech therapist and hospital personnel	9.3	Report only obvious
Colorado	All (emotional neglect implied)	All	22	Report most
Connecticut	All but emotional neglect and "at risk of abuse"	All but speech therapist	5-15 (est.)	Report only obvious

State			
Delaware	All and "exploitation"	12.6	Report only obvious
D.C.	All	5-15 (est.)	Report only obvious
Florida	All	9.7 (birth to 18 yrs.) 15 (age 5 and older)	Report only obvious
Georgia	Only school administration (new law proposed)	15-30 (est.)	Report most
Hawaii	All	5-15 (est.)	Report most
Idaho	All but emotional neglect	5-15 (est.)	Report most
Illinois	All	7.3	Report only obvious
Indiana	All	15-30 (est.)	Report most
Iowa	All but emotional neglect	15-30 (est.)	Report most
Kansas	All	5-15 (est.)	Report only obvious
Kentucky	All but hospital personnel	0-5 (est.)	Report only obvious
Louisiana	Only teachers, school nurses, social workers, and any person responsible for care of child	5-15 (est.)	Report only obvious
Maine	All	5-15 (est.)	Report only obvious

Continued

Table 1 (continued)

Reporting state	Types of abuse law requires reported	School personnel required to report	% of reports originating with school personnel	Rated degree of compliance with reporting abuse of school personnel
Maryland	All	All	35	Report most
Massachusetts	All but general maltreatment	All	15-30 (est.)	Report only obvious
Michigan	All	All but psychologist, speech therapist, consulting psychologist and teachers	12	Report only obvious
Minnesota	All	All but administration and consulting psychologist	15-30 (est.)	Report only obvious
Mississippi	All but abandonment	Only principal and teacher	15-30 (est.)	Report only obvious
Missouri	All	Law states teacher, principal, or other official—interpreted to mean all	15-30 (est.)	Report only obvious
Montana	All	All but speech therapist	45-60 (est.)	Report only obvious
Nebraska	All	All	10	Report only obvious

Nevada	All but speech therapist	14	Report most
New Hampshire	All	19	Report only obvious
New Jersey	All	12-4	Report only obvious
New Mexico	All	10—Teachers (2)	Report only obvious
New York	All	11	Unknown
North Carolina	All	5-15 (est.)	Report only obvious
North Dakota	All but speech therapist and counselor	5-15 (est.)	Report only obvious
Ohio	All but hospital personnel	5-15 (est.)	Report only obvious
Oklahoma	All	5-15 (est.)	Report most
Oregon	All but emotional neglect, abandonment	15-30 (est.)	Report most
Pennsylvania	All	15-20	Report only obvious
Rhode Island	All	0-5 (est.)	Report most
South Carolina	All	22	Report most
South Dakota	All	45-60 (est.)	Report only obvious
Tennessee	All	5-15 (est.)	Report only obvious
Texas	All	5-15 (est.)	Report only obvious
Utah	All and exploitation	5-15 (est.)	Report only obvious

Continued

Table 1 (continued)

Reporting state	Types of abuse law requires reported	School personnel required to report	% of reports originating with school personnel	Rated degree of compliance with reporting abuse of school personnel
Vermont	All but emotional neglect	Only school nurses (proposed to include all)	10	Report only obvious
Virginia	All	All	5-15 (est.)	Report only most
Washington	All and exploitation	All but speech therapist	15-30 (est.)	Report most
West Virginia	All	All	5-15 (est.)	Report only obvious
Wisconsin	All but emotional neglect	All	20	Report most (except for sexual abuse)
Wyoming	All	All	5-15 (est.)	Report most

Table 2. presents the frequency, percentages, and mean for school-originated reports of child abuse. The mean (15.5%) was computed by using actual statistics provided by the state or using the midpoint of the estimated range.

Only 1 state indicated that school personnel were consistently unwilling to report cases of child abuse. However, 65% ($N = 33$) of the states indicated that school personnel tend to report only obvious cases of abuse, while 31% ($N = 16$) felt school personnel were reporting most of the appropriate suspected cases.

The second phase of the study, a follow-up comparison of states with a "high" percentage of school-originated reports versus those with "low" percentages, yielded an unsurprising result. The offices responsible for child abuse programs in the "high" states had active programs reaching out to the schools, providing materials, and encouraging liaison relationships. The "low" states tended to have more passive school programs, responding only when requests for information, consultation, etc., were directed to their offices. Among the activities in the active "high" states were:

1. regular newsletters from the state office sent to schools;
2. general workshops and conferences on child abuse that are open to school personnel, among other professionals (some states also go out to local school districts and provide specific workshops/inservice training for school personnel);
3. child abuse publications and lists of available publications provided to schools (some states provide publications specifically developed for school personnel);

Table 2

REPORTED FREQUENCY OF SCHOOL ORIGINATED REPORTS

Range	N	% Age
0-5%	2	4
5-15%	30	59
15-30%	15	29
30-45%	1	2
45-60%	2	4
Above 60%	0	0
No report	1	2
$\overline{X}$ = 15.5%	51	100

4. formation of county child abuse teams that include school personnel;
5. audiovisual programs on child abuse made available to the schools; and
6. a state child abuse specialist who has part of his or her job role specifically designated as school liaison activities.

Discussion

The implications of this survey are clear for the counselor as well as for other education-related professionals. School personnel should be aware of their particular state laws on child abuse, not only to be more effective practitioners, but also to protect themselves legally. On a general level, the laws are clear on mandatory reporting of a variety of types of abuse, and in all cases some school (public and private) personnel are mandated to report abuse with the guarantee of "in good faith" reporting.

Failure to follow established guidelines for reporting suspected cases of child abuse would most likely result in a misdemeanor charge. A sampling of states indicates conviction on these charges would take the form of a fine (under $500) and/or a brief imprisonment (up to 6 months). State employees may be subject to some additional disciplinary action.

From the view of state officials responsible for child abuse programs, school personnel do not appear to be reporting suspected abuse cases with a high enough frequency, although few officials indicated a total lack of compliance. Most state officials indicate that only the "most obvious" cases are reported by educators. Given that schools should account for half or more of abuse referrals, it is surprising that only an estimated 8% to 17% of suspected child abuse cases originate from the schools (Broadhurst, 1978). These figures are consistent with this survey, which indicated a national average of slightly over 15%. This appears to be a function of limited awareness and reluctance on the part of school personnel. In addition, it suggests that state child abuse programs have failed to reach out and educate school personnel on child abuse. The present survey yields a number of implications and recommendations for the pupil personnel professional:

1. Professionals should obtain and become familiar with the child abuse laws in their particular states.

2. Schools should designate a staff member to be a resource and coordinator with regard to suspected child abuse. The school counselor is best qualified for this task. Child abuse is not the type of problem that can be put on the "back burner" or referral list. Immediate intervention is important. The "coordinator" must be versed in legal issues and requirements and have knowledge of procedures in identifying and recognizing possible child abuse.

3. Counselors can function on three levels with the problem of child abuse. The first level involves direct work with the child. This includes conducting interviews with the child to assess the problem as well as to intervene, when appropriate, to provide support from the school for the child. The second level is work with teachers. This may involve developing inservice programs, acting as a resource with regard to the law, helping to assist teachers in identifying child abuse, and providing classroom consultation with regard to helping the abused child. Counselors may also help teachers with the difficult emotional struggle that often accompanies coming to the decision whether to report a case. The third level involves counselors' roles as liaison with community agencies that deal with child abuse. At each level, counselors must be aware of the delineation and appropriate school responses to child abuse and what more appropriately lies in the domain of the public agencies.

4. Counselors and other specialists should encourage the reporting of the more "borderline" or less obvious cases. The purpose of the reporting is not to prosecute or charge; rather, the reporting allows an investigation to ascertain whether a child has been abused or is at risk for further abuse.

5. Counselors should become active with local groups or agencies that deal with child abuse. Where state or local agencies do not seem to be reaching out to the schools, school-based professionals should initiate and encourage these contacts. Counselors could assist in initiating training programs for various professional groups (Volpe, 1981).

6. On a more general theme, it would be interesting to see the Swoba et al. (1978) study on the awareness of child abuse laws among mental health practitioners replicated with educators, particularly pupil personnel specialists. Practitioners may want to conduct "mini" studies of awareness levels in their own settings.

References

Antler, S. Child abuse: An emerging social priority. *Social Work*, 1978, January, 58–60.

Broadhurst, D. What schools are doing about child abuse and neglect. *Children Today*, 1978, January–February, 22–36.

Cincinnati Enquirer. Everyone did his job, but Alan is dead. *Cincinnati Enquirer*, 1981, January 29, A-3.

Gelles, R. The social construction of child abuse. *American Journal of Orthopsychiatry*, 1976, *46*, 580–590.

Griggs, S.A., & Gale, P. The abused child: Focus for the counselor. *Elementary School Guidance and Counseling*, 1977, *11*, 187–194.

Light, R. Abused and neglected children in America: A study of alternative policies. *Harvard Educational Review*, 1974, *43*, 556–598.

Miller, K.A., & Miller, E.K. Child abuse and neglect: A framework for identification. *The School Counselor*, 1979, *26*, 284–287.

Moore, H.B., & McKee, J.E. Child abuse and neglect: The contemporary counselor in conflict. *The School Counselor*, 1979, *26*, 288–292.

Solomon, G. Child abuse and developmental disabilities. *Developmental Medicine and Child Neurology*, 1979, *21*, 101–108.

Swoba, J.S., Elwork, A., Sales, B.D., & Levine, D. Knowledge of and compliance with privileged communication and child-abuse-reporting laws. *Professional Psychology*, 1978, *9*, 448–457.

Volpe, R. The development and evaluation of a training program for school-based professionals dealing with child abuse. *Child Abuse and Neglect*, 1981, *5*, 103–110.

Legal Issues in Child Abuse: Questions and Answers for Counselors

David N. Sandberg, Susan K. Crabbs, and *Michael A. Crabbs*

> *Editors' Note:* David Sandberg is a researcher and practitioner of law relating to children's issues. His law practice includes representation of children in civil and criminal child abuse proceedings, termination of parental rights cases, delinquency petitions, guardianship cases, and divorce and custody cases. He is also a presiding judge in involuntary commitment proceedings. Before his training as an attorney, he was involved with children's issues from a mental health perspective as chairman of a state commission on children and youth, program director, and therapist.
>
> We first contacted David Sandberg for information regarding his book, *Chronic Acting-Out Students and Child Abuse* (1987, Lexington Books). After two lengthy telephone conversations, he agreed to provide written answers to questions about child abuse issues for school counselors. A written interview was chosen to allow him an opportunity to research and accurately represent the legal issues.

ESG&C: *How would you generalize, across all 50 states, the school counselor's legal responsibility in reporting suspected abuse?*
D.S.: Virtually every state has a child abuse reporting law requiring school counselors and others to report suspected abuse. School counselors should insist that they have a very clear understanding of what their state law does and does not require. Given the extreme importance that state legislators have given to reporting laws as well as potential liability for nonreporting, I believe that school districts have an obligation to have legal counsel available so that

all school personnel understand and feel secure about the scope of their legal obligations.

ESG&C: *To what extent should counselors document their involvement and intervention with an abused child (e.g., photographs, audio recordings, anecdotal records, case notes)?*

D.S.: "Document" suggests an investigatory process. Keep in mind that child abuse statutes assign a reporting role to school counselors and an investigatory role to child protection services and, in some cases, to the police. This may sound pedantic, but it's a central and important premise of our child protection system. The counselor is reporting only a suspicion of abuse, not proof of abuse.

Consistent with this is the wisdom of counselors utilizing reasonable methods to document their suspicions of abuse. A foremost methodology is good note taking, (e.g., the date a suspicious black-and-blue mark was first noticed). Often, counseling explanations and dates relative to a child's injury emerge during a child protective services investigation, and it is very helpful if counselors can provide precise items and a sequence of events.

ESG&C: *In some states, school counselor interviews may benefit from a privileged communication statute. In what way does this help or hinder the counselor's reporting of suspected cases of child abuse? Do abuse-related laws supersede any privileged communication statutes?*

D.S.: Our legal system has historically protected several types of relationships deemed to be very important: doctor-patient, priest-penitent, and attorney-client. One layer of legal protection is confidentiality, which restricts or limits third parties from having access to important information arising within the context of these relationships. A second layer is the law of privileged communications, which acts as a bar to the professional being forced (or volunteering) to testify about a client's statements. Whereas the law of confidentiality is general and flexible, allowing for some exceptions, the law of privilege is specific and inflexible.

The basic policy consideration justifying the laws of confidentiality and privilege is simple: People are not apt to come forward with sensitive information, an essential prelude to problem resolution, if others are going to be told.

These laws worked well until the rise in public awareness of child abuse in the 1970s and 1980s. Society's concern has been so great that an exception has been made to both the law of confidentiality and privilege in many states. In New Hampshire where I practice law, the only privileged relationship the child abuse reporting statute recognizes is attorney-client (please don't ask me to explain this exception). The clear import of the New Hampshire law is that if a penitent confesses abuse of his child to a priest, for example, the priest must make a report to child protective services.

In effect, society has made a value judgment that there is greater public good in protecting children against abuse than in guaranteeing confidentiality and privilege.

ESG&C: *Some counselors fail to report suspected abuse because of a fear of reprisal directed at the child. What do you suggest the counselor do when this is a real and immediate concern?*

D.S.: Again, I may come off sounding pedantic and a bit detached from the front lines, but my advice is to report because that is what the law requires. However, the reporter should stress to child protective services and the police, if need be, that there is a very real possibility of reprisal against the child.

Let me add that there is something troubling about not reporting a case of abuse due to fear of reprisal. In some cases, I suspect that the prospective reporters are more concerned about reprisals against themselves than the children involved. Also, an abused child lives in a world of violence, threats, and coercion, so it is difficult for me to see that a reprisal would constitute something new and different.

My intention here is not to make light of the reprisal concern. Instead, I am suggesting that there may be more to a reporter's hesitancy than meets the eye. No matter how the reprisal issue is looked at, the question of how the abuse is to terminate if a report is not made has to be answered. I know of no other way than through state intervention.

ESG&C: *For whatever reason a professional person (e.g., counselor, educator, mental health worker) might fail to report a suspected abuse, have you discovered any cases in which these individuals have been prosecuted?*

D.S.: I am aware of several cases, nationally, in which physicians have been criminally prosecuted for failure to report. No doubt there have been more cases, but, overall, it seems that states with failure-to-report statutes have seldom enforced them.

On the other hand, there has been a growing number of private (civil) suits for monetary damages brought on behalf of victims against mandated reporters who failed to report. In a California case, a failure-to-report suit was brought against four doctors and a police chief, and was eventually settled for $600,000. The victim was a 3-year-old boy who suffered permanent brain damage after being beaten constantly by his mother's boyfriend.

ESG&C: *Most statutes contain a phrase about reporting "in good faith." Would you elaborate on this?*

D.S.: The "good faith" provision grants immunity from legal suit to reporters who file an abuse report in good faith. Such a provision protects just about everyone who reports except the person who did not have a reason to suspect child abuse and was principally motivated to report by a desire to attack someone. The policy consideration underlying good faith is that people who comply with a legislative command should not be vulnerable to suit.

ESG&C: *What are the investigatory responsibilities of a school counselor before reporting suspected abuse?*

D.S.: If we can agree that counselors basically report and that child protective services workers investigate, I can go on to say that counselors, in my opinion, have a duty to remain alert and make discreet inquiries in cases where there is little hard evidence but a strong feeling persists that abuse is occurring. Even more than this, anyone working with chronic problem children should have child abuse in mind as a possible contributory factor. This duty becomes distorted and trouble begins when a counselor progresses to a zealous crusade in the search for evidence.

In other cases where there is "reason to suspect" abuse or there is a "suspicion" of abuse, which inferentially implies some specific evidence such as a black-and-blue mark or behavioral indicators, there is no duty to investigate further. At this point, a report is compelled.

ESG&C: *At times, school counselors may be faced with principals, administrators, or district policy that demands proof of abuse before reporting. What advice would you provide to a counselor in this position?*

D.S.: First, I am concerned about any reporting protocol that has not been reviewed by an attorney with experience in the child abuse field. Second, a "demand proof" procedure suggests that mandated reporters must overcome a legal burden having to do with the requisite amount of evidence that is required before a report can be filed. I know of no child abuse reporting law which operates in this manner. Moreover, it is up to the child protective services, not to the school, to determine whether there is adequate evidence to warrant an investigation.

Frankly, I am worried about school personnel who are working in a "demand proof" atmosphere as they may be at risk for civil or even criminal liability. This should be sufficient motivation for them to take steps to correct the situation and protect themselves.

ESG&C: *In talking with counselors around the country, we have* *found that most will meet individually with a child prior to completing a report of abuse. First, is it appropriate for the counselor to make this contact? And second, if it is, what types of questions should be asked of the child?*

D.S.: If the intent is to explain that a report is going to be made and to give the child a lot of support, I think that meeting with the child is a good idea, probably essential. If the intent is to learn more about the abuse, then I think that it depends upon several factors including the child's age and rapport with the counselor. In any event, filing a report is in no way pre-conditioned on the child acknowledging that abuse is occurring.

As for types of questions a child should be asked, I prefer a general question such as "Is there anything going on at home that bothers you?" As a general rule, this conveys caring, provides the child an opportunity to disclose, yet does not trap the child who is not ready to disclose. In cases where a counselor has developed a strong rapport with a child a more specific question about abuse is appropriate, provided there is some basis for asking the question.

ESG&C: *In many instances, other individuals on a school campus may become involved in the reporting of suspected abuse. As an example, the school nurse may take pictures of the injured child. Or, the school principal might request that the report proceed through the administrative office. In your opinion, when a counselor has information about an abused child, who within the school system has a "need to know" about the specific facts?*

D.S.: This varies from school to school, depending upon the size of a school and its organizational structure. I find it difficult to understand any system in which the principal, the child's primary teacher, and the counselor are not made aware that a report has been filed. As for specific facts about the abuse, I'm not sure that anyone other than the child's counselor needs to know.

ESG&C: *Newspapers and magazines have begun to report what appears to be an increase in the number of false reports of abuse. From your perspective, has the incidence of false reports increased over the years? If so, what factors do you believe have contributed to this?*

D.S.: By "false reports," I presume you are referring to cases where the report is fabricated rather than reported in good faith but no finding of abuse is made. Although the child protection system (which allows for reporters to remain anonymous) would seem ripe for misuse, I have no direct knowledge of someone using the reporting system for the sole purpose of "getting someone." I have not even read about such a case, although, surely, some exist.

Increasingly common are allegations of sexual abuse in divorce/ custody disputes. Unquestionably, such an allegation can be a devastating weapon in these disputes, surpassing all others in terms of charged emotions. I have been in the middle of a number of these cases, usually as a guardian ad litem, but not one involved simple fabrication. What is going on is much more complex, involving the convergence of angry, hurt, and suspicious feelings of the custody litigants within the context of new public awareness about child abuse. In several of the cases in which I have been involved, I am satisfied that the children were never abused. I also believe that because of his/her extreme emotional condition, the parent making the accusation distorted things the child did or said but did not deliberately fabricate them.

So, if we want to call these false reports, yes, the number has increased and particularly in the divorce and custody context. The explanation for the increase would seem to be that most adults today have some general awareness of child abuse, some of its possible symptoms, and that it is a common phenomenon. If one divorcing spouse is enraged at the other and hears a child complain about an irritation "down there," today you are apt to hear a child abuse allegation. I would caution anyone about making general assumptions as to whether such allegations are "false reports." Each case must be looked at carefully without prior bias one way or the other.

ESG&C: *Counselors are frequently admonished to "err on the side of the child" when reporting suspected abuse. How might this contribute to false reporting?*

D.S.: Now I'm hearing "false report" more in the sense of unfounded cases following a good faith report. So, perhaps I should add a comment to the preceding question first. As a practicing attorney, I am only involved with more serious cases which are in court. From this perspective, I see very few cases where no judicial determination of abuse is made. But, keep in mind, I am only seeing the more serious cases.

As for "erring on the side of the child," such an approach is apt to result in more unfounded cases than if reporting is only done when there is a strong suspicion. The more cases that are reported, the more unfounded cases there will be. That's predictable.

But, I'm not particularly troubled by this because broad reporting will also result in detecting some serious abuse cases that otherwise would have continued. I realize that a broad approach also results, at times, in traumatic state intervention when no abuse exists. That is regrettable, but it is a price we necessarily have to pay for protecting far more children who are being abused. Show me a better way. I'm willing to listen.

ESG&C: *To what extent should the counselor, who reports suspected abuse, be provided with periodic follow-up information by child protective services? What legal provisions exist to improve the communication between the service agency and the counselor?*

D.S.: This continues to be a major bone of contention between child protective services agencies and mandated reporters, especially professionals including educators. Typically, a teacher or counselor files a report and never hears back from child protective services concerning the investigation's outcome. When a call is made to child protective services, the response is that confidentiality prevents disclosure of the outcome.

This is crazy, and some states such as Maine have amended their child abuse statutes to allow child protective services personnel to disclose investigatory information to professional reporters. Even in states which do not expressly permit this, child protective services' claim of confidentiality may be more deeply rooted in self-protection than in law. Why disclose the outcome of an investigation to a school counselor who may tell the parent who, in turn, will probably swiftly launch an attack on the child protective agencies involved? It's an understandable reaction if you are looking at the world through the eyes of a child protection agency, but not good policy. People who are instrumental in a child's development, including professionals, must have all vital information about a particular child.

ESG&C: *What advice would you give counselors who might be called upon to testify in suspected abuse cases?*

D.S.: The best advice I can offer is to request that the administrators make school legal counsel available. After all, everyone else involved is represented by counsel. More than this, counsel can prepare counselors for their testimony, and can intercede if opposing counsel gets a little too aggressive.

ESG&C: *If all 50 states have a statute which requires mandatory reporting by any individual who has a suspicion of abuse, do school districts need a written policy on child abuse reporting procedures for their staff? If so, what are the essential ingredients of such a policy?*

D.S.: Given the extreme importance legislatures have given to child abuse reporting statutes, yes, school districts should have a written policy on reporting procedures. These procedures should be reviewed by legal counsel prior to being implemented. Counsel, in turn, may want to consult with one of the large, national child abuse organizations such as the C. Henry Kempe National Center in Denver.

As for essential ingredients of reporting policy, let me suggest several. First, the policy must track with state statutory and any regulatory requirements. Second, there needs to be a direct chain from the person suspecting the abuse to child protective services (i.e., trouble increases as additional administrative layers are imposed between the person suspecting and child protective services). And third, a feedback loop between the school and child protective services and within the school is needed to maintain confidence in the reporting system.

Beyond this, I believe it is very important for schools to involve themselves with abused children in addition to just reporting. Abused children usually require special services and their educators must ensure that they receive them. If these children have a chance in this world, it is principally through meaningful educational opportunity.

ESG&C: *Since a significant part of the school counselor's role is consultation with school personnel and coordination of services to benefit children, it would seem that counselors have a responsibility to be directly involved in any attempts to write, revise, or implement a policy on child abuse reporting. What steps should a counselor follow in this process (i.e., meet with child protective services representatives and school attorney, inform/train teachers and other staff about the policy)?*

D.S.: I agree that school counselors can play a significant role in shaping good child abuse reporting procedures. Two of the more important things they can do is meet with school counsel to clarify any ambiguities in the procedures, and develop a good working relationship with a child protective services worker. Nothing is accomplished by being a child protective system "basher." Spend a day at the nearest child protection agency. I guarantee it will be an eye-opener.

ESG&C: *Based upon what you have seen happen in legal proceedings, what changes do you anticipate will occur in the reporting of suspected abuse cases over the next few years?*

D.S.: Well, some people contend that the present reporting system is not working because of child protective services case overloads and the impossibility of properly investigating all reported cases. Many child protective services agencies, it is suspected, screen-out or give low priority to reports having to do with maltreatment other than sexual abuse or serious physical abuse. As the argument goes, this de facto policy should be codified in the form of amended reporting statutes, significantly narrowing the type of cases that would have to be reported.

I don't think there is much doubt that the child protective services system is overloaded. Workers are supposed to have 20 cases. Typically, they have 50 or more. But I have trouble concluding that the entire system is not working. That's to discount completely the hundreds of thousands of children who are protected against further abuse, not to mention the helpful services the children and their parents sometimes receive.

Neglect, psychological abuse, and even so-called minor physical abuse are all harmful to a child's development. Why should we as a society tolerate these forms of maltreatment? Under what rationale do we justify discontinuing protection and supportive services for these children? I strongly believe that our nation's first priority should be the healthy maturing and development of our young people. Call it idealistic, call it naive, but I am convinced that this is the only policy which offers any long-range hope insofar as significantly reducing crime, delinquency, and many of society's other more costly ills.

So, I am not sure what changes are likely to take place, but it looks like the central debate will focus on whether to narrow reportable conditions.

Child Abuse Hysteria and the Elementary School Counselor

Lawrence D. Spiegel

Across the country, helping professionals have failed to become accurately informed about the problem of child abuse and have been caught up in the public hysteria that surrounds this sensitive issue. Because investigations of alleged child abuse cases are besieged with complex yet subtle problems, helping professionals, especially school counselors, need to be well informed on this topic.

Personal Involvement

As a practicing clinical psychologist for more than a decade, I have worked with a fair share of abused children, as well as with adults who themselves had been abused as children. I knew the complexities, subtleties, and traumas inherent in the problem of abuse. What I was not aware of, however, was the developing trend of false accusations of abuse, especially those emanating from divorce and custody disputes. My initiation into the problems of false accusation was a novel one.

The story began the day I was arrested in the parking lot of my office in Morris County, New Jersey. That day, December 9, 1983, I was a successful clinical psychologist with a growing private practice. That afternoon, I was escorted to a waiting police car, charged with sexually molesting my then 2½-year-old daughter, handcuffed, and taken to police headquarters. Suddenly, my work, my dreams, my life—everything I had struggled for—were shattered. The confusion, disbelief, fear, and anguish I had experienced at that moment became an ongoing nightmare which continued for over two years. This

182

charge was filed by my ex-wife about 2 weeks after our divorce was finalized. (Spiegel, 1986, p. 1)

More than 2 years went by before I was able to clear my name and once again see my daughter, from whom I had been denied access for the entire time. Finally, after a series of court battles, which ended in the New Jersey Supreme Court, I was acquitted by a jury in January 1986. Yet the questions remained: How could such a thing have happened? What evidence existed to justify the charge? And what fueled the fires of those prosecutors who pursued the charges? It has taken well over 4 years for me to develop answers to these questions. During this process, I became more aware of the general trend of false accusations and the public hysteria about abuse. As a result, I set out to understand the genesis of both. The irony of my own situation, both as a psychologist and a victim of a false accusation, enabled me to develop a unique dual perspective, which I now seek to share in this article.

Recently, an identifiable set of behaviors was defined and described that could account for the epidemic rise in reports of child abuse (Spiegel, 1987). By enumerating the problems associated with overreporting and overreacting to alleged child abuse, in this article I challenge the validity of many child abuse cases. For those in the helping professions, especially those in the elementary school settings, an understanding of the hysteria that surrounds this issue is important, lest counselors allow themselves to become unwitting participants. My purpose in this article is to summarize the history of the current public hysteria while describing the child abuse phenomenon itself.

Overreaction and Bias

The trend of unusually high numbers of false reports of child abuse and neglect has skyrocketed. In 1976, approximately 35% of all reports of child maltreatment were determined to be unfounded (Besharov, 1985). In 1985, that number had swelled to 65%, involving approximately 750,000 children whose alleged abuse was reported without substantiation (Besharov, 1985). The tendency of both the lay and professional public to react overzealously has resulted in a host of new problems. These problems include good faith but overzealous reporting, professionals looking for abuse in otherwise innocuous behaviors, and parents using accusation of sexual abuse in divorce and custody proceedings (Spiegel, 1986).

Counselors have an obligation to be cognizant of each of these three problems and to develop strategies to deal with them. With a sensitive issue like child abuse, however, some counselors may overlook that most issues have two sides. Not surprisingly, some individuals who think of themselves as child advocates have been extremely susceptible to public pressure to do something about abuse. Consequently, school counselors' beliefs, opinions, and re-actions must be carefully guarded to maintain objectivity while avoiding overzealous attempts to protect children, which do more harm than good.

The dangers of professional overreaction have not gone un-noticed in the literature. Schuman (1986) stated, "In some quarters there is such a degree of sensitivity or outrage about possible child abuse that a presumption exists that such abuse has occurred when-ever it is alleged" (p. 1). Other articles call for therapeutic inter-viewing of alleged abuse victims, in an effort to guard against such bias. As an example, McIver (1986) quoted a mental health prac-titioner who concluded that, "most of the abuse professionals are not in touch with their real motives and are masquerading tyranny as charity" (p. 4).

Indeed, given the current climate and its historical evolution, counselors must consider themselves vulnerable to this bias. Within this context of public pressure, sensitivity, and hysteria came the mandatory and anonymous reporting laws that have a direct impact on a community in general and educators, including elementary school counselors, in particular.

The Climate of Hysteria

Fueling the current climate of hysteria are a variety of vehicles, none more insidious than sensationalized media accounts quoting government figures depicting an epidemic of child abuse (Dor-schner, 1985). Communities have been barraged with attempts to heighten awareness through televised public service announce-ments, newspaper feature articles, pictures of missing children on milk cartons, and prime time television movies. These efforts have succeeded in generating a frenzied public response to do something about the problem. Other approaches designed to capture public interest include books and movies on such topics as good touches, bad touches (Freeman, 1986; Hart-Rossi, 1984), puppet shows (Chapman, Baird, & Kile, 1986), lectures, and even groups of traveling actors, all portraying the dangers of abuse.

A special feature article titled "Teaching Fear" appeared in *Newsweek* (Kantrowitz & Leslie, 1986) and provided documentation of the novel approaches to educating children and adults about child abuse. In addition to the flood of books and pamphlets, which include titles such as *It's Okay To Say No*, the *Newsweek* article also discusses some new offerings, which now include board games, *Safe City, USA*, and one developed by a former Illinois state prosecutor titled *Strangers and Dangers*. One of the most popular children's story writing teams, Stan and Jan Berenstain, have written a new book titled *The Berenstain Bears Learn About Strangers* (Berenstain & Berenstain, 1985). Although the titles don't always suggest it, the message goes far beyond the old adage, "don't talk to strangers."

Indeed, if figures compiled by the National Center on Child Abuse and Neglect (NCCAN) are accurate, the proliferation of this type of material may be justified. According to these official figures, the number of reports of child abuse have skyrocketed from 510,000 reports in 1972 to 1.3 million in 1982 (Besharov, 1985). Not surprisingly, this proliferation of literature has been interdisciplinary. From the abundance of legal articles that led to the 1974 Child Abuse Prevention and Treatment Act to the fields of social work, psychiatry, and psychology, the response has reflected the public climate. Each of these fields has seen the development of new theories and syndromes seeking to explain, diagnose, and treat child abuse in general and sexual abuse in particular.

Many writers in other disciplines have contributed a wide array of fundamental works on the topic of abuse that have come to form the backbone of the child-saver movement. Sgroi, Porter, and Blick (1982); Summit (1983); and White (1986) are just a few of the many authors developing theories that attempt to define syndromes of abused children. New tools such as anatomically correct dolls and other diagnostic aids are being touted as the cutting edge of the field. All of these professional attempts to address the issue of child abuse have been spurred by the public passion and, paradoxically, seem to contribute to it.

The Backlash

Perhaps the most telling sign that public reaction has reached epidemic proportions has been the abundance of "backlash" literature (Coleman, 1986; McIver, 1986; Schuman, 1984; Underwager, 1986). These works have sought not only to identify the public hysteria but to point to the resulting problem of overreporting. Many of these authors cite the same government figures mentioned previously but add a crucial dimension: While the number of abuse reports has skyrocketed, so has the percentage of unfounded reports. Many believe this secondary problem, false reports, to be as damaging as abuse itself (Underwager, 1986).

Indeed, since the publication of the book, *A Question of Innocence: A True Story of False Accusation* (Spiegel, 1986), I have received a deluge of articles, court decisions, books, and research projects that document the tumultuous problem of overreporting of alleged child abuse. The attention this book has garnered has led to invitations to participate in conferences and symposiums conducted by the American Psychological Association, the American Medical Association, the American Academy of Psychiatry and Law, the American Association of Social Workers, and the Ortho-Psychiatry Association. Moreover, I have been called upon to testify in both civil and criminal cases of child abuse while consulting with literally hundreds of law firms across the country.

Again, the backlash literature has been interdisciplinary and equally vociferous. One legal expert, Besharov (1985), the first director of the NCCAN, reported that the percentage of unfounded reports increased 30% in one 10-year period (i.e., from 1975 to 1985). Some practicing attorneys (Gordon, 1985; Hertzog, 1986) have expressed vigorous concerns about the growing legal trend that has stretched the rules of evidence precariously thin. During the past 2 years there has been an explosion of articles on the problem of false reports. Social work specialists (Shultz, 1985) as well as psychological and psychiatric experts (Coleman, 1986; Green, 1986) have responded. Taken together, these articles have provided a myriad of warnings about the dangers facing the clinician through the epidemic of false reports.

Most of these experts have addressed specific problems arising from the recent modifications in court procedure. They have limited themselves, however, to points that only refute expert testimony from the state's witnesses. Some experts have attempted to neutralize evidence resulting from the use of anatomical tools. Each expert agrees that there must be more controlled studies and rigorous protocol developed before anatomical dolls can achieve credibility.

Coleman (1986) and Green (1986) have responded to abuse syndromes by methodically picking them apart and, in an effort to balance the issue, some experts have presented their own syndromes. A credible effort in this regard is the Sexual Allegations in Divorce (SAID) Syndrome postulated by Blush and Ross (1987). Other authors (e.g., Benedek & Schetky, 1984; Schuman, 1986) have discussed even broader problems, including competency of children to testify and biased interviews by social workers and prosecutors. Many of these same issues are discussed in the False Accusation Syndrome that I developed (Spiegel, 1986). By far, the most comprehensive treatment of the problem of false accusation is the work by Underwager (1986). This author addresses all of the aforementioned areas and provides in-depth treatment of the problems of suggestibility, cognitive development, and interrogation.

The backlash phenomenon has not escaped the media's attention. Within the past 2 years, a grass roots organization, Victims of Child Abuse Laws (VOCAL), has garnered considerable press coverage. Composed of parents who believe they are victims of a witch-hunt mentality, VOCAL has more than 3,000 members nationally (Besharov, 1985). In the past year, virtually every network, newspaper, major magazine, and radio station in the United States has covered the problem of false accusations and referred to these false accusations as epidemic (Dorschner, 1985).

That the media have begun to report the backlash is further substantiation of the national hysteria. On a recent segment of *Donahue*, Phil Donahue characterized the attitude of hysteria prevalent in the audience with the statement, "show me a man who is accused of child abuse, and I'll show you a child abuser" (Harrell, 1987). News correspondent Bernard Goldberg (1987) summed up the paradox that society is facing. In his report on the *CBS Evening News with Dan Rather*, Goldberg commented that the efforts to do something about child abuse are "not only overdue, but overdone as well." The inherent paradox is that along with endangering innocent people, false reports also endanger children who need protection by misdirecting the resources of child protective services. In part, the very dissonance that this creates has heightened the hysteria.

The Child Abuse Hysteria Syndrome

Much of the backlash literature documents the climate of hysteria, or witch-hunt mentality that predominates. Yet, nowhere is this syndrome defined as a cohesive and comprehensive issue, as a condition unto itself. That is, even when it is accepted that such hysteria exists, an adequate explanation of how it affects the whole process of abuse investigation is lacking. Though the results are

clear—unwarranted intrusion into the family and possible conviction of innocent people—the problem itself is not.

It is this point that the child abuse hysteria syndrome (Spiegel,
1987) seeks to explain. To understand the uniqueness of the current
phenomenon, it is necessary to integrate information from several
different disciplines. This syndrome is composed of a three-stage
process that draws from the fields of sociology and social psychology, cognitive psychology, and psychiatry. As a result of the exchange of information from each of these areas, there emerges a
recognizable set of behaviors that explains the complex processes
through which false reports of abuse are taken as fact by professionals and the public alike. The constructs from these disciplines
explain the manner in which hysteria spreads, creating a contagion
that predisposes both parents and children to misinterpret, mis-
construe, and overreact, which results in false reports of abuse that
might otherwise have been seen as innocuous behaviors.

Stage 1 of the child abuse hysteria syndrome involves an understanding of the constructs of collective behavior that have communicated and enabled overzealous attitudes toward abuse to become
so widespread. These constructs include specifically the phenom-
enons of congregated and uncongregated collective behavior, as
well as groups psychology and the notion of mass hysteria (Brown,
1986).

In Stage 2, the cognitive capacities that make children so
suggestible (Underwager, 1986) are exploited either consciously or
unconsciously by the reporting adult, helping professionals, and
investigators. The alleged child victim is often subjected to repeated interviews and interrogations by overzealous, and sometimes, poorly trained case workers. Throughout this process, the
child, in effect, learns the story. These perceptions are then reinforced by a biased adult eager to find abuse and save the child.

In the third stage, a psychiatric disorder known as folie a deux
(Kaplan & Kaplan, 1981) or shared paranoid disorder often develops. It is characterized by a symbiotic relationship of a dominant-
submissive nature, in which the submissive partner takes on the
ideas, delusions, and behavior of the dominant partner. For a child,
such a relationship with a parent or other adult can easily develop,
because children are normally submissive to adults. In addition,
by unconsciously imitating the adults' behavior, the child seeks
love and approval, two powerful reinforcers.

The results of this syndrome can been seen in the alarmingly
high rate of false reports and irrevocable damage (Underwager,
1986) to hundreds of thousands of innocent people, adults and

children alike (Besharov, 1985). These false reports and subsequent investigations not only misdirect resources and ravage families, but they are the reason many children believe they have been abused when they have not. By setting the stage for the onset of psychosis for these children, helping professionals are confronted with a unique problem: Whereas many counselors have the training and skills to deal with the problems of a child who has been abused, how should counselors approach a child who believes the abuse has occurred when it has not?

The irony is that helping professionals, who want so much to assist children, become unwitting participants in this syndrome. Faced with mandated reporting laws in most states, a school counselor is often the first individual to hear a child's statement and complete the required report. Although well intentioned, counselors go too far in trying to provide support by encouraging the child to describe the situation. Therapeutic skills are used to reinforce what is expected, yet many counselors are naive regarding the effects of these interviews and diagnostic aids on children. Frequently, counselor observations are based on the misconception that children don't lie about abuse. Although it may be true that children rarely make up premediated lies, frequently they describe what they think the truth is. Many counselors have been taught to play it safe and err on the side of the child. Is the child being served, however, when the counselor unknowingly completes a false report? In my view, the false report can often be just as damaging to the child as an actual abuse situation.

Recommendations and Conclusions

Second only to parents, educators in general and school counselors specifically play a crucial role in protecting the health and well being of children. In addition to providing essential services to children, counselors are expected to manifest professional responsibility while being both knowledgeable and objective. Although it is often difficult to stay knowledgeable in so diverse a field, counselors must assume special responsibility to become aware of important societal issues. This professional mandate, to develop understanding as well as objective intervention strategies, must be directly communicated to parents, school administrators, and community leaders.

Counselors must be more discerning in their recommendations of guidance service programming for children. In the case of abuse, a balance must occur between sensitizing children to the problem of abuse and avoiding the hysterical climate that exists today. Counselors need to study abuse program materials (e.g., books, kits, community-based lectures) to determine which ones exceed this balance and should be limited in their use. All materials designed to acquaint children with this issue must meet acceptable standards of objectivity.

Most of all, counselors must recognize the important pivotal role that they play during investigations of abuse. The first step is to be aware of the child abuse hysteria syndrome. Second, once a suspicion is reported, counselors must communicate with case workers and ensure that all invloved parties are contacted. No longer can counselors simply file a report, excuse themselves of subsequent involvement, and assume that the investigation will be timely and complete. Third, school counselors need to keep in mind that child protective workers and members of law enforcement agencies may be overburdened, undertrained, and biased. Because suspicions are often turned into realities, counselors must establish criteria for what constitutes a suspicion as well as delineate steps for their own involvement in the investigation before reporting occurs. At a minimum counselors must impress on those caseworkers who take over the investigation their own doubts and concerns and urge those individuals to exercise caution in forming conclusions.

Counselors and educators must stay informed in this sensitive area by becoming familiar with the writings of the authors mentioned previously in this article. Most make very specific recommendations and suggestions that establish the "red flag" indicators for abuse as well as the false reporting of abuse. Avoiding bias and using appropriate interview techniques is a must in abuse situations. Recommendations regarding the initial interview, case referrals, and information safeguards (e.g., video or audio-tapes of interviews) must be considered and implemented as appropriate.

Ultimately, counselors must make a commitment to stay informed while avoiding the public hysteria on this issue. To do any less is to abdicate the primary responsibilities of a professional. No longer should counselor intervention be dictated by simplistic approaches like "err on the part of the child." Because the counselor's role as a helping professional dictates the standards that must be met, counselors cannot afford to err at all. Each must assume the personal and professional obligation to see that investigations are completed thoroughly and competently. This commitment—to intervene in an effective, objective manner to preserve the welfare of the child—is the key for elementary school counselors to avoid the public hysteria surrounding child abuse.

References

Benedek, E., & Schetky, D. (1984, October). *Allegation of sexual abuse in child custody cases.* Paper presented at the annual meeting of the American Academy of Psychiatry and the Law, Nassau, Bahamas.

Berenstain, S., & Berenstain, J. (1985). *The Berenstain Bears learn about strangers.* New York: Random House.

Besharov, D. (1985). Doing something about child abuse. *Harvard Journal of Law and Public Policy, 8,* 540–588.

Blush, G.L., & Ross, K.L. (1987, March). *Sexual allegations in divorce: The SAID syndrome.* Detroit: Oakland County Bar Association.

Brown, R. (1986). *Social psychology.* New York: Free Press.

Chapman, D., Baird, K., & Kile, D. (1986). *BodyRights.* Circle Pines, MN: American Guidance Services.

Child Abuse Prevention and Treatment Act, 42 U.S.C.

Coleman, L. (1986, January/February). False allegations of child sexual abuse: Have the experts been caught with their pants down? *Forum, 13*(1), 12–22.

Dorschner, J. (1985, July 25). A question of innocence. *Miami Herald,* pp. 10–15.

Freeman, L. (1986). *Loving touches.* Seattle, WA: Parenting Press.

Goldberg, B. (1987, February 23). *The CBS Evening News with Dan Rather* [Television program]. New York: Columbia Broadcasting Systems.

Gordon, C. (1985). False allegations of abuse in child custody disputes. *Minnesota Family Law Journal, 2*(14), 225–228.

Green, A. (1986). True and false allegations of sexual abuse in child custody disputes. *Journal of American Academy of Child Psychiatry, 25,* 449–456.

Harrell, J. (Producer). (1987, March 17). *The Phil Donahue Show* [Television program]. New York: National Broadcasting Company.

Hart-Rossi, J. (1984). *Protect your child from sexual abuse.* Seattle, WA: Parenting Press.

Hertzog, P. (1986, May). *Some important aspects of pre-trial investigtions and motions.* Paper presented to North Carolina Academy of Trial Lawyers Seminar, Fayetteville.

Kantrowitz, B., & Leslie, C. (1986, March). Teaching fear. *Newsweek,* p. 14.

Kaplan, S.L., & Kaplan, S.J. (1981). The child's accusation of sexual abuse during a divorce and custody struggle. *The Hillside Journal of Clinical Psychiatry, 3*(1), 92–93.

McIver, W. (1986). The case for a therapeutic interview. *The Oregon Defense Attorney, 6*(4), 3–4.

Schuman, D. (1984, October). *False accusations of physical and sexual abuse.* Paper presented at the annual conference of the American Academy of Psychiatry and the Law, Nassau, Bahamas.

Schuman, D.C. (1986). *Psychiatric and psychological evidence.* Colorado Springs, CO: McGraw-Hill.

Sgroi, S.M., Porter, F., & Blick, L. (1982). *Handbook of clinical intervention in child sexual abuse.* Lexington, MA: Lexington Books.

Shultz, L. (1985, November). *The social worker and the sexually abused minor, where are we going?* Paper presented to the National Victims of Child Abuse Laws conference, St. Paul, MN.

Spiegel, L.D. (1986). *A question of innocence: A true story of false accusation.* Parsippany, NJ: Unicorn Publishing.

Spiegel, L.D. (1987). *The phenomenon of child abuse hysteria as a social syndrome.* Unpublished manuscript.

Summit, R. (1983). The child sexual abuse accommodation syndrome. *Child Abuse and Neglect, 7,* 177–193.

Underwager, R. (1986). *Child sexual abuse.* Unpublished manuscript.

White, S. (1986, August). *Mental health evaluators' role in child sexual abuse assessments.* Paper presented to the American Psychological Association, Washington, DC.

Overstating the Issue: A Reaction to Spiegel

Richard D. Krugman

The article written by Spiegel cautions elementary school counselors to be "well informed" and " to avoid the public hysteria surrounding child abuse" (Spiegel, 1988, p. 282). Unfortunately, his article is filled with serious inaccuracies and, for the most part, seems to be a follow-up to his own book (Spiegel, 1986) in which he stated he was wrongly accused of sexually abusing his child. Before elementary school counselors follow Spiegel's recommendations and advice, careful consideration should be given to the following points.

Unfounded Versus False Reports

The linking of unfounded reports to false reports is misleading and inaccurate. In my experience, departments of social services conclude that some reported cases of child abuse are unfounded for a variety of reasons. One of those reasons is that adequate data on which to make a decision are unavailable (the most common reason why reported cases end up unfounded [Jones, 1987]). Additionally, cases may become unfounded when a child has symptoms that are initially suggestive of sexual abuse but turn out later to be symptoms that can be attributed to something else (i.e., similar to a negative throat culture for a child with a sore throat).

Finally, a report may be unfounded because it is a fictitious report. These may arise from either an adult or a child. In Jones's (1987) study, published in the *Journal of Interpersonal Violence*, he established that the majority of reports that were unfounded were deemed so because of inadequate data. Of the 576 cases of sexual abuse in Denver involved in this analysis, 34 (8%) were fictitious or false, with 26 (4.5%) cases judged to be clearly false reports by adults. Only 8 (1.5%) of these 576 cases were fictitious reports made by a child. Because elementary school counselors most often hear allegations of sexual abuse from children, this very low incidence of false reports by children should be considered.

The Backlash

Counselors should be cautious in accepting Spiegel's references to "backlash" (Spiegel, 1988, p. 278) literature. For the most part, the citations do not come from peer-reviewed journals, and those that are reported are generally single case reports. None provide any type of adequately controlled prospective study to address the problem he says exists.

Further caution should be employed in accepting Spiegel's allegations that "the media have begun to report the backlash" (p. 279) and that it is evidence of a "national hysteria" (p 279). In my opinion, the media attention that presently exists is just as likely to have resulted from a concerted effort by Victims of Child Abuse Laws (VOCAL) to draw such attention to its own particular problem. Studies completed by the Association of Family Court Counselors (N. Theonnes, personal communication, November 2, 1987) have indicated that the prevalence of false reporting of child sexual abuse in custody disputes is only 10% of all cases. Again, a staggeringly small statistic compared with what Spiegel and VOCAL would have counselors believe.

A Question of Innocence

Personally, I would be more accepting of Spiegel's innocence and the VOCAL members' allegations that they have been wronged if each would open up his or her entire social service and civil court records to public scrutiny. In my own experience of dealing with a number of cases in which members of VOCAL have claimed that they have been wronged, this perception has arisen because a juvenile court found enough evidence to order them into treatment for sexually abusing their children, although the criminal court was unable to prove beyond a reasonable doubt that they were guilty.

The criminal justice system requires a much higher standard of proof as to guilt or innocence than does the juvenile system, which itself requires only a preponderance of evidence. A judgment of not guilty in a criminal court does not mean innocent; this may merely mean that evidence to prove guilt beyond a reasonable doubt was lacking. Contrastingly, evidence in juvenile court is kept confidential, to protect the child (and, paradoxically, to protect the abusive adult). Requiring only a preponderance of evidence, these courts may order that visitation rights be suspended until evalu-, ations and treatment occur to ensure the child's safety. This is not backlash, this is not hysteria, and this is not a violation of the adult's constitutional rights. It is an effort to protect children and gather data in a manner that would be appropriate to ensure the continued protection of the child, as well as the institution of treatment for the family.

Education and Training

Without a doubt, there is a need for continued education and better training for child protective and law enforcement workers, judges, physicians, teachers, and all those involved in a multidisciplinary approach to the prevention and treatment of child abuse and neglect. Elementary school counselors should act as any citizen to ensure that the present system that has been set up to protect children is adequately funded and supported. To label the problems that 3,000 members of VOCAL have called *child abuse hysteria* as epidemic would be greatly overstating the issue. These members of VOCAL, who feel as if they have been falsely accused, do not represent a very large number of complainants when all reports are considered. In the 3- to 4-year period in which VOCAL has been established, there have been well over 4 million reports of child abuse and neglect (American Humane Society, 1987). These reports have overwhelmed child protective service agencies and their staffs. To ignore the fact that the child protective service system is stressed and needs help would also be a great mistake. To change policy because of this so-called "hysteria epidemic," however, would also be a great mistake.

References

American Humane Association (1987). *National study on the incidence of child abuse and neglect.* Denver, CO: Author.

Jones, D. (1987). Reliable and fictitious accounts of sexual abuse to children. *Journal of Interpersonal Violence, 2*(1), 27–45.

Spiegel, L.D. (1986). *A question of innocence: A true story of false accusation.* Parsippany, NJ: Unicorn Publishing.

Spiegel, L.D. (1988). Child abuse hysteria and the elementary school counselor. *Elementary School Guidance & Counseling, 22,* 275–283.

Counselors Need To Be Knowledgeable and Sensitive: A Reaction to Spiegel

Patricia A. Ferris

Two major points have been made by Spiegel (1988) in his article: (a) elementary school counselors must be knowledgeable about the child abuse hysteria syndrome, and (b) an objective process is needed to assist counselors in handling such cases. In my opinion, few elementary school counselors possess sufficient education and understanding regarding the child abuse hysteria syndrome that Spiegel described. Moreover, Spiegel's suggestion that there is a need for further research and clarification of the present knowledge base seems to be sound.

Without doubt, some counselors may become involved with children who believe abuse has taken place when, in fact, it has not. Contrary to what Spiegel may believe, such reports that turn out to be false are not intentional fabrications. Instead, counselors act based upon what they believe to be correct information with the full intent to protect the child in a difficult situation. Yet, I do agree that counselors need to be able to recognize the hysteric reactions Spiegel describes and develop ways to counsel with children who are reacting to this syndrome.

Spiegel has presented an excellent rationale for school counselors to explore, in greater depth, problems associated with false reporting. To date, counselors have neglected this issue while becoming familiar with abuse reporting procedures and the general implementation of state laws of child abuse. Although counselors around the United States continue to improve their skills through participation in workshops and professional reading, an emphasis on the hysteria syndrome described by Spiegel must be included in in-service training experiences and journal articles.

In 1981, the American School Counselor Association (ASCA) adopted a position statement titled, "The School Counselor and Child Abuse/Neglect Prevention," which was revised in 1985 (see Appendix F for a reprint of this statement). It should be noted that this document fails to contain any reference to false reporting or the need for counselors to be cognizant of the child abuse hysteria syndrome. Because false reporting and the child abuse hysteria syndrome are important issues, ASCA must assume leadership and provide information to its members and update the position statement. Certainly, counselors need a better understanding of the syndrome and its characteristics, which will assist them in its identification. All school counselors must guard against a situation that could lead to false reporting. As Spiegel recommended, counselors will need to ensure that a balance is achieved in prevention programs that sensitize children to abuse issues without creating hysteria or fear.

Closely related to the issue of false reports presented by Spiegel, yet somewhat different, is the effect that the reporting law itself has on the counselor's attitude of responsibility in any type of child abuse case. One might ask, "Is the law that requires counselors to report child abuse used as an excuse for abdicating professional responsibility to provide services to these children?" No doubt the answer to the question could be yes in some instances.

It is not unusual to find professionals at all levels who dread the interaction with an abused child and the adult suspected of the abuse. Some counselors may be fearful of the adult and the problems that such an accusation could cause; perhaps they may not want to discuss a topic that society has labeled taboo; or the counselor may feel inadequate in terms of knowledge and experience in dealing with such cases. I agree with Spiegel that, in some situations, helping professionals, including counselors, may act without awareness of their own motivation to avoid this confrontation. A counselor who relies on child protective agencies may not realize the shortsightedness of this decision and the damage that may be done to adults and children alike. Ideally, in cases where no actual proof of abuse exists, or if there are strong doubts, the counselor would decide to clarify the situation through face-to-face contact with the parents.

Without question, the professional counselor must develop adequate techniques to interview the child and parents, establish criteria to judge situations, suggest a specific process for reporting all information objectively, and develop follow-up methods to ensure that all parties are contacted in a timely and appropriate manner. Counselors must be encouraged to approach complicated abuse situations with well-grounded knowledge and skills if the incidence of false reporting is to be avoided.

Reference

Spiegel, L.D. (1988). Child abuse hysteria and the elementary school counselor. *Elementary School Guidance & Counseling, 22,* 275–283.

Shared Responsibility for Reporting Child Abuse Cases: A Reaction to Spiegel

Janet Howell-Nigrelli

Awareness, knowledge, commitment, and effective communication skills are important attributes that school counselors must have when confronted with a suspected case of child abuse. Counselors, however, should also realize that within an educational setting, the reporting of child abuse is a responsibility that is shared with the counselor's school district. On the one hand, the individual counselor must be accurately informed about the applicable state laws and reporting procedures. On the other hand, the school district must provide a written policy for counselors and other employees of the district to follow when abuse is suspected.

In many instances the school counselor may be the designated agent for reporting cases of suspected abuse. Failure to report one's suspicions may lead to subsequent prosecution under state law. In Pennsylvania, where I am an elementary school counselor, this is the case. My school district, however, attempts to minimize inappropriate reports through a team effort. Counselors should consider forming teams of 3 or 4 members of the school community to review suspected situations of child abuse. Meetings must be held in a timely manner, which would enable the counselor, or other designated reporter, to contact the local child protective services as soon as possible. This procedure enables the counselor to review the evidence that has been gathered from a child or adult and clarify any discrepancies with other professional educators before a report is filed. Instead of abrogating responsibility, the process ensures that the report that is filed will be accurate and factual, containing all the accumulated information. I believe the team approach that my counseling department uses also keeps members of the department from becoming unwitting participants in the hysteria surrounding this issue.

Additionally, a team effort has been used in my school district to approach the prevention-awareness issue of abuse with teachers and students. After we on the counseling staff review abuse prevention materials, we discuss their contents as well as student needs with individual teachers or grade level teams. These needs are then shared with local community mental health agencies to involve them in the accurate representation of facts and knowledge to the students. A strong commitment to open communication between school and community professionals has resulted in a greater awareness of child abuse.

In summary, elementary school counselors need to be aware and knowledgeable of issues surrounding child abuse. Furthermore, it is imperative that each counselor has a commitment to report any and all cases of suspected child abuse. Counselors, however, must share this commitment and communicate their needs to the school districts and communities in which they work. The responsibility for accurately reporting cases of child abuse must be shared by all of society.

Recent Research on Child Abuse: A Brief Review

Edwin R. Gerler, Jr.

Child abuse and neglect are major problems throughout the world. In the United States, elementary school counselors are at the forefront of efforts to improve understanding of child abuse and to develop educational programs aimed at preventing and treating child abuse (Downing, 1982; Holtgraves, 1986). The purpose of this brief article is to review some important recent studies showing the harmful effects of child abuse as well as the beneficial effects of educational programs designed to deal with abuse. Elementary school counselors may gain valuable insights about the problem of abuse from recent research.

The Effects of Child Abuse

Child's Perspective of Self and Others

A study by Ney, Moore, McPhee, and Trought (1986) of the child's perspective on abuse resulted in some interesting findings about how children perceive abuse. Using an 84-question structured interview, the researcher asked 57 abused children (ages 5–13) about their perceptions of abuse, views of family, self-concepts, and world views. Mothers of the children also participated in interviews.

The study found that children's perceptions were affected in differing degrees depending on the nature of the abuse. Physically abused children, for example, accepted the blame for mild abuse but not for severe abuse. Also, verbal and sexual abuse seemed to have a larger negative influence on children's perceptions of themselves and the world than did physical abuse. The overall findings of the study, though limited by the problems of small sample size and self-report data, supported the clinical and experimental findings of other researchers, namely, that abused children tend to blame themselves, but the extent of blame is mediated by the type and extent of abuse.

Developmental Effects

Among the most important recent studies on the subject of child abuse was Augoustinos's (1987) review of research findings on developmental effects of abuse. Her review included a summary of pre-1982 research on developmental effects of abuse as well as a careful examination of more recent reviews. Her conclusion was that the research is fraught with definitional and methodological problems, but that, despite these problems of methodology, "there is sufficient empirical evidence to support the widely held assumption that child abuse and neglect have deleterious effects on the physical, neurological, intellectual, and emotional development of the child" (Augoustinos, 1987, p. 15).

She found further, however, that healthy development may occur regardless of maltreatment provided the child is surrounded by strong environmental resources and positive interpersonal interactions.

Research on Child Abuse Programs

Effects of Preventive Programs

Researchers have met with little success in documenting effective programs for preventing child abuse. As Garbarino (1986) noted, measuring the success of preventive programs is a problem of major proportions. The development of preventive programs is equally difficult.

The most successful preventive approach seems to be the health visitor program studied by Olds, Chamberlin, Henderson, and Tatelbaum (in press). Their rigorous study showed that a registered nurse assigned to a family judged to be at high risk for abuse resulted in significant preventive effects. The nurse visited the high-risk mother weekly during pregnancy and visited the family at least monthly for the first 2 years of the child's life. It is clear from the health visitor study that preventive strategies often need to be intensive and highly individualized. Evidence is not yet as clear on the effectiveness of educational programs for groups of potentially abusive parents. Many more group programs need to be developed and studied.

Effects of Preventive Group Programs

A parent education program developed and studied by Golub, Espinosa, Damon, and Card (1987) for groups of abusive parents offers the hope that preventive group programs are within reach. This program, titled "Hugs 'n Kids," incorporates videotapes of 13 episodes depicting typical problem situations between parents and their preschool children. Golub et al. studied 40 parents who participated in pretests and posttests to assess the program's effects. Results indicated that abusive parents and high-risk parents who completed the program had improved their knowledge of alternatives to physical punishment and had changed their attitudes toward children's misbehavior.

Implications for Elementary School Counselors

The current research indicates that abuse has deleterious effects on the self-image of children and often blocks healthy physical and psychological development. Elementary school counselors, therefore, need, first of all, to be advocates for those children who have experienced abuse and, perhaps more importantly, need to be advocates for programs, such as the nurse visitor program, that show promise in preventing high-risk parents from becoming abusive.

Moreover, elementary school counselors should be at the forefront in advocating and developing group programs aimed at preventing abusive behaviors among parents identified as potentially abusive. Interventions like the "Hugs 'n Kids" videotape program are models for elementary school counselors to follow as they develop their own programs. Counselors interested in more information about the "Hugs 'n Kids" program should contact Dr. Judith S. Golub, San Fernando Valley Child Guidance Clinic, 9650 Zelzah Ave., Northridge, CA 91325.

Finally, elementary school counselors need to be attentive to the special needs of children who have been mistreated. In some instances, counselors may need to work with these children individually or in small groups. Some other children, of course, will need to be referred for intensive treatment.

In conclusion, elementary school counselors who have worked with abused children are well aware that preventive programs are much needed. Research supports this need. Counselors should continue to advocate and work toward the implementation of effective treatment programs for abused children as well as the implementation of promising programs of child abuse prevention.

References

Augoustinos, M. (1987). Developmental effects of child abuse: Recent findings. *Child Abuse and Neglect, 11,* 15–27.

Downing, C.J. (1982). Parent support groups to prevent child abuse. *Elementary School Guidance & Counseling, 17,* 119–124.

Garbarino, J. (1986). Can we measure success in preventing child abuse? Issues in policy, programming and research. *Child Abuse and Neglect, 10,* 143–156.

Golub, J.S., Espinosa, M., Damon, L., & Card, J. (1987). A videotape parent education program for abusive parents. *Child Abuse and Neglect, 11,* 255–265.

Holtgraves, M. (1986). Help the victims of sexual abuse help themselves. *Elementary School Guidance & Counseling, 21,* 155–159.

Olds, D., Chamberlin, R., Henderson, C., & Tatelbaum, R. (in press). The prevention of child abuse and neglect: A randomized trial of nurse home visitation. *Pediatrics.*

5

ETHICAL ISSUES IN GROUP WORK

Group counseling presents ethical issues not found in individual interventions with clients. The advantages of a comprehensive group counseling program are numerous; however, school counselors who direct such programs of services need to be familiar with potential ethical problems. Kottler (1982) offers 13 reasons why professionals who engage in group counseling must be aware of special problems.

Corey, Corey, Callanan, and Russell (1982) provide a comprehensive overview of the many issues group counselors face, with a specific focus on implementing group techniques.

Davis and Meara (1982) discuss the special problem of keeping group counseling sessions confidential and offer practical guidelines for fostering confidentiality within a group.

Although group counseling in general presents special problems, providing group counseling for children introduces issues not found when working with adults. Although the ASCA *Ethical Standards for School Counselors* (1984) does not directly addresss group counseling, some specific guidelines are found in the AACD *Ethical Standards* (1988). The ASGW *Ethical Guidelines for Group Work* (1980) provides additional direction upon which Terres aned Larrabee (1985) base their recommendations regarding group counseling programs within schools.

Kottler (1982) calls upon counselors to be more honest with themselves regarding what they say and do in groups. He maintains that counselors often distort information they convey to group counseling clients.

Ethics Comes of Age:
Introduction to the Special Issue

Jeffrey A. Kottler

Ethics is a timely topic, one that everyone would say merits more attention, whether they believe it or not. It has been only in the past decade that ethics has received so much press, perhaps because it has traditionally been considered a boring, esoteric, and largely irrelevant branch of philosophy for modern day practitioners. But then came Watergate, and the public got a crash course in the abuses of leader power. Suspicions worsened still when Charlie Manson and Jim Jones got into the act, proving with casual arrogance how group leaders can effectively use dimensions of trust, cohesion, peer pressure, and reinforcement to induce murder or suicide. The Moonies, Scientologists, and EST-ettes then entered the scene, further demonstrating both the attraction and dangers of group-oriented therapeutic movements. Whether we like it or not, the time has come to close our ranks, to demonstrate our professional character, our responsibility, our integrity. And from such concerns, ethics has finally come into prominence, spawning greater leader effectiveness, our own ethical guidelines, and yes, a special issue of our journal devoted to this timely topic. This special issue treats the subject of ethics from a group practitioner's viewpoint, emphasizing practical implications, controversial issues, and above all, stimulating discussion.

Ethics is a subject of particular importance to group leaders because of the special problems our work presents. These unique issues that are an implicit part of our practice make us more vulnerable to error:

1. Verbal abuse and subsequent casualties are more likely to occur in goups than in individual treatment because of specialized group techniques. (See article by Corey, Corey, Callanan & Russell in this chapter.)

2. The therapist has less control over the proceedings and client behavior. Potentially more things could go wrong before the leader could intervene.

3. The group leader also has more control in the sense of influencing capabilities. This power can be used for better or worse.

4. Confidentiality cannot be guaranteed or enforced since other group members do not necessarily live by the same moral codes that we do. (See Davis & Meara article in this chapter.)

5. Many group leaders practice without benefit of any training, education, or supervision. There are no standardized criteria for acceptable qualifications. In the same city, a psychiatrist, psychologist, astrologer, palm reader, and prostitute can all label their professional activities as "group therapy" of one sort or another.

6. Because groups are such intense environments, the risks for each member are greater. Change and damage are accelerated.

7. The screening of clients is often haphazard. Often they are required to participate involuntarily in the experience.

8. The lines are muddled that separate unethical, incompetent, and inappropriate leader behaviors, and a discrepancy exists between what leaders say they do versus what they actually practice (See last Kottler article in this chapter).

9. Group work presents some special reentry problems for participants when the sessions have ended.

10. Dependency effects are more pronounced in the creation of "groupies."

11. There is no licensure, certification, or regulation that can effectively enforce the practice of responsible group leadership (see articles by Roberts and Gumaer in *Journal for Specialists in Group Work*, 7, 1982).

12. Ethical decision making skills are rarely included in the professional training and development of group leaders (see Paradise & Siegelwaks article in *Journal for Specialists in Group Work*, 7, 1982).

13. It is difficult to document the effectiveness and to evaluate the results of group work progress (see Brown article in *Journal for Specialists in Group Work*, 7, 1982).

Each of these considerations, unique to the practice of group work, makes our task of functioning responsibly and ethically that much harder. Only through further study and dialogue can we hope to refine our ethical decision making skills and improve our competence as practitioners. The articles in this special issue cover a broad range of topics intended to raise as many questions as provide answers to the universal query echoing through the centuries: How ought we to act?

Ethical Considerations in Using Group Techniques

Gerald Corey, Marianne Schneider Corey, Patrick Callanan, and J. Michael Russell

This article presents specific issues in implementing techniques at all the stages of groups. It is designed to stimulate thought leading to ethical practice and the appropriate use of techniques.

The Association for Specialists in Group Work has approved *Ethical Guidelines for Group Leaders* (ASGW, 1980; see article by Roberts, *Journal of Specialists in Group Work*, 7, 1982). These guidelines address the leader's responsibility for providing information about group work to clients and for providing group services to clients. We were influenced by these guidelines in developing our views on the ethical considerations in using group techniques.

Techniques are powerful instruments. Their abuse is not always due to a lack of concern for clients; abuse can also come from a lack of awareness of the potential effects of techniques. Thus in our training workshops for group leaders we encourage spontaneity and inventiveness in the use of techniques, yet we also teach the participants the importance of having a rationale and some theoretical framework for these techniques. We urge group leaders to strike a balance between creativity and irresponsible lack of caution.

We believe that the reputation of group work has suffered from irresponsible practitioners, mostly those who use techniques in a gimmicky, ill-conceived, or inappropriate way. But we surely do not want to foster the myth that there is a tidy body of techniques firmly embedded in clear-cut scientific doctrine guaranteed to lead to highly predictable outcomes when used by omniscient specialists. Neither do we want people to become overly rigid and frightened in their group leadership. Basically, we believe that if the group leader has a sound academic background, has had extensive supervised group experience, has experienced his or her own therapy (perferably including experience as a group member), and has a fundamental respect for his or her clients, that group leader is not likely to abuse techniques.

Preparation of Group Members

Providing Information About the Group

The techniques appropriate for a group depend on the goals and qualifications of the leader. Prospective members and referring agencies should be informed about these goals and qualifications. A group that advertises itself to the general public should make its particular population and purposes clear. Is it a support group for parents without partners, a personal-growth group, or some type of special interest group? Will the group be open or closed? Will the group have a fixed number of sessions, or will it continue as long as there is interest? All these matters should be clearly stated in advance.

Prospective group members have a right to know about the leader's qualifications, including experiences in leading groups. As far as is feasible, the leader must explain to prospective members the kinds of techniques likely to be employed, and these techniques should be congruent with the leader's level of training and experience. Leaders should not suppose that the mere possession of relevant academic degrees and licenses guarantees that they are personally or experientially qualified for employing any technique, and they should not assume that citing such degrees is sufficient for fully informing prospective members about their qualifications. If emphasis is going to be on some specialized or experimental techniques, it is appropriate for leaders to indicate that they have the experience to employ such techniques. Leaders who cannot substantiate their training in the specialized techniques they plan to use in their groups may be misleading their clients.

In setting group goals and identifying proposed techniques, leaders should be aware that the material they wish to explore should connect with issues they have encountered in their own lives. And while they may not have experienced every specific technique they intend to use, they should have personally experienced the general kinds of techniques they want to employ or should have learned about them under the supervision of or in collaboration with someone familiar with them.

Although group members should be informed in advance about the kinds of procedures and techniques that are likely to be employed in the group, it would be unrealistic to try to explain every technique. But group members can be informed about the general style of the leader. Certainly, if the leader intends to employ exotic techniques such as nudity, highly cathartic techniques, or confrontive techniques designed to break down defenses, the client should be fully aware of these intentions.

Freedom of Exit From a Group

One of the ASGW's (1980) ethical guidelines states that group leaders have the responsibility for informing members in advance that their participation in the group is voluntary and that they have the right to exit from the group at any time. It is our position that the leader's attitudes and policies on the issue of "freedom of exit" should be spelled out during the pregroup individual screening interview or at the preliminary group session. Further, we think that group members have a responsibility to the leaders and members to explain why they want to leave. We have several reasons for this policy. It can be deleterious to members to leave without being able to discuss what they considered threatening or negative about the group experience and, in addition, it is unfortunate for members to leave a group because of a misunderstanding about some feedback they have received. On the other side, it can be damaging to other members if they suppose that someone left the group because of something they said or did.

By having the person who is leaving the group present reasons for desired departure to the group as a whole, we give the other members an opportunity to check out any concerns they may have about their responsibility for that person's decision. We tell our members that they have an obligation to attend all sessions and to inform us and the group should they decide to withdraw. If members even consider withdrawing, we encourage them to say so because such an acknowledgement inevitably provides extremely important material with which to work. While we do not seek to subject members to a debate or to undue pressure to stay, we stress the serious impact their leaving will have on the whole group, especially if they do so without explanation.

The Leader's Motivations and Theoretical Stance

Being Aware of Motivations

We are concerned about leaders who use techniques to protect themselves, to meet their own needs for power or prestige, or to control the members of their groups. Leaders who are unaware of their own motivations can easily impose their unmet needs and their values on the members of their groups. One of the ASGW's (1980) ethical guidelines that we see as especially important is the following: "Group leaders shall refrain from imposing their own agendas, needs, and values on group members." There are many ways that leaders can misuse techniques if they are unaware of their motivations. They may apply pressure on certain individuals to get them to perform in desired ways. They may use techniques mainly to impress participants with their therapeutic prowess or to steer members away from explorations of feelings and issues they personally find threatening. They may use highly confrontive techniques and exercises to stir up aggression in their groups.

The potential exists for leaders to hide behind their position. They can camouflage their incompetence, fearfulness, or insecurity by seeking to create the impression that they are all-knowing and all-powerful. They can keep their real feelings hidden and project only what is consistent with the impression they wish to create; and they can choose techniques that perpetuate this illusion.

In all such cases, the leader's needs become primary, while those of the members assume relative unimportance. Even experienced leaders are sometimes slow to recognize such motivations in their use of various techniques. When these become patterns, one hopes they will show up in the leader's own therapy or supervision sessions. Coleaders can also point out these patterns. If leaders do not have supervisors or coleaders, they should make a habit of reviewing group sessions and be alert to ways their own needs and motives may be getting in the way.

Dealing With the Superhuman Image

Group members often attribute exaggerated power and wisdom to leaders, and there is the temptation for leaders who are motivated by a need for power to unethically reinforce this misconception. One way to aviod such reinforcement is to be willing to explain the purpose of a suggested technique. Although it is distracting to regularly explain the point of a technique in advance, it can on occasion be appropriate for a member to ask and for a leader to state the purpose of a technique or an exercise. At times, providing a general explanation or rationale for a technique can lessen the impression that leaders are superhuman wizards.

Having a Theoretical Rationale for Using Techniques

Leaders cannot always predict the exact outcomes of techniques, but they can have some expected outcomes in mind or have an idea of how a technique is connected with the material of the moment. If a supervisor, colleague, or group member asks a leader: "Why did you use that technique: What did you hope to gain from it?" the leader should be able to justify using it. A leader who cannot do so is probably grasping at straws and filling time rather than providing constructive leadership. We are not urging leaders to be so preoccupied with thinking about the rationale for a technique that they become timid and unspontaneous, but being aware of the purpose of a technique can become second nature and does not have to be incompatible with the ability to follow a hunch spontaneously.

Using Techniques to Avoid Leaders' Own Fears

Some leaders introduce techniques to cover up their own fears or unwillingness to explore the themes present in the group. Such diversion frequently occurs with themes relating to lack of closeness and hostility.

Genuine closeness takes time to develop. During some periods in a group's history closeness can often be conspicuously absent. Leaders who feel uncomfortable with this lack of closeness may try to force a false sense of closeness through the use of various techniques. For example, in one group with an apparent lack of closeness, the leader might suggest that members all huddle together. If any technique is to be introduced here, we believe the preferable procedure would be to suggest that members of the group spread out to far corners of the room and then talk about how they feel. In other words, leaders should attempt to make explicit and even exaggerate what is already going on rather than try to overcome their own unease by imposing an artificial solution.

Leaders are sometimes afraid of conflict and thus they introduce some techniques designed to smooth it out, or find some other way to avoid dealing directly with it. Conflict that exists within a group should be acknowledged directly and dealt with openly. If conflict is not brought into the open, it lies dormant and festers and eventually halts productive work in the group. Broadly, this ethical concern could be stated as follows:

> One of the most important things a group can and should teach is that one can learn to face and express what one thinks and feels. If group leaders introduce techniques that detract from or cover up the dynamics of the groups, then they are modeling the idea that feelings are to be avoided.

One should be cautious about using techniques at all if they are artificial substitutes for genuine exploration. When a technique is introduced, it should generally serve to highlight the emotional, cognitive, and behavioral material present in the group and not detract from it because of the leader's unease.

Undue Pressure in Using Techniques

Freedom to Decline Participating in Exercises

Two ethical guidelines developed by ASGW (1980) pertain to the issue of pressuring members to get involved in certain techniques from which they might choose to refrain: They refer to risks involved in group participation and to group pressure exerted on members. One of these guidelines deals with protecting group members from coercion and undue peer pressure insofar as is reasonably possible. The other related guideline provides that group members be informed about the personal risks involved in any group. Surely, one such risk involves the undue influence of group pressure that could cause members to act in ways other than those they might independently choose.

Although group pressure is a realistic and oftentimes therapeutic factor leading to change, undue pressure causes us some concern, especially as it relates to coercing members to join into all exercises and activities during a session. For example, a leader may ask members to pair up and engage in a touching exercise or to otherwise express what they are feeling to their partners in a nonverbal way. If leaders are not careful, they can easily create the impression that all members are expected to participate in all such exercises. Such leaders court the dangers of intruding on members' sensitivities and values, and of not respecting their right to pass, particularly on some of the exercises that they might not want to participate in or might not be ready to handle.

Leaders cannot simply state at the beginning of a group that members have a right not to participate if they choose not to do so, for some members may feel pressured to do what everyone else is doing. Leaders must make it genuinely acceptable for members to pass by mentioning this option periodically when appropriate. To avoid this problem we usually invite members to work on personally meaningful material. If members bring up issues they want to work on, it increases the chance that they can handle whatever might surface.

Further, we typically impress on members that they can decide at what point they wish to stop. Members sometimes open a painful or threatening area and then say that they do not want to go ahead. Generally, we explore their desire for stopping and in this way focus on the factors members find threatening. They may not trust the leader to deal with what will emerge, or they may not trust the group enough to pursue an issue. They may be worried about looking foolish, or they may fear losing control. Even if members decide to stop, we tell them that if at a later time they want to return to the issue we hope that they will announce this desire. The responsibility is then clearly on the members to decide what they will bring out in the group and the level or depth to which they choose to explore the issues they do bring out. Placing responsibility with the members is a built-in safety factor, and it is a sign of our respect for them.

There is another side to this issue. We assume that people who come to a group want some pressure; so the tricky task is to achieve a balance between appropriate pressure and unethical coercion. A leader who is unwilling even to say, "How would it be if you just tried this for a minute, and then we could stop if you like?" may be failing to take some responsibility for maintaining therapeutic leverage. The leader needs to be alert to whether the client is leaving an opening for pursuing the technique, but the leader also has an ethical obligation to respect the client's refusal and yet to attempt to explore the client's reasons for declining.

Pressure From Other Members

Group leaders have an ethical obligation to respond to undue peer pressure on a group member, especially when they have assured the group that no one will be coerced into making disclosures or participating in the activities. The leader can comment on the peer pressure or can offer an interpretation of the seeming need to coerce and thus can turn the spotlight on the people exerting the pressure. The leader can ask them to talk about why they need to pressure another. The point of this type of intervention is to acknowledge the feelings of those who are exerting the pressure and to see what productive work might be done with those feelings, while reminding the group of the need to respect the wishes of an unwilling member.

Misuse of Confrontational Techniques

Leaders may abuse their power by inappropriately focusing on a member they select. Some leaders derive a sense of power from putting members on the spot, bombarding them with questions, deliberately putting them in a defensive position, or applying pressure on them to open up. One group leader we observed opened a session by calling on a particular member and staying with the same person for the entire session. He believed this was an effective technique to use with resistant members and assumed such pressure would crack their stubborn defenses. We have seen another leader ask question after question, relying on this technique to give the group the appearance of movement. Although we think confrontational techniques can be used to work through members' resistances or defenses, we do not think it appropriate to endlessly interrogate members. Confrontation needs to be handled with care and concern for the member being confronted; it is not to be used by leaders as a club to beat members into submission.

Forced Touching

There are several facets to the ethical issue of using touching as a technique. In some cases leaders use touching techniques to fulfill their own needs or fantasies and are not sensitive to the needs of the members. Leaders may have a lack of touching and physical contact in their own lives, and they compensate for this lack through their work with groups.

Another ethical aspect of touching techniques has to do with their potential artificiality; they can often be used as a short cut to intimacy. Although increasing ease with physical contact is therapeutically important, this need should be balanced by respect for the readiness and values of the participants. Although we do not discourage spontaneous touching in our groups, we rarely introduce a technique that explicitly directs clients into a physical intimacy they do not want. As a group develops intimacy and risk taking, touching tends to increase; but touching has by then become spontaneous rather than imposed by some artificial technique.

Inappropriate Catharsis

Some leaders evaluate the success of their groups by the degree of emotional intensity they evoke; they are too eager to push people into a cathartic experience for its own sake. Highly emotional sessions are exciting for their drama, and the expression of emotion is certainly an important part of the group process; the danger lies in losing sight of what one hopes would emerge from these cathartic incidents. It is also dangerous to make members believe that they are good members only when they engage in catharsis.

Among the ethical issues brought to the fore by the use of catharsis in group work are the following:

- Whose needs are being met by the catharsis—those of the leader, the group, or the individual member?
- Is the leader clear about what the catharsis is supposed to mean or to what it is supposed to lead?
- Is the leader capable of handling the intensity of the catharsis or to what it might lead?
- Is there enough time in the group session to work with the emotions that arise and to arrive at some resolution?
- Will the group leader have subsequent sessions with the client to deal with the repercussions of the catharsis?
- Is the leader sensitive to the subtle line between invoking catharsis for its therapeutic potential and involving catharsis for the sake of drama?

Leaders should be especially aware of times they use catharsis to fulfill their own and not their clients' needs. For example, leaders may like to see people express anger because they would like to be able to do so themselves, and so they unethically push members to get into contact with angry feelings by developing techniques to bring out anger and to focus the group on anger. Although anger and its expression and exploration is surely appropriate in groups, the issue is the degree to which the leader's needs become central in the selection of techniques designed to bring out certain feelings in members.

Ethical Aspects of Using Physical Techniques

As with touching, the encounter group movement fostered many techniques to help people express their aggressive feelings— hitting pillows, arm wrestling, pushing and shoving, breaking in or out of a circle. These techniques are often unpredictable in outcome. The symbolic release of aggression can obviously be therapeutically valuable, but one should take relevant precautions. Leaders who introduce such techniques should protect the client and other group members from harm and should be prepared to deal with the unforeseen directions the exercise may take. The concern here is not simply for the physical safety of the clients. If a client has restrained emotion for a long time out of fear of the consequences of expressing it, that fear tragically gets reinforced if the emotion does indeed get out of control when it is finally expressed and proves damaging to others. In general, we avoid physical techniques involving the whole group for safety reasons. We prefer to introduce physical techniques only when pursuing work with an individual with whom we are familiar.

Leaders who introduce physical techniques should have enough experience and training to deal with the consequences. While we encourage leaders to try a variety of techniques, we also see a danger in their foolishly or unthinkingly using techniques they have not experienced themselves or techniques that easily generate material that they have no idea how to handle. Merely reading about techniques and then trying them out is not sufficient. Beginning leaders should use them only with direct supervision or when they are coleading with an experienced counselor.

In addition, leaders should never goad or push members into physical exercises. In inviting members to participate in an exercise the leader must state clearly that members have the option to refrain. Leaders who explain to members the exercise they have in mind, ask them whether they want to try it, and take safety precautions minimize the chances for negative outcomes.

Coleadership Issues

We favor coleadership for a number of reasons. Having more than one leader increases the ways in which a group can function; for example, a female–male team gives members the benefit of having two role models. Members can also benefit from the differing perceptions of different coleaders. One of the coleaders may have the ability to contact and work with certain difficult members, while the other leader might be unable to reach them.

From the viewpoint of the coleaders, each can build on the other's style, and they can complement and extend each other's work with individuals. Coleaders can provide each other with valuable feedback after each session, and they can share impressions of what occurred in the group. They can talk about what they think the group needs or a direction in which they think the group should move. They can plan and evaluate sessions. They can bring two perspectives to the understanding of certain individuals or particular relationships in the group.

An ethical issue arises when coleaders form a relationship that inhibits the group's progress. For instance, group leaders who have sharp differences may cause group members to polarize. Coleaders who are competitive may push the members into using techniques designed simply to prove the prowess of one or the other leader. To avoid these problems coleaders need to establish a relationship based on trust and respect; one in which each leader can function as an individual, yet one that is characterized by harmony and teamwork wherein both coleaders work for the good of the members. In such a relationship, the primary aim is not to fulfill the needs of the leaders but to provide diversity for the members.

Concluding Comments

We have limited ourselves to discussing important ethical questions connected with the use of techniques in groups. Other crucial ethical and professional issues in group practice that we have not addressed include: recruiting, screening, selecting, and preparing group members; involuntary participation in groups; issues pertaining to confidentiality; issues concerning termination and reentry; controversial issues in group practice; and specific issues concerning the group leader's training, supervision, and level of competence. We have explored these topics in more detail else-where (Corey, 1981; Corey & Corey, 1982; Corey, Corey, & Callanan, 1979)

The most important point we hope we have conveyed is that techniques can be harmful if used inappropriately or insensitively. They can injure group members physically or emotionally. Ethical concerns arise when techniques are used simply as gimmicks and are not designed to serve the needs of the participants. The negative popular image of groups has come from the abuse of techniques, from using them to replace what a group fundamentally is—an arena for genuine and caring human interaction.

References

Association for Specialists in Group Work. *Ethical guidelines for group leaders.* Falls Church, Va.: Author, 1980.

Corey, G. *Theory and practice of group counseling.* Monterey, Calif.: Brooks/Cole, 1981.

Corey, G., & Corey, M.S. *Groups: Process and practice (2nd ed.).* Monterey, Calif.: Brooks/Cole, 1982.

Corey, G.; Corey, M.S.; & Callanan, P., *Professional and ethical issues in counseling and psychotherapy.* Monterey, Calif.: Brooks/Cole, 1979.

Corey, G.; Corey, M.S.; Callanan, P.; Russell, J.M. *Group techniques.* Monterey, Calif.: Brooks/Cole, 1982.

Recommended Readings

Corey, G. Description of a practicum course in group leadership. *Journal for Specialists in Group Work.* 1981, 6, 100–107.

Corey, G.; Corey, M.S.; Callanan, P.; & Russell, J.M. A residential workshop for personal growth. *Journal for Specialists in Group Work*, 1980, 5, 205–211.

So You Think It Is a Secret

Kathleen L. Davis and *Naomi M. Meara*

Group confidentiality is difficult to enforce. A hypothetical situation is presented to illustrate how members might violate confidentiality. Group cohesiveness and certain leader skills can help to maintain confidentiality norms.

When seeking help with a problem, people choose a person they can trust. They assume that the helper they have chosen is able to keep a secret. Clients seeking professional help expect that their secrets are safe. Perhaps, of all the ethical responsibilities that professional helpers have, clients are most concerned about confidentiality.

Confidentiality in individual or group counseling means the counselor or psychologist is not allowed to disclose anything said in the interview without the client's permission (American Personnel and Guidance Association, 1981; American Psychological Association, 1981). In the individual counseling session only two people, the client and the counselor, focus on the client's concerns. The client has the freedom to tell anyone what was said or what happened during the session. This freedom is generally accepted by the counselor as the client's personal decision. In the group counseling session there are more than two people, the members and the leader or leaders, focusing on many members' concerns and interactions. If members are free to tell anyone what happened or was said in the group session, there is a good chance that they will divulge personal information about someone other than themselves. Therefore, most leaders do not support the members' freedom to talk about the group or its participants to nongroup members (Davis, 1980; Gazda, 1978).

The recent APGA Ethical Standards (1981) specify: "In a group setting, the counselor must set a norm of confidentiality regarding all group participants' disclosures" (p. A). According to this standard, the group leader is ethically bound to state the expectation that information revealed in the group is not to be disclosed outside

223

the group. If this expectation is not accepted by the group, then it will not become a norm for the group. If the leader's expectation is accepted by a majority of group members, then it will become a group norm (Shaw, 1981). There is no way to guarantee that confidentiality will be honored by every group member, however. The Association for Specialists in Group Work (1980) recognizes that confidentiality is difficult, if not impossible, to enforce. Davis (1980) found that group members do reveal information learned in the group to others and that the leader's presentation of confidentiality affects members' disclosures outside the group. Groups whose leaders talked about disclosures to other people had a lower percentage of members breaking confidentiality.

Usually, the first opportunity a group leader has to discuss confidentiality with a potential group member is in the screening interview. The American Psychological Association (1973) suggests the inclusion of a statement about confidentiality expectations in the written contract given to each potential participant before the group begins. During the initial screening interview it needs to be made clear that the general expectation for confidentiality includes the leader as well as the members. Also at this time, several other aspects of confidentiality need to be discussed; for example, early termination, discussions with the leader outside the group, and legal protection. Even if a member leaves the group, that member is still expected to honor confidentiality. If a member talks with the leader about the group outside the sessions, the member is expected to inform the group about the conversation at the next meeting. If a group member is involved in a court action, the leader cannot guarantee legal protection for what is revealed in the group (Foster, 1975).

In the first group session, the leader needs to review his or her expectations and discuss confidentiality with members. The leader may ask the members whom they would like to tell about what happens in the group, what they would like to tell these people, what the purpose is of talking to others, and how they would feel if they learned another group member was talking about them. A few members may state that they have no secrets and they are not going to say anything they would not say to anyone else. Some members may question how deep the group will get into their personal concerns. Many times these questions will be an indication of participants' fears that they will be pressured to reveal things in the group that they do not want others to know. A controversial issue that is usually initiated by members during the discussion of confidentiality is whether they will be permitted to talk to other members about the group outside the sessions. After responding to these issues and concerns, the leader needs to help the group reach a consensus about the limits of confidentiality for their group. Even if a majority accepts a rule for confidentiality, this does not mean that everyone has accepted the norm and there may be variations in participants' interpretations of the norm. At least through the discussion, the members may become aware of how other members view confidentiality.

After this initial discussion the group members may think that they have a clear agreement about what is expected. While a general discussion may sensitize members to the issues, it is not until a group member discloses personal information that differences in interpretation may arise. For instance, assume the leader has discussed confidentiality in the screening interview and initial session. Near the beginning of the second session, Mary says:

> I really don't like it when my boss makes sexual advances toward me. This afternoon he asked me to go to dinner with him, just the two of us. I really felt uncomfortable. Thank goodness I had this group tonight so I got out of it.

While Mary may not consider this information confidential, the group must. In fact she may have already told a friend about her boss, or may be planning to do so. As long as Mary does not refer to the group, this is her prerogative and in no way violates group confidentiality.

Some breaches in group confidentiality may occur when a member (a) has an emotional reaction to a statement or a session; (b) seeks enhancement with others; (c) wants to help another group member; (d) does not feel he or she is a group member; (e) does not trust other members; and (f) needs more support or understanding than what is offered in the group. For instance, Mary's statement may elicit from some members the following cognitive reactions that illustrate, in order, these reasons.

> *Bob*: My wife was late coming home three times this month. I better ask her if her boss is suggesting things to her. I wonder if she's afraid to tell me.
>
> *Jane*: I was telling my women's group, sexual harassment was going on in town. Here's the proof I need.
>
> *Ted*: I think I'll speak to the personnel director at my plant. Mary seems to be a nice person and she probably wants a new job. I'd like to help her.

> *Hazel*: I don't know why I joined this group. Mary and most of these people are so young. My friends and I have talked about our husbands being surrounded by younger seductive women all day. I'd better warn Betty that John's flirting with Mary.
> *William*: Mary is just like Sue. I'll bet she's leading her boss on.
> *Patrick*: I've been accused of that. I've tried to be careful lately, I'd better check it out.

The leader must be aware that there is a high probability some members are reacting to Mary's statement. If the leader does not encourage these members to voice their thoughts and reactions, there is a good chance that confidentiality will be broken.

To decrease the likelihood of confidentiality violations, the leader must have a good command of individual counseling skills, which can be used with the group or individual members, as well as some specific group skills. The group leader must be aware of members' nonverbal reactions to a member's statement. The leader may acknowledge members' nonverbal reactions in a specific manner (e.g., "Bob, you looked worried," or "Patrick, your face turned red when Mary was talking") or with a general statement (e.g., "A number of you seemed to have a reaction as Mary was talking. Who would like to share their reactions?").

A counseling skill used with more intentionality in groups than in individual counseling is modeling. The leader models communication and interpersonal skills to give members examples of how they are to function within the group (Trotzer, 1977). The leader may model by reflecting a member's feelings, clarifying, going first in an exercise, or self-disclosing perceptions or personal material. If the leader were to give a personal reaction to Mary's statement, the other group members might follow by sharing their reactions.

Pointing out commonalities in members' statements or perceptions is labeled *linking* (Corey & Corey, 1977; Trotzer, 1977). Linking is a skill that must be in the group leader's repertoire to promote interaction among group members. Since the example occurs in an early session, there is a slim chance that the leader will be able to link together Mary's concerns with those of other members. If Jane has said something about her feminist affiliation, the leader might say: "Jane, you and Mary seem to share a concern about women being placed in difficult positions by their employers." Hazel, William, and Patrick may have different perceptions of the employee-employer relationship than Mary and Jane. To ensure that all sides of the issue are heard, the leader could make a moderating response (Trotzer, 1977). An example would be:

> We've heard how female employees have a difficult time dealing with their employers. What about those of you involved from the employer's side? Any employers having a difficult time dealing with their female employees?

If the leader were aware of the differences in the members' views, a linking response would be even more appropriate. The leader might say:

> Mary and Jane seem to share a concern about employers making advances toward women employees, while Hazel and William seem to be concerned about the other side of the issue—the employers being enticed by younger female workers.

Toward the end of this session, the leader should suggest that members discuss their thoughts and reactions to the meeting (Corey & Corey, 1977). Ted might disclose how he was hoping to help Mary. The leader would tell Ted to ask Mary if she wanted a new job. Mary could then decide for herself whether to apply for a new position at Ted's plant and confidentiality would not be broken.

The leader also could remind the members about the importance of confidentiality. Periodic reminders should be initiated by the leader (Corey & Corey, 1977; Gazda, 1978) to decrease the probability of members talking about the group between sessions with others and to clarify members' interpretations of the confidentiality norm.

The leader alone cannot force the group to adhere to the confidentiality norm. The members have to enforce it themselves. Research indicates conformity to group norms occurs in cohesive groups (Shaw, 1981). The more cohesive the group, the more likely it is for members to conform to the confidentiality norm and to exert pressure on other members to conform.

Group cohesiveness requires opportunities for interaction and takes time to develop. Obviously, the leader cannot focus on just building a cohesive group; the group is meeting for other purposes. There are some leader skills that will help the group work toward its goal(s) and at the same time encourage group cohesiveness. Structuring the group so members understand how they will attain their goals is one way to do both (Shaw, 1981). Providing feedback with the positive feedback preceding the negative (Schaible & Jacobs, 1975) and linking members' attitudes and concerns (Corey & Corey, 1977; Trotzer, 1977) are useful skills that can serve dual purposes.

Even in a highly cohesive group, the confidentiality norm might be violated. If this happens, the members will first try to talk directly to the violator(s) before applying other types of pressure toward conformity, such as name calling, ridiculing, ignoring, and excluding. Many times the violation is the result of a personal misinterpretation of group confidentiality. The leader must assist the members in clarifying the restrictions the confidentiality norm places on them because the group process will be affected if confidentiality violations continue.

At the last session, the leader should remind members that what was said or happened in the group is still to remain secret. Confidentiality is even more difficult to enforce once the group has terminated. Although the group members may honor the norms they have agreed on, there is a lack of legal protection. If Mary decided to prosecute her boss for sexual harassment, her lawyer could subpoena every group member. The members and leader would probably have to testify as witnesses concerning the psychological discomfort she was experiencing during the group meetings.

The ideal for group confidentiality is that members do not share with nongroup members any information learned in the group. This ideal is seldom realized. Members who learn something new about themselves want to share it with family members and friends with whom they feel a close affiliation. The members may decide that such sharings do not violate confidentiality unless information about others in the group is also revealed. Members need to be very careful when talking about themselves to others that they do not disclose group information. It is very tempting to attribute a new insight to the group, a particular member, or the leader. Confidentiality is violated if the conversations or actions of others leading to the insight are repeated.

If the group agrees that members may talk to other members outside the sessions, it should be with the understanding that the conversation will be discussed at the next meeting. Confidentiality is essential to the group's productivity and cohesiveness (Gazda, 1978), which in turn are dependent on members' self-disclosures, trust levels, and interactions with one another.

Group members cannot assume that anything they say or hear in the group will be kept secret. They should be able to make an informed choice about how much they reveal to the group; therefore, they need to know about the difficulties in enforcing confidentiality.

Often, leaders briefly discuss confidentiality in a screening interview and an initial session. Since issues of confidentiality will arise over the course of the group sessions, leaders must spend more group meeting time on this issue. Leaders also need to use techniques to intervene in situations that harbor the potential for breaches in group confidentiality.

There are many reasons members break confidentiality and the leader cannot prevent all violations. If confidentiality becomes a norm for a cohesive group, there is a greater likelihood that members' secrets will remain in the group; however, there still are no guarantees.

References

American Personnel and Guidance Association. Ethical standards. *Guidepost*, March 19, 1981, Supplement A-C.

American Psychological Association. Ethical principles of psychologists. *American Psychologist*, 1981, 36, 633–638.

American Psychological Association. Guidelines for psychologists conducting growth groups. *American Psychologist*, 1973, 28, 933.

Association for Specialists in Group Work. *Ethical guidelines for group leaders* (1980 rev.). Falls Church, Va.: American Personnel and Guidance Association, 1980.

Corey, G., & Corey, M.S. *Groups: Process and practice.* Monterey, Calif.: Brooks/Cole, 1977.

Davis, K.L. Is confidentiality in group counseling realistic? *Personnel and Guidance Journal*, 1980, 59, 197–201.

Foster, L.M. Group psychotherapy: A pool of legal witnesses? *International Journal of Group Psychotherapy*, 1975, 25, 50–53.

Gazda, G.M. *Group counseling: A developmental approach* (2nd ed.). Boston: Allyn & Bacon, 1978.

Schaible, T.D., & Jacobs, A. Feedback III: Sequence effects: Enhancement of feedback acceptance and group attractiveness by manipulation of the sequence and valence of feedback. *Small Group Behavior*, 1975, 6, 151–173.

Shaw, M.E. *Group dynamics: The psychology of small group behavior* (3rd ed.). New York: McGraw-Hill, 1981.

Trotzer, J.P., *The counselor and the group: Integrating theory, training, and practice.* Monterey, Calif.: Brooks/Cole, 1977.

Ethical Issues and Group Work With Children

Cynthia K. Terres and Marva J. Larrabee

Group work became extremely popular during the 1960s and early 1970s. Professional issues associated with group counseling and therapy emerged as professional organizations such as the American Association for Counseling and Development (AACD, formerly American Personnel and Guidance Association [APGA]) and the American Psychological Association (APA) struggled with questions concerning ethical problems of group work (Van Hoose & Kottler, 1978). Van Hoose and Kottler indicated that much of the professional literature implies that the general confusion regarding group counseling and therapy has now been resolved; they concluded, however, that among professionals and among the general public problems, confusion, and doubt about ethics still exist. It seems clear that elementary and middle school counselors using group work with children must resolve any confusion if their work is to provide the highest quality service in school settings.

For elementary and middle school counselors who work with groups, several ethical issues need particular attention. Over 10 years ago Zimpfer (1971) reminded us that because groups are a powerful force, they demand special consideration for ethical practice. Because children and adolescents are especially influenced by peer pressure, group leaders "should take into account . . . each individual's level of ability for taking responsibility for his own decisions and actions" (p. 282). The Ethical Guidelines for Group Leaders, approved by the Association of Specialists in Group Work (ASGW) in 1980 (reprinted in Callis, Pope, & DePauw, 1982; Corey & Corey, 1982), are the acceptable guidelines for group work practice for counselors working with elementary and middle school students. In this article these guidelines are applied particularly to group work with minors in elementary and middle school settings. Specifically, the article focuses on the ethical standards for counselor competence and the planning and implementation of group work in schools.

Students have the right to a competent counselor in a group situation. Eberlein (1977) called attention to client rights and acknowledged that these "rights have often been ignored by counselors and their employers" (p.219). Leader competence is a primary issue in ensuring that consumers are protected against inferior counseling services. Unfortunately, the competence of group leaders and the competence of individual counselors are not synonymous (Larrabee & Terres, 1984). Elementary and middle school counselors should be guided by the ASGW ethical guidelines in assessing their own competence as group leaders.

The only ASGW standard that deals specifically with leader competence is B-7, which states, "Group leaders shall not attempt any technique unless thoroughly trained in its use or under supervision by an expert familiar with the intervention" (Callis et al., 1982, p. 173). When elementary and middle school counselors consider leading counseling groups or conducting other types of group work, they need to be aware that "they can't lead all kinds of groups or work with all kinds of clients" (p.36). Rossberg (1980) stated that "group leaders have a responsibility to limit their group practice to developed levels of competence and skill, and to reveal those limits to their clients" (p.565).

Counselors must be responsible for assessing their own competence as group leaders. Often competence is assumed until an involved adult complains about a counselor's methods of practice either in the press or in the courts. Counselors may be surprised to find that their beliefs about consumer rights and counselor responsibilities are inaccurate and that ignorance of the law and of ethics is no protection (Eberlein, 1977).

Corey and Corey (1982) suggested that counselors be familiar with the special ethical considerations of group leadership and with their own personal limitations. The following questions can help counselors assess their limitations as group leaders:

1. Am I qualified to lead this specific group?
2. What criteria can I use to determine my degree of competence?
3. Perhaps I am "technically qualified," but do I have the practical training or experience necessary to conduct this group?
4. How can I recognize my limits?

5. If I am not as competent as I would like to be, what
    specifically can I do? (Corey, 1981, p. 408).

Another critical issue when assessing competence is the ability
of elementary and middle school counselors to determine the appropriateness of group experiences for specific children. The ASGW
guidelines address this issue in Standard A-2, which states in part:
"select group members whose needs and goals are compatible with
the established goals of the group; who will not impede the group
process; and whose well-being will not be jeopardized by the group
experience" (Callis et al., 1982, p. 173). Thus, counselors of children must be knowledgeable of the developmental stages and the
tasks of each age level to comply with this guideline for group
member selection. It cannot be assumed that all group experiences
will be good for all children.

Further assessment of competence is generally determined by
a counselor's educational experience and training in group process.
The guidelines clearly state that supervised practice in group work
is essential (Corey & Corey, 1982). Although experience as a participant in a therapeutic group is recommended by some authors
(Corey, 1981), the ASGW guidelines do not specify this criterion
for competence. School counselors who are planning to incorporate
more group work in their guidance programs may find discussions
of the kinds of groups that enhance group leader training to be
beneficial (e.g., Corey, 1981; Corey & Corey, 1982).

Counselors in elementary and middle schools are often the
only professionals in their work settings with any mental health
expertise. They may find that they are assumed competent to conduct all group experiences for their clientele. It is crucial that
counselors carefully examine their skills both in developmental
group guidance and in group counseling. It seems that certified
school counselors should have little difficulty with group guidance
activities, but they may not have the expertise needed to lead
specific group counseling experiences (e.g., alcohol and drug use,
death and dying, divorce and family conflicts). Although counselors
may believe their skills are applicable to all types of groups, the
ASGW guidelines raise questions about that conclusion.

The needs of students in any school setting may vary over
time. Therefore, it seems reasonable and professional to recommend that counselors seek additional training in group leadership
that will qualify them to deal with specific counseling topics and
procedures. In fact, according to the AACD Ethnical Standards
(APGA, 1981), to function ethically a counselor must make contin-

uous efforts to improve professional practice by participating in professional growth experiences throughout his or her career. Elementary and middle school counselors cannot afford to neglect these guidelines. The conscientious school counselor must take advantage of professional workshops, additional graduate course work, and other professional meetings on a regular basis.

Planning for Groups in Schools

Several ASGW guidelines have implications for planning group work in elementary and middle school settings. Issues related to student and parent rights and to the internal and external constraints of the school setting must be considered in planning group work.

Section A of the ASGW guidelines focuses on the group leader's responsibility to provide information about group work to clients. Counselors have an ethical responsibility "to inform group members, in advance and preferably in writing, of the goals in the group, qualifications of the leader, and procedures employed." (Callis et al., 1982, p. 173). This ethical guideline (A-1) requires the counselor to understand the additional responsibilities of group leaders who are employed as counselors in schools. To inform group members of these criteria, counselors in elementary and middle schools must expand this guideline to include responsibility to provide information to parents and guardians of minors.

Neither the AACD or ASCA ethical standards deals fully with students' rights versus parents' rights (Nugent, 1981; Wagner, 1978), and neither addresses appropriate procedures related to group participation. In this issue of *Elementary School Guidance & Counseling* Cooney thoroughly discusses one aspect of the standard for providing information about groups. Counselors must understand and be prepared to deal effectively with the constraints of the school counselor's role when he or she works with minors and encounters the interaction between student rights and parent rights. Such constraints may be either internal or external to the school.

The work of elementary and middle school counselors is affected by external constraints that are focused primarily on legal issues and community expectations. Of course, conflicts with individual parents will occur, but competent school counselors must be aware of the federal and state regulations regarding the rights of minors (Talbutt, 1980) and be knowledgeable about local school district policies to avoid potential conflicts inherent in the group counseling situation in schools. Because school counselors have responsibilities to students, parents, and society (Burgum & Anderson, 1975), guidelines are essential to address the potential legal and ethical conflicts that arise when working with minors. Recently, attempts to inform counselors of these conflicts and to interpret the positions held by professional organizations have addressed medical rights (Talbutt, 1980), confidentiality (Wagner, 1978), child abuse, drugs, and pregnancy issues (Kennedy & Reynolds, 1977). Remley's article in chapter 3 of this book also sheds light on these matters.

A counselor's adherence to the law is not always a suitable solution in conflict situations. It is clear that community expectations may be ignored in some conflicts concerning student-parent rights and that entire guidance programs could be jeopardized by negative community responses to a particular counselor's decision in a conflict situation. For example, Nugent (1981) reported that minors in some states have legal rights to see doctors or other professionals about drug use, abortion, or contraceptives without parental consent. Although it may be suitable and legal to address these student needs in a group setting, community reactions to such efforts must be anticipated and adequately addressed by counselors in their program planning efforts. (See Remley's article for additional information.)

Counselors have an added responsibility to prepare school personnel for implementation of group counseling by establishing group procedures compatible with the school philosophy and respectful of student privacy. Corey and Corey (1982) recommended developing a program in which the counselor is in continuous contact with the students' teachers, principal, and parents. This contact will enable groups to be established based on the needs of students. An advisory group, composed of a representative from separate groups of parents, teachers, and students, would allow everyone to help plan the kind of groups offered in a guidance program. With this consensus the counselor can describe group experiences that are compatible with his or her experience and training. Outside resources may be tapped when counselors judge themselves inadequately prepared for a specific kind of group.

It is clear that group leaders must state their limits of competence to clients when initiating group counseling (Rossberg, 1980). In the case of elementary and middle school counselors, the term *clients*, as used by Rossberg, may refer to the advisory group described because children would not be expected to understand these concepts. When a counselor states his or her limitations according to the ethical standards, the advisory planning group can help develop outside resources for meeting the specific needs of the age group of the students with whom the counselor works. This consultation group can also help in acquisition of funds for the professional development experiences that a counselor desires for updating his or her skills in group work or any other area important to guidance program leadership.

Implementing Group Work in Schools

Group services may be initiated in the school setting after the counselor's competence for conducting groups in schools has been determined and after the necessary planning has occurred. ASGW ethical standard A-2 directs the counselor to "conduct a pre-group interview with each prospective member . . . " (Callis et al., 1982, p. 173). In the elementary or middle school, counselors may already have a well-defined program of guidance established in the school. Thus, through classroom contact counselors may believe that they know students well. It is essential, however, that a pregroup interview be conducted no matter how well the counselor knows the child. This interview enables the counselor and student to establish firmly the goals of the group experience and the student's reasons for participating. It also allows the counselor to protect the student's well-being and determine if the group process will be impeded by the student's participation in the group.

According to the ASGW standards, counselors "shall protect members by defining clearly what confidentiality means, why it is important, and the difficulties involved in enforcement" (Callis et al., 1982, p.173). In elementary and middle schools it is essential that this standard (A-3) be implemented during the pregroup interview and also at the initial meeting of the group. This standard may seem particularly difficult to explain to elementary and middle school students. Ohlsen (1974) listed 14 questions commonly asked by students about groups. Two of these questions address the issue of confidentiality—"What can I say in the group?" and "Can I really trust others in the group with personal problems?" If confidentiality is to be maintained, it is essential to state initially, and at every group session that follows, the need to talk about issues within the group and to keep the information that is shared by others private.

Counselors must recognize that they can guarantee only their own adherence to the confidentiality guidelines (see Olsen, 1971).

It would be a serious counselor error to assume that because confidentiality has been discussed once in the group it will be understood. All group members need to be reminded regularly of the confidentiality principle (Corey, Corey, & Callanan, 1984). Thus, in helping youngsters to understand the positive results of interaction with peers and the advantages of privately sharing concerns, feelings, and problems with others, counselors will be more likely to ensure that group members adhere to confidentiality by regularly repeating the advantages associated with the confidentiality standard.

Section B of the ASGW guidelines and the Preamble of the American School Counselor Association Ethical Standards for School Counselors (1984) focused on the counselor's responsibility to provide services to clients or pupils. Specifically, ASGW Guideline B-1 and ASCA Preamble Statement 4 recognized that within the structure of the school program student rights must be preserved by protecting the student from "physical coercion, and undue peer pressure insofar as is reasonably possible" (Callis et al, 1982, p. 173). To adhere to this standard counselors must be aware of the place where group sessions are held. The structure of the physical environment must include the space and privacy that are essential for effective group work. Physical structuring, such as determining group size and the length of each session, has received attention in the literature on elementary and middle school groups (Corey & Corey, 1982; Muro & Dinkmeyer, 1977). The rationale for these decisions has often revolved around the developmental growth stages of the student.

There are ethical reasons to consider when establishing space, privacy, age and number of participants, and length of sessions. Conducting counseling groups with twelve 6-year-olds sitting on the floor of a 5- by 7-foot room may not provide the best atmosphere for counselors to protect group members from physical threats and coercion as specified in the the ASGW standards. It is more likely that a group of five or six 8-year-olds seated in comfortable chairs for 30 minutes might allow greater "opportunity to utilize group resources and interact within the group" in accordance with ASGW standard B-3 (Callis et al., 1982, p. 173). Thus, the basis for structuring the environment of a counseling group is found in the ethical standards. When questioned about the rationale for a private group room, a specified number of students for a group, and the length of time needed per session, a counselor should refer to the professional standards for support in seeking adequate facilities.

When determining the number of sessions necessary for a group, counselors again may refer to the ethical standards. Standard B-6 states that "group leaders shall help promote independence of members from the group in the most efficient period of time" (Callis et al, 1982, p. 173). The number of group sessions should not be determined because there are 6 weeks in the grading period or because the music teacher comes for one semester and some of the pupils can miss this class to attend the group. The number of sessions should be determined by the goals the group wishes to accomplish using the most efficient period of time.

In addition to determining group goals, the counselor, according to ASGW Guideline B-9, also has a responsibility to "make every effort to assist clients in developing their personal goals" (Callis et al., 1982, p. 173). Therefore, once group goals have been decided, the counselor may also consider the time needed for individual goals to be met before determining the number of sessions for the group. Because ASGW Guideline B-10 indicates that it may be necessary to have "between session consultation to group members and follow-up after termination of the group, as needed or requested" (Callis et al., 1982, p.173), counselors must consider these factors when determining how long services will be extended. The ethical standards related to physical structuring of group work may be quite helpful to elementary and middle school counselors when communicating to parents, teachers, administrators, and other school personnel the principles of group work with children.

When conducting groups, particularly in middle schools, counselors may be confronted with student use of alcohol or drugs. Standard B-8 states that "group leaders shall not condone the use of alcohol or drugs directly prior to or during group sessions" (Callis et al., 1982, p.173). This standard is likely to concur with most school system guidelines on the use of alcohol or drugs. The guideline does not exclude discussing the issues or assisting youngsters who may be using drugs. It does specify clearly that counselors should discourage the use of these substances before or during group sessions. To comply with this standard, counselors need to be knowledgeable of physiological signs of drug use and develop a suitable way to check the group's compliance with this standard. Certainly, counselors should include discussion of this standard in pregroup interviews and initial group meetings with middle school students. If a group member discloses information about drug use, the counselor must restate his or her position on drugs and alcohol and the conflict between the ethical standards of confidentiality and school policy. To gain the respect necessary for effective group leadership, counselors need to challenge students who come to a group session inebriated or under the influence of drugs (Corey et al., 1984).

Conclusion

Several aspects of implementing group work in elementary and middle schools are specified clearly in professional ethical standards. These aspects, such as the requirements for pregroup interviews, continuous attention to confidentiality, and physical structuring conducive to assuring group member safety and growth, are essential to implementing group work with minors in the school setting. It is imperative that a thorough review and a basic understanding of the ASGW and AACD ethical standards be accomplished by elementary and middle school counselors before they conduct group counseling and guidance sessions in schools.

References

American Personnel and Guidance Association. (1981). *Ethical standards*. Falls Church, VA: Author.

Association of Specialists in Group Work. (1980). *Ethical guidelines for group leaders*. Falls Church, VA: Author.

American School Counselor Association. (1984). *Ethical standards for school counselors*. Alexandria, VA: Author.

Burgum, T., & Anderson, S. (1975). *The counselor and the law*. Washington, DC: American Personnel and Guidance Association.

Callis, R., Pope, S. K., & DePauw, M. E. (1982). *Ethical standards casebook*. Falls Church, VA: American Personnel and Guidance Association.

Corey, G. (1981). *Theory and practice of group counseling*. Monterey, CA: Brooks/Cole.

Corey, G., & Corey, M. S. (1982). *Groups: Process and practice* (2nd ed.). Monterey, CA: Brooks/Cole.

Corey, C., Corey, M. S., & Callanan, P. (1984) *Issues and ethics in the helping professions* (2nd ed.). Monterey, CA: Brooks/Cole.

Eberlein, A. (1977). Counselors beware! Clients have rights. *Personnel and Guidance Journal, 55*, 219–223.

Kennedy, B. C., & Reynolds, C. (1977). Ethical issues for the middle school counselor: One counselor's point of view. *Elementary School Guidance & Counseling, 11*, 302–306.

Larrabee, M. J., & Terres, C. K. (1984). Group: The future of school counseling. *School Counselor, 31*, 256–264.

Muro, J. J., & Dinkmeyer, D. C. (1977). *Counseling in the elementary and middle schools.* Dubuque, IA: Brown.

Nugent, F. A. (1981). *Professional counseling—An overview.* Monterey, CA: Brooks/Cole.

Ohlsen, M. M. (1974). *Guidance services in the modern schools.* New York: Harcourt Brace Jovanovich.

Olsen, L. D. (1971). Ethical standards for group leaders. *Personnel and Guidance Journal, 50,* 288.

Rossberg, R. (1980), Issues and guidelines in ethics and training. In J. C. Hansen, R. W. Warner, & E. J. Smith (Eds.), *Group counseling theory and process* (2nd ed.) (pp. 553–575). Chicago: Rand McNally.

Talbutt, L. C. (1980). Ethical standards. Assets and limitations. *Personnel and Guidance Journal, 60,* 110–112.

Van Hoose, W. H., & Kottler, J. A. (1978). *Ethical and legal issues in counseling and psychotherapy.* San Francisco: Jossey-Bass.

Wagner, C. A. (1978). Elementary school counselors' perceptions of confidentiality with children. *School Counselor, 25,* 240–284.

Zimpfer, D. (1971). Needed: Professional ethics for working with groups. *Personnel and Guidance Journal, 50,* 14–24.

Unethical Behaviors We All Do and Pretend We Do Not

Jeffrey A. Kottler

The author highlights common unethical behaviors that occur in groups and argues for more honest self-monitoring in group work practice.

One would expect that a set of articles such as those contained in this special issue would include a warning to the practitioner about certain unethical practices; that the clinician would be admonished to watch one's p's and q's, stay out of trouble, and follow certain guidelines described therein. Actually, there are several existing sources that do just that (Corey, Corey, & Callanan, 1979; Gazda, 1978; VanHoose & Kottler, 1977). In these publications, clinicians are urged to study their ethical codes, familiarize themselves with relevant law, debate issues with colleagues, and closely monitor their behavior as well as the actions of peers since ethics is virtually unenforceable from existing sources (Kottler, 1978).

After all the hoopla and threats are over, professional organizations, licensing boards, and courts can actually do very little to scrutinize what goes on within the privacy of a therapist's office—unless, of course, there is a complaint filed. Even in that case, it is quite difficult to do anything to halt the destructive behavior.

Naturally, the advanced group leader is expected to operate much more ethically than those with less experience. No longer can we claim we are acting responsibly just because we do not happen to be breaking any laws or professional codes. Ethics is not an all-or-none phenomenon, no matter what the judges and Moral Majority would like us to believe. Most of the field, and indeed most attention, is directed toward the grosser forms of misconduct—sexual improprieties, breach of confidentiality, incompetence, negligence, and malpractice. Much indignation occurs among professionals, also, whenever a colleague is caught doing something that is inappropriate. The attitude that prevails is that ethics is applied to "them," not "us." Yet, to some extent, we all act unethically at times. All of us in the field of group leadership are human beings prone to biases and weaknesses, vulnerable to deception and deceit on a small scale. Occasionally we even make mistakes. To make the subject of ethics more instantly relevant to every group leader, this article discusses some common unethical behaviors of a less significant nature that usually go unchecked.

In this regard, Sheldon Kopp (1976) solicited testimony from a number of prominent therapists as to their most embarrassing mistakes made during illustrious careers. The contributions collectively portrayed the clinician as a fallible being, a wise fool, a person who acts "just plain silly from time to time" (Kopp, 1976, p. 222). The ethical transgressions reported by these famous therapists included: (a) developing inappropriate social relationships with clients as friends; (b) deliberately lying to save face (and getting caught); (c) acting seductively; and (d) seeing clients who really could not be helped. There are many, many other "slightly" unethical behaviors in which we commonly engage, never giving a moment's hesitation. Some of these follow.

No pressure will be put on you to participate unless you want to. Ah! Now there is one of the great lies of our time, similar to the promise made to creditors around the world: "The check is in the mail." Do these promises sound familiar to anyone? They certainly do to me. There is not a group I begin without making that claim. Only later do I catch myself more honestly admitting that no matter how I attempt to protect the rights of each member, incredible pressure—subtle, unconscious, sneaky, and overt—will come to bear on those reluctant to get involved. Occasionally we will jump on the bandwagon, temporarily ignoring our previous promise, and use all our skills to manipulate the reluctant clients to join in even against their will. Are we excused from such transgressions? Certainly. We are, after all, only human. But copping a plea does not diminish the nature of an unethical act.

There are constant tugs pulling on every member to conform, to contribute, to be one of the guys and gals. There are also many good reasons why we underplay these forces and attempt to reassure clients that their privacy will be respected. Realistically, we could not even begin a group unless we successfully convinced participants that their freedom of choice would be encouraged. Nevertheless, is lying for the client's own good a moral act?

Nothing you say will leave this room. Here is another distortion that appears necessary if we are going to get any work done. Confidentiality cannot be enforced absolutely in a group. In all probability, no matter what safeguards are taken, no matter how careful we are to button our lips, no matter how much we stress the importance of privileged communication, there will be those who slip up. Some clients will inadvertently disclose confidential information during a mindless moment, while others will deliberately run home with a pocket full of juicy details to spill.

What then is the alternative? To be truly honest and above-board, we would have to report to our groups:

> There is every reason to believe that any secret you share in here, any private thought you disclose, will be privy only to the people you see here. And, oh yes, perhaps a few of their spouses and friends. Perhaps a few others who overhear.

I neither like nor dislike you; you're a client. Inevitably a group member, or usually more than one, will ask quite directly how we feel about them. Recognizing the dangers of saying what we really think (whether the reactions are positive or negative), we pretend that we do not feel at all. And most of the time, during actual sessions, we do guard against letting our personal feelings get in the way of our therapeutic actions. Again the therapeutic options seem fairly limited: (a) we could respond honestly but risk being seductive if the feelings are positive, or being perceived as hostile if the feelings are negative; (b) we could employ therapeutic maneuvers

4208 ("How would that be helpful for me to tell you?"),

4209 ("What difference would it make to you?"), or

4210 ("I'm sorry. I didn't hear you. Does anyone else have something to say?"); or (c) we could share our problem: "I feel uncomfortable telling you my feelings because then I compromise my neutrality." But then members might wonder why they should be honest if their leader is being so evasive.

Each of these responses creates potential problems we would prefer to leave alone. So, instead we resort to the little white lie, "But it's for their own good," without being quite certain that the excuse is valid.

I bet your mother was a meticulous housekeeper. How many times do we make interpretations not to help the client but to check out the accuracy of our predictions? We occasionally like to play "super sleuth" at the expense of wasting valuable group time. We have formulated a hunch about why people act the way they do, and even though this hypothesis may be completely unrelated to what the group members are currently working through, we broadcast the interpretation and then smugly wait for confirmation. Naturally, we feel good because our investigative skills have proved once again to be accurate, but the whole episode was actually an exercise in self-indulgence.

I remember the time when . . . Inappropriate self-disclosure is another way in which group leaders keep the focus on themselves and waste time. Unless a therapist has a specific, defensible rationale that can be articulated, it is more likely than not that sharing stories from one's life may be digressive or downright abusive. Each time a group leader engages in long-winded anecdotes that are not specifically intended to deliver an important message or to help a group member work through the presenting concern, then the action is unethical because it negates the client's importance and wastes time.

Facilitative self-disclosure that is well-timed and appropriately implemented satisfies certain criteria mentioned by Corey, Corey, and Callanan (1979):

> How crucial is it for group members to perceive you as being human?
>
> What specific intentions do you have for revealing your personal life?
>
> How might clients' progress be hindered as the result of your self-disclosure?

Only after these questions are addressed may the group leader be reasonably certain that self-disclosing interventions are indicated.

I know I can help you. In an effort to plant favorable expectations for success, we sometimes exaggerate what we really can deliver. We are never actually certain that we can keep our promises but we nevertheless understand that such claims are necessary to keep up morale.

Group members enjoy hearing this little lie; they want optimistic assessments desperately. So, for the same reason that a physician might prescribe a placebo in the belief that it will make the patient feel better, we justify our little deceits in a similar vein.

I wonder what would happen if I try _____. Another one of those irreconcilable ethical conflicts centers around using clients as guinea pigs on which to practice an experimental treatment procedure. Are we justified in trying out new technologies before we are sure they are safe and before we have had sufficient supervision in their execution? After returning from a workshop or course, we find many new therapeutic ideas floating around in our heads, itching to be applied. There is no other way after all to determine if an idea is worth its weight until we try it out for ourselves. But where do we experiment? Can we counsel a group of white rats and then observe their behavior before we try it out on human subjects? Do we wear warning stickers on our foreheads reading: "Caution. The surgeon general has determined that these procedures may be hazardous to your health?"

The only alternative to stagnation is to cautiously and critically experiment with new group strategies, fully aware that they may not work out as we had intended. "Group work is a risky business anyway," we reason. "If the technique does not do the job, we will remember not to use it next time in similar circumstances. Let us just hope that no one is hurt too badly."

If you work hard enough you can be like me when you grow up. Are we justified in creating miniature disciples, surrogate selves? So much of what constitutes group work involves great potential for clients to become dependent on the leader or on the group process. Many "groupies" do become addicted to group work, unable to function without a support system. Alcoholics Anonymous, for instance, operates on just that premise—that members must stay as addicted to AA meetings as they used to be to their liquor.

If we are perfectly honest, we recognize that there are those among us who deliberately create dependencies in clients by sending out clear messages: "You need me. You cannot get along without this group. This will take years of intensive treatment. By the way, do you have Blue Cross insurance?" On a smaller scale, most of us are sometimes guilty of seeing clients longer than absolutely necessary, particularly professionals whose livelihoods depend on client fees. It is easy for me to rationalize that anyone could profit from a group experience no matter how long they attend the sessions. But there usually is a point of diminishing returns when the money a group member invests no longer results in significant products, except further dependency on the leader.

Everyone in this group will be treated equally. The foundation of the U.S. Constitution guarantees that all people regardless of age, sex, race, religion, appearance, and hairstyle will have equal status. The reality of the world, however, is that human beings have definite preferences as to the sort of people they would like to be around. Group leaders, of course, are no different. Holding all things constant, we like the group members more who are sexually attractive, who think like we do, who come from similar backgrounds. In spite of our restraint, we may give more attention to those who smile and laugh more at our witticisms. Although we attempt to hide our biases, there are those in the group to whom we give less time and patience. In fact, it is no more possible to treat all clients the same as it is for parents to love all their children equally.

The inevitable conclusion during a rare moment of honest vulnerability is that we all act unethically. We are all imperfect beings, inconsistent and hypocritical. We muddle in the dark doing our level best to be genuinely helpful, knowing full well that we cannot possibly please everyone all of the time.

The experienced group leader understands thoroughly that naked confidence and a few primitive helping skills are about all that is necessary to practice this craft, besides a well-integrated ego and a strong sense of ethical convictions. With all the lip service paid to legislating more stringent laws to enforce competence, more specific ethical codes to regulate behavior, peer monitoring, review boards, licensing exams, and other external watchdogs, the fact is that these efforts are more of a smoke screen to convince the public we are trying to police our own ranks than an actual deterrent to immoral behavior.

Ethical codes and laws are all very fine for publishing in professional journals, posting on walls, or presenting to graduate students. There is, naturally, great confusion as to whom the group leader is primarily responsible when often the sources have conflicting demands. Professional codes, institutional policies, legislative mandates, state and federal laws, peer practices, societal expectations, client needs, and parents' wishes all have legitimate claims. The awesome responsibility of group leadership is that practitioners must answer ultimately to themselves for their actions.

References

Corey, G.; Corey, M. S.; & Callanan, P. *Professional and ethical issues in counseling and psychotherapy.* Monterey, Calif.: Brooks/Cole, 1979.

Gazda, G. M. *Group counseling: A developmental approach* (2nd ed.), Boston: Allyn & Bacon, 1978.

Kopp, S. *The naked therapist,* San Diego: Edits, 1976.

Kottler, J. A., A question of ethics. *Journal for Specialists in Group Work,* 1978, 3, 2, 24.

Van Hoose, W., & Kottler, J. A. *Ethical and legal issues in counseling and psychotherapy.* San Francisco: Jossey-Bass, 1977.

6

SPECIAL ISSUES

Computers and computer products are increasingly present in school counseling offices. School counselors have made attempts to understand and utilize this modern technology, but many counselors are still unaware of the ethical issues involved in the use of computers. Sampson and Pyle (1983) explore ethical issues and trends in computerized guidance and counseling services and testing. Childers (1985) suggests that the use of microcomputers in the counseling office demands certain ethical precautions. Authors of both articles call upon the profession to develop ethical standards regarding computer use, and all three stress the importance of direct counselor-client contact in conjunction with the use of computers.

School counselors have a responsibility to provide services for all students, including those from other cultures. The counseling profession is a Western culture phenomenon; however, school counselors constantly interact with families and children who speak languages other than English, adhere to values different from those of the counselor, and conform to social expectations that may seem odd to the American school environment. The majority of practicing school counselors have not had the opportunity to take courses in multicultural counseling that are becoming more prevalent in modern counselor education programs. Cayleff (1986) explores some of the ethical issues that counselors face when they work with populations different from their own.

There is an increasing demand for school counselors to engage in field-based research. Documenting program effectiveness can do more to promote school counseling than all public relations efforts combined. But even if school counselors never conduct research themselves, they need to know the rights of students involved in research projects and the responsibilities of researchers. Robinson and Gross (1986) summarize the ethical issues involved in research.

Sexual intimacy with clients is perhaps the most pressing ethical problem in the counseling profession. School counselors are involved less often in sexual relationships with clients than are their colleagues who counsel adults. Nevertheless, clients, no matter what their age, often introduce sexual dimensions into the counseling relationship. Coleman and Schaefer (1986) offer suggestions for counselors who are faced with sex and intimacy boundary issues in their professional counseling roles.

Ethical Issues Involved With the Use of Computer-Assisted Counseling, Testing, and Guidance Systems

James P. Sampson, Jr. and *K Richard Pyle*

This article discusses (a) the growing use of computers in counseling, testing, and guidance; (b) potential ethical problems; and (c) principles for ethical use of computer applications.

An 18-year-old freshman experiencing frustration with her courses and having difficulty making the adjustment from high school to college, walks in the counseling and career planning center. There she sees a sign that tells students how they can take a battery of tests at a computer terminal. She sits down and proceeds to take a personality test on-line. After completing the test the results are interpreted via videotape. The student walks away with a printout of the test results.

A student assistant in the computer center is working late into the night regarding a task provided him by his supervisor. He accidentally accesses a file that provides him with test and personal information on a number of students whom he knows personally.

A senior comes into the career planning center to gain assistance with a career choice. He goes through a computer-assisted guidance program and makes a number of decisions regarding his career direction on the basis of the information provided him. A year later he discovers that much of the information that he used in making his decision was out of date and inaccurate.

A doctoral student, anxious to have data that will allow him to overcome the dissertation hurdle, accesses the data bank of a computer program that has stored student values profiles. He proceeds to get printouts on their profiles which he is to make use of in his research. This is done without checking with the students concerning their willingness to participate in such a research endeavor.

Trends That Have Impact on the Use of Computers in Counseling, Testing, and Guidance

One of the most significant developments of the past decade has been the impact of information technology on our daily lives. Beginning in science and business, information technology has become an important component of education, communications, and recreation. At the center of this revolution we find the computer. Two facts principally account for the increased use of the computer. First, there has been a steady reduction in the unit cost of computing (Dertouzos & Moses, 1979). Recent dramatic cost reductions in small electronic calculators and digital watches is a prime example. Second, the overall computing power of individual computers has increased (Atkinson, 1978). For example, the average large (mainframe) computer today is approximately 10 times faster in operation and stores 30 times more information in main memory than the average mainframe computer of 10 years ago. In essence, computers have become less expensive while at the same time becoming more powerful.

Two other trends are influencing the expanding use of computers. First, small, inexpensive, and easily maintained microcomputers (sometimes referred to as personal computers) are becoming a common feature in many businesses, homes, and schools. These microcomputers are used for either general computing, which involves many applications, or are used for special applications involving a few limited functions (e.g., accounting, analysis of laboratory specimens, or games). Microcomputers are designed for use by persons with little or no background or expertise in computer programming. The ease of technical operation and the wide variety of existing programs to operate various applications places the power of the computer in the hands of the general public. As average persons become proficient in programming, their ability to utilize the capabilities of their computer increases as well.

The second trend involves the use of computer networks. Improvements in communication technology have resulted in the connection of computers in various locations by telephone lines or by satellite. Using a communication device called an acoustic coupler modem it is possible, with proper permission, to access through a computer network a specific data file or program in a computer that is hundreds of thousands of miles away. As a result the data, programs, and computing power available to the individual has increased significantly over what is available on any one computer.

The net effect of the above developments is that computers are being used in applications that before now were the domain of person-to-person interaction. The use of automated 24-hour bank tellers is a prime example. Computer applications in counseling, testing, and guidance is another example. Functions of problem-solving, test administration, scoring and interpretation, information dissemination, and instruction in decision-making strategies are being carried out by an individual interacting with a computer.

Use of Computer Applications in Counseling, Testing, and Guidance

The advent of computer use in counseling, testing, and guidance came about as a result of the realization that there were aspects of the helping process that could be more effectively handled by a computer than by a counselor. These aspects are generally repetitive and are not viewed by many counselors as the most challenging or satisfying part of their work. Aspects of the helping process that are repetitive, as in information dissemination, or that follow a uniform sequence of steps, as in decision making instruction or administration of assessment instruments, are more effectively handled by a computer. Aspects of the helping process that involve exploring the nature of client concerns, facilitating an understanding of the factors involved, and identifying and following up on various action-oriented strategies are more effectively handled by a counselor. By using the computer for repetitive tasks, counselors are free to spend more time completing tasks that are well suited to their expertise, while avoiding tasks that are more efficiently completed by a computer. A secondary benefit of this approach is that after using the computer the client and the counselor share a common vocabulary and frame of reference for dealing with various concerns.

The widest computer applications in the helping professions have historically occurred in career counseling and guidance. At present, 25 computer-assisted guidance systems are available (Shatkin, 1980). These systems are available to a wide range of individuals in various age groups through public schools, colleges, libraries, public employment offices, and private agencies. The goal of these systems is to facilitate rational career decision making on the part of the individual. Katz and Shatkin (1980) categorize computer-assisted career guidance systems as providing either career information or a combination of career information and guidance functions. The guidance functions in the latter type of system include assessment of values, skills, and interests as well as instruction in decision making. These systems tend to require more time to complete and model the complete decision making process as opposed to systems emphasizing only career information.

Computer-assisted testing and assessment have traditionally involved computer scoring of interest, ability, and values instruments at a remote location. With the advent of microcomputers, programs have been written that allow for administration, scoring, and generalized interpretation of test results in one session at the computer. There are several advantages to this approach. First, microcomputer-controlled equipment is available that allows persons with various visual, auditory, and physical disabilities to take tests with minimal staff assistance. This reduces the chance that a staff member might influence an individual's results. Second, a generalized interpretation of test results on microcomputer-controlled videotape can better prepare the client for discussing specific results with a counselor. Generalized interpretations introduce terminology, stress basic concepts, and provide some indication of test results in broad terms. This approach may not be appropriate for some instruments. Third, the traditional time lag and clerical work in scoring tests is eliminated. Fourth, potential scoring errors are significantly reduced.

Computer-assisted academic counseling is designed to assist individuals in enhancing their motivation and study skills as well as assisting individuals in eliminating behaviors that limit academic performance (e.g., test anxiety and procrastination). The Computer-Assisted Study Skills Instruction system (CASSI) (Sampson, 1980) is an example of one such approach. After it is determined that CASSI is an appropriate resource, individuals complete various assigned lessons and are then provided with assistance in implementing the concepts into their academic work. It is recommended that a counselor or a learning skills instructor assist individuals who are using this system.

Computer-assisted personal counseling is generally designed to assist individuals in solving personal problems. These systems are used as part of the counseling process with a counselor or are used without counselor intervention as an independent client-controlled resource. The specific purpose and design of existing systems vary considerably according to the therapeutic orientation of the developer. The systems developed by Weizenbaum (1965, 1976) were based on a client-centered approach while the systems developed by Colby, Watt, and Gilberg (1966) and Taylor (1970) were based on a psychoanalytic approach. These systems were designed more for demonstration purposes than for providing a complete computer-assisted counseling system. Greist (1973) developed a system that evaluated an individual's clinical state and their potential for attempting suicide. The most comprehensive computer-assisted personal counseling system was developed by Wagman and Kerber (1978). PLATO DCS operates from a theoretical framework that is cognitive in nature and models the logic pattern of the computer. The system is designed to assist in resolving personal dilemmas by having the client progress through the following five sequenced and interrelated processes:

> (a) formulating the original case problem as a psychological dilemma; (b) formulating the extraction route for each dilemma component; (c) formulating the creative inquiry for each extraction route; (d) generating solutions for each creative inquiry; and (e) ranking and evaluating solutions. (Wagman, 1980, p. 18)

Individuals are referred to PLATO DCS by a counselor or are self-referred to the system. Follow-up counseling is available if requested by the individual.

Future Trends

In general the impact of information technology through the use of computers will continue to grow. Reductions in the cost and improvements in the performance of computers is projected to continue throughout this decade. Microcomputers will become more common in education, business, and the home. Individuals will have increasingly wider access to data and computer programs available at other locations through the use of computer networks. Computer applications in counseling, testing, and guidance will also grow as computers (especially microcomputers) become more affordable to institutions and agencies providing services and as more systems are developed to meet specific individual needs. It is also likely that public acceptance of using a computer to assist in solving career, academic, and personal problems will increase as computers become a more accepted part of daily life.

Ethical Issues

Computer applications have the potential to augment the efforts of counselors in ways that enhance the growth, decision making skills, and problem solving abilities of individuals. Research evidence cited by Harris (1974), Pyle and Stripling (1976), Sampson and Stripling (1979), Katz (1980), and Wagman and Kerber (1980) support this conclusion. Computer applications also have the potential to undermine the client-counselor relationship and influence clients in ways that limit growth, decision making skills, and problem solving abilities. The potential negative impact of computer applications occurs when these applications are used in a manner that violates sound ethical principles for the provision of counseling and guidance services. Ethical principles are generally stated in a professional code of ethics. McGowen and Schmidt (1962) state that an ethical code, among other things, provides standards of practice to guide professionals when possible conflict situations arise in their work and help to clarify the responsibilities of the counselor toward the client.

At the present the *Ethical Standards* (American Personnel and Guidance Association, 1981) and the *Ethical Principles of Psychologists* (American Psychological Association, 1981) do not specifically address the ethical issues relating to the growing use of computer applications in counseling, testing, and guidance. The only exception to the above statement involves Principle 8e of the *Ethical Principles of Psychologists* which includes automated interpretation services under Assessment Techniques. Since it appears that the availability, use, and acceptance of computer applications will continue to increase, it seems important to revise existing ethical standards to include guidelines for appropriate use of such systems. Specific topics that need examination in terms of ethical standards include: (a) confidentiality of client data maintained on a computer; (b) use of computer-assisted testing and assessment; and (c) the need for counselor intervention with clients using computer-assisted counseling, testing, and guidance systems.

Confidentiality of Client Data

Confidentiality is generally regarded as an essential element in the provision of counseling and guidance services. Several unique problems exist in maintaining the confidentiality of client data stored on a computer.

First, the advancements in computer technology described previously make it cost effective to keep large amounts of data on an individual (Gambrell & Sandfield, 1979; Lister, 1970). Large quantities of data may or may not be necessary for the provision of services. Also, as more data are available the potential for abuse grows as well.

Second, technological advances also make it cost effective to keep records for longer periods of time in comparison with existing paper records (Gambrell & Sandfield, 1979). Data can be maintained even though they are no longer of any value in providing services; for example, test results that are out of date or personal problems that no longer exist.

Third, as data are transferred from test report forms or paper record forms into a computer record file mistakes or omissions can be easily made. The resulting inaccurate or incomplete information can be damaging to the individual, especially in view of the perception held by the general public that computer data have a high degree of value and reliability (Lister, 1970).

Fourth, the increased availability of microcomputers as well as remote terminals connected with large computers increases the possibility of unauthorized access to confidential data. Super (1973, p. 303) states: "Non-computerized records have occasionally been abused. But computerized records lend themselves to larger scale abuse." This problem has led Denkowski and Denkowski (1982) to suggest that counselors "not provide sensitive client information for entry into electronic data storage systems" (p. 374).

Fifth, the existence of computer networks described previously makes it possible to access confidential information stored in a computerized data bank. Confidentiality can be compromised if the data can be identified with a particular individual (Ad Hoc Committee on Ethical Standards in Psychological Research, 1973).

Sixth, many computer-assisted counseling and guidance systems can collect research data while the individual is at the terminal. It is possible to collect the data without the individual's knowledge or permission, thus violating established ethical principles of research.

In view of these problems the following ethical principles are suggested:

1. Ensure that confidential data maintained on a computer are limited to information that is appropriate and necessary for the services being provided.
2. Ensure that confidential data maintained on a computer are destroyed after it is determined that the information is no longer of any value in providing services.
3. Ensure that confidential data maintained on a computer are accurate and complete.
4. Ensure that access to confidential data is restricted to appropriate professionals by using the best computer security methods available ("appropriate professionals" are described in existing ethical standards).
5. Ensure that it is not possible to identify, with any particular individual, confidential data maintained in a computerized data bank that is accessible through a computer network.
6. Ensure that research participation release forms are completed by any individual who has automatically collected individually identifiable data as a result of using a computer-assisted counseling, testing, or guidance system.

Use of Computer-Assisted Testing and Assessment

Testing and assessment is an important part of providing many counseling and guidance services. Computer applications in this area can be effective or lead to the following unique problems.

First, microcomputers can be programmed to score a wide variety of tests accurately. It is possible that occasional equipment failures or problems with the program that scores the test will invalidate the client's results. The error may or may not be readily apparent.

Second, generalized interpretations of test results presented by microcomputer-controlled videotape may or may not accurately reflect the meaning of the scales as developed by the test author. At best, confusion may result from viewing a videotape containing inaccurate information; at worst, erroneous conclusions may be reached.

In view of these problems the following ethical principles are suggested, in addition to the six mentioned earlier:

7. Ensure that computer-controlled test scoring equipment and programs function properly thereby providing individuals with accurate test results.
8. Ensure that generalized interpretations of test results presented by microcomputer-controlled audiovisual devices accurately reflect the intention of the test author.

Need for Counselor Intervention

Existing computer applications in counseling and guidance use a variety of formats for counselor intervention. In some systems the counselor is involved before, during, and after an individual uses a computer system. In other systems the counselor serves as a consultant on an as-needed basis with the computer application operated as a stand-alone service. Considerable variation exists between these two options. Counselor intervention is typically provided in individual and group counseling formats. In some settings counselor intervention functions are divided between professional and paraprofessional staff. Sampson and Stripling (1979) indicate that advantages exist for providing counselor intervention in a structured as opposed to a nonstructured manner. The structured approach includes a systematic introduction and follow-up of computer use. Research conducted with the counselor intervening and managing the computer-assisted guidance process has demonstrated significant change in career maturity (Pyle & Stripling, 1976). Devine (1975) found no changes in career maturity when the student worked only with the computer without counselor intervention or management.

Several unique problems result from inadequate counselor intervention with individuals who are using computer-assisted counseling, testing, and guidance systems.

First, some individuals who are experiencing substantial emotional problems initiate their contact with a service agency by asking for specific information such as communication skills, motivation, or career choice. Individuals experiencing a moderate to severe crisis are unable to use a computer application effectively. The individual who fails at using such a system may be too embarrassed or discouraged to seek additional counseling. A related assessment problem occurs when, owing to a lack of adequate initial evaluation, an individual who is experiencing substantial emotional problems draws inappropriate conclusions from a generalized test interpretation.

Second, problems can result when clients are not adequately introduced to the process involved in using a computer application. Anxiety concerning the use of a computer has a negative effect on an individual's performance (Rohner & Simonson, 1981; Schraml, 1981). This anxiety relates in part to concerns that an inordinate amount of skill or mathematical expertise is required for successful operation of the computer or that a simple error made while using the system will result in damage to the computer equipment or the program being used. This anxiety tends to intensify the existing anxiety clients often have about the problem that led them to seek help. A related problem concerns client misconceptions about the nature of computer applications (e.g., the computer will provide a quick solution to the problem). The recent dramatic achievements in computer technology have led some individuals to believe that computers can accomplish tasks that are in fact presently impossible. Another related problem involves clients who fail to understand the basic concepts or procedures involved in using a computer application. When an introduction to a computer application is not provided, excessive anxiety, misconceptions, or misunderstandings may severely limit an individual's ability to benefit from using the resource.

Third, problems can result when a follow-up of the client's use of a computer application is not provided. For example, potential misunderstandings and misconceptions may not be corrected. Also, potential inappropriate use of a computer application may not be identified. Finally, the client's subsequent needs may not be examined. The lack of an appropriate follow-up may limit the beneficial results of using a computer application.

Fourth, the information contained in a computer-assisted career counseling and guidance system is only as good as its source. Career information from some sources may be inaccurate or formerly accurate information may be out of date.

Fifth, a computer application may, after a period of successful operation, fail to operate properly due to problems with equipment or computer programs. As a result clients may become so anxious or frustrated by an inoperative computer application that they discontinue the entire counseling process.

In view of these problems the following ethical principles are suggested:

    9. Ensure that a client's needs are assessed to determine if using a particular system is appropriate before using a computer-assisted counseling, testing, or guidance system.

10. Ensure that an introduction to using a computer-assisted counseling, testing, and guidance system is available to reduce possible anxiety concerning the system, misconceptions about the role of the computer, and misunderstandings about basic concepts or the operation of the system.

11. Ensure that a follow-up activity to using a computer-assisted counseling, testing, and guidance system is available to correct possible misconceptions, misunderstandings, or inappropriate use as well as assess subsequent needs of the client.

12. Ensure that the information contained in a computer-assisted career counseling and guidance system is accurate and up-to-date.

13. Ensure that the equipment and programs that operate a computer-assisted counseling, testing, and guidance system function properly.

14. Determining the need for counselor intervention depends on the likelihood that the client would experience difficulties that would in turn limit the effectiveness of the system or otherwise exacerbate the client's problem. It is the counselor's responsibility to decide whether the best approach to avoiding the above problem for a specific client population is direct intervention or indirect intervention through the use of work-books, self-help guides, or other exercises. In general, academic counseling systems and career guidance systems that primarily provide information can be used effectively with less direct counselor intervention than personal counseling, testing, and assessment systems or career guidance systems that provide assessment and guidance functions. In spite of the fact that some academic and career systems may need less direct counselor intervention, the individuals who use these systems can still benefit from direct intervention when counselors are available.

The ethical principles presented in this paper have implications for the training of counselors, psychologists and career development specialists. One way of increasing the likelihood that computer applications are used in an ethical and appropriate manner is to ensure that students in training have a knowledge of: (a) the rationale for using computer applications; (b) common operational procedures; (c) common counselor intervention strategies; (d) strategies for implementing computer applications into existing services (including staff training); and (e) related ethical issues. Beyond the general competencies described above, the student in training has an obligation to be familiar with the specific theoretical basis, operational procedures, and counselor intervention strategies of any computer application used by a client. This obligation also extends to any professional who is providing computer-assisted services to clients.

The ethical problems resulting from the use of computer applications in the helping professions are complex. The increasing use of computer-assisted counseling, testing, and guidance systems necessitates a thorough examination of the issues involved. These systems can be effective or ineffective depending on the way in which they are used. It is the responsibility of the profession to develop ethical standards that encourage effective and responsible use of computers in providing counseling, testing, and guidance services.

References

Ad Hoc Committee on Ethical Standards in Psychological Research. *Ethical principles in the conduct of research with human participants.* Washington, D.C.: American Psychological Association, 1973.

American Personnel and Guidance Association. *Ethical Standards.* Washington, D.C.: American Personnel and Guidance Association, 1981.

American Psychological Association. Ethical principles of psychologists. *American Psychologist,* 1981, *36,* 633–638.

Atkinson, R.C. Futures: Where will computer-assisted instruction (CAI) be in 1990? *Educational Technology,* 1978, *18,* 60.

Colby, K.M.; Watt, J.B.; & Gilbert, J.P. A computer method of psychotherapy: Preliminary communication. *Journal of Nervous and Mental Diseases,* 1966, *142,* 148–152.

Denkowski, K.M., & Denkowski, G.C. Client-counselor confidentiality: An update of rationale, legal status, and implications. *Personnel and Guidance Journal,* 1982, *60,* 371–375.

Dertouzos, M.L., & Moses, J. (Eds.). *Future impact of computers: A twenty year view.* Cambridge, Mass.: MIT Press, 1979.

Devine, H.F. *The effects of a computer-assisted career counseling program on the vocational maturity of community college students.* Unpublished doctoral dissertation, University of Florida, 1975.

Gambrell, J.B., & Sandfield, R.E. Computers in the school: Too much too soon? *High School Journal,* 1979, *68,* 327–331.

Greist, H.J. A computer interview for suicide-risk prediction. *American Journal of Psychiatry,* 1973, *130,* 1327–1332.

Harris, J. The computer: Guidance tool of the future. *Journal of Counseling Psychology*, 1974, *21*, 331–339.

Katz, M.R. SIGI: An interactive aid to career decision making. *Journal of College Student Personnel*, 1980, *21*, 34–40.

Katz, M.R., & Shatkin, L. *Computer-assisted guidance: Concepts and practices* (ETS RR-80-1). Princeton, N.J.: Educational Testing Service, 1980.

Lister, C. Privacy and large-scale personal data systems. *Personnel and Guidance Journal*, 1970, *49*, 270–211.

McGowan, J.F., & Schmidt, L.D. *Counseling: Readings in Theory and Practice.* New York: Holt, Rinehart & Winston, Inc., 1962.

Pyle, K.R., & Stripling, R.O. The counselor, the computer and career development. *Vocational Guidance Quarterly*, 1976, *25*, 71–75.

Rohner, D.J., & Simonson, M.R. *Development of an index of computer anxiety.* Association for Educational Communications and Technology Convention, Philadelphia, April 1981.

Sampson, Jr., J.P. CASSI: A computer-assisted approach to improving study skills. *NASPA Journal*, 1981, *18*, 42–47.

Sampson, J.P., Jr., & Stripling, R.O. Strategies for counselor intervention with a computer-assisted career guidance system. *Vocational Guidance Quarterly*, 1979, *27*, 230–238.

Schraml, M.L. The psychological impact of automation on library and office workers. *Special Libraries*, 1981, *72*, 149–156.

Shatkin, L. *Computer-assisted guidance: Description of systems.* (ETS RR-80-23) Princeton, N.J.: Educational Testing Service, 1980.

Super, D.E. Computers in support of vocational development and counseling. In Borow, H. (Ed.) *Career guidance for a new age.* Boston: Houghton Mifflin Co., 1973.

Taylor, K. *Computer applications in psychotherapy: Bibliography and abstracts* (PHS No. 1981). Washington, D.C.: U.S. Government Printing Office, 1970.

Wagman, M. PLATO DCS: An interactive computer system for personal counseling. *Journal of Counseling Psychology*, 1980, *27*, 16–30.

Wagman, M., & Kerber, K.W. *Dilemma counseling system.* Minneapolis: Control Data Corporation, 1978.

Wagman, M., & Kerber, K.W. PLATO DCS, an interactive computer system for personal counseling: Further development and evaluation. *Journal of Counseling Psychology*, 1980, *27*, 31–34.

Weizenbaum, J. ELIZA, a computer program for the study of natural language communication between man and machine. *Communications of the Association for Computing Machinery*, 1965, *9*, 36–45.

Weizenbaum, J. *Computer power and human reason: From judgment to calculation.* San Francisco: Freeman, 1976.

The Counselor's Use of Microcomputers: Problems and Ethical Issues

John H. Childers, Jr.

Review of current counseling literature reveals a dramatic increase in the use of microcomputers and other technological advances by counselors (Daniel & Weikel, 1983; Sampson & Pyle, 1983), a trend that is predicted to continue (Daniel & Weikel, 1983). Several factors have contributed to this trend.

First, microcomputers are common in many work settings because they are small, relatively inexpensive, easily maintained, and powerful. A second factor is the availability of "user friendly" software. Numerous software programs that are easy to use and relatively inexpensive are currently available for various uses: vocational guidance, study skills, testing and assessment, statistics, word processing, spelling, educational programs, scheduling, record keeping, individualized educational plans, and many other uses.

The evolution of the microcomputer and related software packages is leading to a second computer revolution (Leveson, 1980). Cornish (1981) and Hald (1981) suggested that by the 1990s the capabilities of the microcomputer are likely to increase at least a thousandfold. There is little doubt that its impact will greatly affect how we work, relate, and gain information as well as numerous other life-style areas (Cianni-Surridge, 1983). The question is no longer "Will counselors find useful strategies for computer technology?" but "Will counselors use this technology in a responsible, ethical manner?"

Microcomputer technology has the potential to augment as well as to undermine both the relationship between client and counselor and the client's growth, decision-making skills, and problem-solving abilities (Sampson & Pyle, 1983). Counselors need to examine the possible problems and ethical issues of using micro-computer technology. Currently, the *Ethical Standards* of the American Personnel and Guidance Association (1981) and the "Ethical Principles of Psychologists" (American Psychological Association, 1981) do not specifically address ethical issues related to microcomputer technology. Because of the prediction that there will be an increased use of computers and other technological advances by counselors, it is important to consider revising existing ethical standards to include guidelines for appropriate use of such technology (Sampson & Pyle, 1983).

A first step toward establishing such standards may be to identify and discuss representative problems and ethical issues. In this article I identify and discuss 11 issues that may have ethical implications for counselors and the counseling profession.

Confidentiality

Confidentiality is perceived as essential in the delivery of effective guidance and counseling services. Several special problems arise regarding how to maintain confidentiality of client data stored on a computer.

First, data stored on a computer, unless restricted to appropriate personnel, can be obtained by anyone. This suggests the importance of computer security procedures as well as identification of those who have authorized access to confidential data.

Second, confidentiality can be compromised if the data can be linked with a particular individual. Confidential data maintained in a computer should not identify a particular individual.

Third, many software programs collect and store data while the individual is at the terminal. As a result, it is possible to gather information without the individual's knowledge or permission. This suggests the importance of guidelines regarding informed consent and release forms for individuals storing identifiable data.

Data Storage

The issue of data storage is closely related to confidentiality. Several areas require the development of guidelines to protect client welfare.

First, the computer has made it cost effective to store large amounts of data. These data may or may not be necessary for the effective delivery of guidance and counseling services. Guidelines should be established to ensure that the information stored is appropriate and necessary for the services to be delivered.

Second, the computer has made it possible to store data for a long period of time even though it may no longer be useful in providing services. Thus, consideration should be given to establishing guidelines regarding the length of time data will be stored as well as what types of information will be retained.

Software Issues

Inadequate software is cited throughout the literature as the single greatest impediment to the computer revolution (Benderson, 1983). Benderson (1983) suggested that 95% of the available software on the market is not worth having. Critics point out that much of the existing software is mainly drill-and-practice and tutorial routines full of spelling and typographical errors and bugs that prevent the programs from working properly under certain conditions. Several issues involving software may require specific guidelines.

First, counselors face the important issue of selecting high-quality software. The majority of magazines dealing with computers provide evaluations of software, but the evaluations vary in quality and reliability. There is a need, therefore, for independent educational organizations to evaluate software programs. The two most widely recognized programs for screening and reporting on the quality of educational software are the Northwest Regional Education Laboratory's MicroSIFT Clearinghouse and the Education Product Information Exchange (Benderson, 1983).

The validity and reliability of software programs are also significant considerations. Software programs need to be evaluated by their users as well as by programmers, instructional designers, content experts, and clients to determine whether they meet various educational or therapeutic objectives.

Finally, counselors need to be concerned about procedures for updating information in software programs once they are on the market. The dissemination of outdated information to individuals seeking input for decision making is a major ethical issue.

Counselor-Assisted Software Programs

Most software programs in the area of guidance and counseling are designed to be used in conjunction with a counselor rather than by clients independently; thus, they should not be perceived as "stand alone" programs. Counselor-assisted software programs were not designed to replace contact with a counselor; therefore, when they are used by clients independently, an issue of professional concern arises.

Client-Screening Procedures

Although research generally supports the effectiveness of computer-assisted instruction, counselors should seriously consider establishing client-screening procedures for microcomputer use. There are several specific issues related to client-screening procedures.

First, a certain degree of skill in microcomputer technology is required for clients to be able to use microcomputers. This is the issue of computer literacy. There is no agreement in the professional literature on the definition of computer literacy. With software becoming increasingly user-friendly, clients will not be required to have an intimate knowledge of the computer or programming. The issue for counselors is not only what is computer literacy, but what degree of skill is required to use specific software programs. Consideration must eventually be given to matching clients and software programs according to the consumer's degree of skill. Mismatching a client and software will probably increase the client's feelings of low self-esteem, anxiety, sense of failure, helplessness, and frustration.

Second, microcomputer technology may result in a "hypervigilant" decision-making style (Janis & Mann, 1977) in which a person makes an almost obsessive attempt to take in all data before making a decision. This decision-making style often causes high anxiety because the individual fears an important piece of information still remains to be gathered before making a decision. This style often results in information overload. The hypervigilant client is aware of the many possibilities that exist but is so emotionally or intellectually involved that key issues may be missed. This client could be described as overly stressed. Screening procedures should be designed to identify hypervigilant clients.

Screening procedures for highly anxious clients should also be considered. Such clients may need to reduce their level of anxiety before being introduced to the microcomputer. This type of technology may only increase the anxiety level of certain clients.

Finally, screening procedures should be developed to help determine which services are most appropriate for which clients. Clients in crisis situations may turn to this technology when direct contact with a counselor would be more appropriate.

Use by Affluent Versus Poor Clients

Microcomputers may only increase the division between the rich and the poor in this country. Affluent school districts can afford microcomputer literacy programs, whereas many low-income districts lack the resources to support such programs. High technology and its related benefits belong to the more affluent. This trend has societal implications. For example, if society becomes increasingly characterized by high-technology innovations, people more familiar with the technology will have greater opportunities for better jobs and better education and will exercise more personal freedom in decision making.

Sexism

Becker (1983) reported that relatively few girls elect to take computer classes in high school. He suggested that by the time students reach high school, computers have become linked with the male sex. This may exclude girls from many future jobs. One solution would be to introduce microcomputer technology to students during the elementary grades, thereby possibly eliminating any sex role bias. Counselors should ensure that both sexes have equal opportunities to use computer technology.

Computer Literacy with Poor Socialization Skills

Advocates of computer education suggest that to be properly prepared for the future, people will have to achieve computer literacy. Today many people are becoming computer literate, but some of them may spend so much time interacting with technology that they do not develop effective socialization skills. Such individuals may be as inadequately prepared for living in a rapidly changing world as those lacking computer literacy. Counselors should consider guidelines that would help in the development of the whole person.

External Locus of Control

Locus of control is a personality variable involving an individual's general expectancies of reinforcement or gratification (Rotter, 1966). Individuals with an internal locus of control believe that reinforcements are contingent on their own behavior, capacities, or attributes. Individuals with an external locus of control believe that reinforcements are not under their personal control but are under the control of powerful others, luck, fate, or chance (Joe, 1971).

Clients with an external locus of control may be more likely than are clients with an internal locus of control to reach a decision because "the computer told me this is the correct choice." That is, externally oriented clients may perceive that the microcomputer has power that is not under their personal control.

Procedures that ensure that a client accepts personal responsibility for his or her own decisions should be considered. The counselor and client should examine the array of potential solutions and make a commitment to action based on an examination of the solutions and their possible consequences. The client then can decide which solution he or she is willing to assume responsibility for implementing. This would help develop a client's internal locus of control.

Left-Brain Thinking

The left hemisphere of the brain has been associated with logical, rational, and digital thinking (Springer & Deutsch, 1981); the right hemisphere involves intuitive, metaphorical, and analogical thinking (Springer & Deutsch, 1981). Computer technology and its related software programs, which consist mainly of drill-and-practice and tutorial routines, reinforce left-brain thinking. Right-hemisphere thinking receives little or no reinforcement; consequently, consumers of technology may come to value left-brain thinking over right-brain thinking. The goal of counseling is development of the whole person. This goal suggests that, with increasing emphasis on left-brain thinking, counselors may need to develop strategies that enhance and validate right-brain thinking.

Counselor Preparation

Most counselors and counselor educators have not been trained to use computer technology. Often counselors know less about computer technology than do many of their clients. This raises several issues at both the preservice and inservice training levels.

First, computer literacy is rapidly becoming a criterion for employment. Currently there is no specific requirement in the professional training standards (Commission on Standards and Accreditation, Association for Counselor Education and Supervision, 1977) that require counselors in training to be computer literate before graduating. If graduates of counseling programs are to be competitive for employment in the future, consideration should be given to including computer literacy in the professional training standards.

Second, few new counselor positions are being announced in school districts; thus, most of the counselors who will be in the schools during the next decade are already there. Probably these counselors are not computer literate. This lack of computer literacy suggests the importance of inservice training in school districts. Many existing inservice programs are designed for the classroom teacher. Counselors share many of the same needs as this group, but they also have unique professional needs. Counselor education programs should consider implementing inservice programs to prepare counselors for using microcomputers in their work environment. Although it is not necessary for counselor educators to deliver these inservice programs, they should provide input concerning the hardware and software needs of counselors.

Third, counselor educators need to be computer literate. Those who are not will have less opportunity to influence computer technology and how that technology affects their professional field. Counselor educators may want to consider becoming computer literate as part of their continuing professional development plan.

Fourth, professional organizations should be responsive to membership needs. These professional organizations need to provide inservice computer literacy programs for counselors and counselor educators.

Conclusion

Many counselors and counselor educators are frightened by computer technology. The computer is often perceived as a substitute for the counselor. Wrenn (1973) suggested that if a counselor is only performing the functions of information retrieval and cognitive analysis, he or she should be worried because a computer can perform these functions better. He stated that computers cannot completely substitute for counselors, but they will enable counselors to capitalize on human qualities, such as sensitivity to verbal and nonverbal cues and responsiveness to group interactions.

The effective use of microcomputers by counselors will mean that less time will have to be devoted to information retrieval and cognitive analysis. Counselors will be able to focus on the unique needs of their clients. For this to happen, it will be necessary to change the perceptions of many counselors toward technology and to redesign many guidance and counseling programs.

The counseling profession is now on the periphery of computer technology, but the use of computer technology by counseling professionals will increase. This technology can be used effectively or ineffectively. It is the responsibility of professional counselors to examine problems and to develop ethical standards that encourage the responsible use of computer technology in the delivery of guidance and counseling services.

References

American Personnel and Guidance Association. (1981). *Ethical standards.* Washington, DC: Author.

American Psychological Association. (1981). Ethical principles of psychologists. *American Psychologist, 36,* 633–638.

Becker, H.J. (1983). *Microcomputers in the classroom: Dreams and realities.* Eugene, OR: International Council for Computers in Eduation.

Benderson, A. (1983). Computer literacy. *Focus: Educational Testing Service, 11,* 1–32.

Cianni-Surridge, M. (1983). Technology and work: Future issues for career guidance. *Personnel and Guidance Journal, 61,* 413–416.

Commission of Standards for Accreditation, Association for Counselor Education and Supervision. (1977). Standards for the preparation of counselors and other personnel services specialists. *Personnel and Guidance Journal, 55,* 596–601.

Cornish, B.M. (1981). The smart machines of tomorrow. *Futurist, 15*(4), 5–13.

Daniel, R.W., & Weikel, W.J. (1983). Trends in counseling: A Delphi study.

Personnel and Guidance Journal, 61, 327–331.

Hald, A.P. (1981). Toward the information-rich society. *Futurist, 15*(4), 20–24.

Janis, I., & Mann, L. (1977). *Decision making: A psychological analysis of conflict, choice, and commitment.* New York: Free Press.

Joe, V.C. (1971). Review of the internal-external control construct as a personality variable. *Psychological Reports, 25*, 619–640.

Leveson, I. (1980). Technology and society in the next thirty years: We have manageable choices. In C.S. Sheppard & C.D. Carroll (Eds.), *Working in the twenty-first century.* New York: Wiley.

Rotter, J.B. (1966). Generalized expectancies for internal versus external control of reinforcement. *Psychological Monographs, 80*(1, Whole No. 609).

Sampson, J.P., & Pyle, K.R. (1983). Ethical issues involved with the use of computer-assisted counseling, testing, and guidance systems. *Personnel and Guidance Journal, 61*, 283–286.

Springer, S.P., & Deutsch, G. (1981). *Left brain, right brain.* San Francisco: Freeman.

Wrenn, C.G. (1973). *The world of the contemporary counselor.* Boston: Houghton Mifflin.

Ethical Issues in Counseling Gender, Race, and Culturally Distinct Groups

Susan E. Cayleff

This article addresses the complex ethical and cultural issues that arise with counseling women, Blacks, ethnic minorities, poor people, lesbians, and gays. Common dilemmas arising from the social context of the counselor-client relationship, the need to respect client autonomy, and the imperative for ethical and quality health care are outlined and discussed, and management strategies are suggested.

> *Dilemma for Special Focus Section.* Maria Gonzalez is a 32-year-old, first-generation, Mexican-American woman. She is married (3 years), has two children, and has been diagnosed as having uterine cancer. She adamantly refuses a hysterectomy, arguing (through an interpreter) that her husband will leave her, or if he stays, it will be the end of their marital and sexual relations. Even after repeated conversations with residents and clinical faculty in obstetrics and gynecology, she is unpersuadable. These practitioners refer her to a counselor, hoping that the counseling relationship will result in Maria's informed consent for the procedure.

The counselor-client relationship operates as a microcosm of the larger American social structure. It reflects the beliefs, stratifications, tensions, and injustices that exist in American society. In addition to reflecting American beliefs, counselors validate theories that determine general perceptions of women, minorities, and poor people. Like the physician-patient relationship in the medical model, the counselor-client relationship is hierarchical and thus replicates the power dynamics evidenced in other nonpeer relationships. Because professional counseling personnel have only nonspecific ethical guidelines by which to conduct their interactions with culturally nondominant populations (the *Ethical Standards* of the American Association for Counseling and Development [AACD, formerly American Personnel and Guidance Association, 1981]), counselors should be aware that their own place within the larger culture—their social status, sex, and race—will probably influence both what they perceive as problems and dilemmas and how they respond to them (Cayleff, 1984).

For example, women, minorities, and poor people have been (and at times continue to be) labeled "sick" or mentally ill when in fact they have only varied from "normal" patterns of behaving and feeling as defined by others who take White, male, middle-class beliefs as the normative measure or the rule of health and desirability (Ehrenreich & English, 1978; Kristeva, 1982; Raymond, 1982; Scully & Bart, 1973; Smith-Rosenberg & Rosenberg, 1973). Examples include the widely documented labeling of women's physiological illnesses as psychogenic (Lennane & Lennane, 1973) and the frequent diagnostic errors made when psychiatric disorders are labeled psychoses more readily in Black patients than in White patients (Carter, 1983).

In these instances, counselors perpetuate cultural definitions of health and illness that can be used to stipulate acceptable social roles for women and minorities (Schur, 1984; Smith-Rosenberg & Rosenberg, 1973). Further examples include the 19th-century "disease" of drapetomania—the "illness" of Blacks running away to the North, the circumscription of women's social role in 19th-century America on the ground that women were biologically "weak," and the still widely held stereotypes that surface when counseling persons in same-sex love relationships, including denial or exaggeration of the clients' sexual orientation (Jones, 1974; Messing, Schoenberg, & Stevens, 1984).

In short, the professionals' definition of health and illness—in essence their power to name (Schur, 1984)—is a crucial factor in determining both perceptions of mental and physical capability and definitions of acceptable social roles for clients.

In this article I address the complex ethical and cultural issues that arise when counseling women, Blacks, ethnic minorities, poor people, lesbians, and gays. Common dilemmas arising from the social context of the counselor-client relationship, the need to respect client autonomy, and the imperative need for ethical and high-quality health care are outlined and discussed, and management strategies are suggested.

Client Autonomy and Welfare

Clients are products of their own cultural milieu. Their sex, race, ethnicity, social class, and sexual orientation determine when and how they seek help, their compliance with the recommended regimen, and, to a significant degree, the therapeutic outcome (Eisenberg, 1976). Consequently, when counseling ethnic and racial minorities, certain belief systems of the client must be considered if quality care is to be given (Eisenberg, 1976). This entails understanding and honoring folk belief systems such as (a) the humoral hot-cold theory of physical and mental disease (in which a wet, warm body is seen as healthy. Food, herbs, and medication, which are also classified as wet or dry and hot or cold, are therapeutically applied to restore the body to its supposed natural balance. This is still seen as relevant by many Puerto Ricans and Mexican Americans) (Harwood, 1971), (b) *Curanderismo* (the frequenting of folk healers self-taught in native and traditional healing arts) and belief in folk diseases among Mexican Americans in the Southwest (Martinez & Martin, 1966; Mull & Mull, 1981), and (c) religious healing rituals and practices (Hufford, 1977).

If counselors fail to integrate an appreciation for a client's own belief system, the ethical principle of beneficence is violated. *Beneficence*, defined as "doing good" by preventing harm to the patient and, furthermore, acting in such a way as to benefit the patient, is a principle that governs the counselor-client relationship. In this instance, the patient's welfare is intrinsically tied to his or her own belief system; in short, beneficent treatment ensures that the patient is not harmed through a disregard for his or her belief system and does, in fact, benefit from the counselor-client relationship. For example, among Mexican patients using an urban California clinic in 1980, 23% believed that expressing admiration for babies without touching them could make them ill. Of the residents and physicians who treated this clinic population, however, 60% reported not having encountered this belief. Similarly, 85% of these clinic patients attached great relevance to *susto* (i.e., fright sickness, the belief that causes fright illness). Of particular importance to counselors, this belief was not encountered by 60% of the residents (Mull & Mull, 1981). In this example two equally serious weaknesses in counseling overlap—ineffective treatment and, potentially, unethical treatment (violating the principle of beneficence and the patient's welfare).

Like ethnic factors, race contributes to the goals and values of a client and to the counselor's ability to provide effective care (see Casas article in the *Journal of Counseling and Development, 64,* 1986). Counselors must abandon preconceived notions of Black family structure, which may be seen as sociopathological, taking the two-parent patriarchal model as the desired norm. Furthermore, awareness of the pivotal role played in female-headed Black households by community resources, such as church, extended family, and clubs and schools, allows the counselor to address the patient's welfare through a realistic, therapeutic approach (Wilkinson, Connor, & Daniels, 1979).

Other common issues for counselors of Black clients include stressful and conflicting demands on Black women to emulate White standards of behavior and beauty, which have destructive effects on their psyches (Black Women's Community Development Foundation, 1975; Hull, Scott, & Smith, 1982; Morrison, 1970), and pressure for the sterilization of adolescent Black mothers. This pressure often conflicts with the clients' own morals, denies them an important source of self-worth (Black Women's Community Development Foundation, 1975; Cayleff, 1984), and fails to consider the extended kin network that figures so prominently in child rearing and mothering among Black women (Hale, 1980; McAdoo, 1980).

Furthermore, evidence suggests that Black patients may be treated differently than White patients with regard to medication, diagnosis, and politeness of treatment (Carter, 1983; Coles, 1969; Levy, 1985; Wood & Sherrets, 1982). This evidence raises ethical questions regarding respect for persons and ethical principles that assert that counselors treat people with respect when they view them as autonomous agents who are entitled to decide for themselves, to the extent that they are capable, what is in their best interest. Furthermore, treating Black clients differently impedes the ethical principle of distributive justice—the most defensible definition of which indicates that clients are entitled to similar treatment for similar cases, regardless of extraneous social, racial, and economic factors. Finally, research reveals that Blacks are likely to be counseled differently when making career decisions because of counselors' beliefs that they should pursue specific avenues of employment. For example, Black medical school graduates report being urged to choose primary care family medicine over a less service-oriented specialty on the presumption that they do or should want to "serve their own" (Suntharalingam, 1983).

This approach to counseling, in which the counselor slants information, is paternalistic. Paternalistic behavior reflects the counselor's belief that he or she is acting in the client's best interest; to this end the counselor may withhold or distort information. This behavior, in turn, compromises (a) the autonomy of clients, their ability to act in their own best interests in keeping with their cultural self-definition, and (b) rational decision making based on informed consent and awareness of viable options and their likely outcomes.

Like ethnic and racial factors, cultural dictates surrounding sex also affect the counselor-client relationship. Stereotypical sex roles prohibit strong disagreement between authority figures and clients. These roles are often reflected in the power-laden relationships between practitioner and client in the counseling setting (Raymond, 1982). Genuine communication with and autonomous decision making by women are thus often undermined by sex-specific factors. To discern the true autonomy of women, it may be necessary to establish women's own beliefs, as opposed to their socialized, sex-specific propensity to accommodate and attempt to please others (Gilligan, 1982; Kristeva, 1982). This necessitates a counselor-client relationship that is not paternalistic, stresses the client's welfare, and validates a desire for autonomy. In short, counseling women with an eye toward making them compliant to limited pursuits specific to their sex upholds neither their autonomy nor their welfare.

The necessity of developing and maintaining ethical and professional relationships based on the principles of beneficence, autonomy, justice, and welfare has been delineated. More specifically, strategies for coping with the dilemma in which a counselor finds himself or herself unable to respond with a reasonable degree of knowledge to the client's own cultural background include (a) helping the client choose an appropriate counselor; (b) if this is not possible, encouraging peer counseling situations; and, finally, (c) self-directed reading to increase understanding, coupled with consultation with indigenous community liaisons (e.g., women's centers, gay advocacy groups, Hispanic community groups).

Conclusion

Because of the many roles they are asked to serve, counselors face many ethical and cultural dilemmas. Counselors may misunderstand clients who are of a different sex, race, social class, or

sexual orientation than themselves. These cultural misunderstandings, in turn, may precipitate difficulties in communication, ob-
scure expectations, affect the quality of care dispensed, and
dramatically alter a patient's willingness or ability to maintain a
therapeutic program (Roth, 1976). In short, the sex, race, class,
and sexual orientation of the client must be considered, understood, and honored to prevent doing harm, serve the client's welfare, respect autonomous principles, and, ultimately, to provide
effective counseling. Failure to integrate these factors into professional relationships infringes on the client's cultural autonomy,
impedes the likelihood of an effective therapeutic relationship, and
constitutes unethical behavior, because respecting the integrity and
promoting the welfare of the client "through awareness of the negative impact of both racial and sexual stereotyping and discrimination" is the basis of an ethical counselor-client relationship (AACD,
1981, Section A.8).

The influence of cultural factors on counseling is complex. If
counselors recognize that cultural beliefs affect responses, goals,
and decision making within the counselor-client relationship, they
will understand the force and influence of these cultural factors.
This knowledge will, it is hoped, encourage counselors to develop
research and training techniques as well as ethical guidelines for
counseling racial and ethnic minorities (see Casas article in the
Journal of Counseling and Development, 64, 1986) and ethical
standards for cross-cultural counseling practice, counselor preparation, and research (see Ibrahim article in the *Journal of Counseling and Development, 64,* 1986). These guidelines, ideally, would
caution counselors against using sex, race, ethnicity, class, or sexual
orientation as a basis for imposition of culturally dominant beliefs,
paternalism, condescension, misunderstanding, and even misla-
beling of such clients as sick. By considering the impact of a client's
cultural background on the contemporary counselor-client relationship, counselors can let the client's self-definition and belief
system guide the course of the counseling relationship.

Dilemma Response

The counselor, with full knowledge of the extreme importance
placed on mothering and reproduction in the social status, self-
perception, and derivation of personal meaning for Mexican-Amer-
ican women like Maria Gonzalez (Mirande & Enriquez, 1979), acts
and counsels as follows:

1. Tries to find a competent counselor who is also a fluent speaker of the client's language (an interpreter should be used only as a last resort).
2. Does not try to convince Maria that she must undergo the hysterectomy (this would compromise Maria's autonomous decision making and informed consent; it would be paternalistic and, possibly, would compromise her future familial welfare).
3. Emphasizes the aspects of mothering through which Maria will still be able to find pride, fulfillment, and self-definition.
4. Elicits the husband's participation in this situation so that (a) Maria does not feel as if she is being buffeted about between well-meaning health care workers and an uninformed, uninvolved, and anxious husband, and (b) Maria's husband comes to see it as their problem and not hers alone.
5. Uses a peer-support network (e.g., Hispanic women who have faced this situation).
6. Enlists the counseling intervention of Maria's minister, whose opinion she respects greatly and who might mitigate the husband's reaction.

Successful resolution of this case involves not only the prolonging of biological life but the maintenance of the client's welfare and autonomy as well. Furthermore, her understanding of the hysterectomy itself should be explored because informed consent measures physician disclosure and not patient understanding. The counselor should use enough support persons and facilities so that Maria returns to her cultural context with the prospect of self-esteem and familial relations left intact. The ultimate decision about whether to consent to the surgery is hers alone. In cases in which this type of psychosocial counseling is not provided, the woman most often, but not always, agrees to the surgery. This counseling, however, would acknowledge Maria's concerns and seek to use existing familial and community resources to minimize the realization of her fears.

Counseling Research: Ethics and Issues

Sharon E. Robinson and *Douglas R. Gross*

This article focuses on the areas of ethics and issues that relate to counseling research. The authors identify three global areas for research study: (a) clinical studies, (b) counselor training investigation, and (c) evaluation. Issues such as competency, informed consent, confidentiality and privacy, cooptation and manipulation, no treatment controls, validity and generalizability of results, and authorship are discussed.

> *Dilemma.* A researcher, wanting to measure the effect of shame and guilt on participants' willingness to self-disclose, used a tachistoscope to subliminally present messages such as, "You smell awful" and "We hate you." Such research, which focuses on the induction of negative affect, confronts the researcher with an ethical dilemma. Is it possible to protect the dignity and worth of the participant when using aversive stimuli? How can researchers satisfy their need to know and at the same time ensure the welfare of participants?

The desire to know is one of the special, unique characteristics of human beings. Ever since people first learned to talk, the word *why* has been prevalent in our thoughts and conversations. For many, this curiosity has intensified with age and education, and as adults they like to refer to themselves as researchers or scientists. Under the sanctity of such dignified titles, they pursue answers by designing research studies to discover "Why?" "What would happen if . . . ?" or "What does it look like . . . ?"

This picture of the researcher is incomplete, especially if the researcher is also a professional in the field of counseling. Presumably, as Bersoff (1978) pointed out, "Most research counselors engage in can be appropriately characterized as having therapeutic intent. Counselors are interested in data-gathering to benefit the participant as well as future services" (p. 365). Counselor researchers make judgments about the individual therapeutic value of their research, but they must also weigh the cost-benefit ratio of the value of the research to society. There are times when a certain research project has potential for enhancing society at large but has no direct benefit for the participants. Finding a balance is not always simple. Fox (1975) suggested that

> some kind of dynamic equilibrium between the promises and perils of research, between individual and societal considerations, should ideally be struck—an equilibrium that does not immoderately embolden investigators and their subjects, unduly fetter them, or relegate them to an irresolute state of limbo. (p. 59)

Counselors doing research should be trained to design studies that attempt to answer research questions in an ethical and professional manner. Counselors also need training in various research methodologies to enable them to consider alternate approaches. Participants in research must be able to assume that the researcher is competent to conceptualize, to design, and to conduct the project within established professional standards. Researchers need to be aware that such participant reliance and trust may establish a fiduciary responsibility on the part of the investigator (Schwitzgebel & Schwitzgebel, 1980). If investigators violate their obligations to participants, they are liable for malpractice (Bersoff, 1978).

Having the necessary research knowledge and skills to conduct research often means that counselors have had formal classwork in research designs or methods and have had supervised experience in conducting research. The quality and quantity of this education itself may well become an ethical and professional issue. Furthermore, even if counselors do not want to conduct studies personally, they must be able to understand and to implement research findings. "In order to make choices not only about what to do to be an effective counselor, but also who or what to believe, one must be able to understand and to analyze methods, arguments, and conclusions" (Remer, 1981, p. 568). According to Remer, if one does less than this, one "cannot be a professional counselor" (p. 567).

Assuming that the counselor is competent to perform research activities, whether in clinical studies, counselor training investigations, or evaluation research, the following four ethical issues are relevant: (a) informed consent, (b) coercion and deception, (c) confidentiality and privacy, and (d) reporting of results.

Informed Consent

Most counselors are employed in settings in which they provide direct service to clients or client systems. In such settings, both the client and the client system are potential research participants. If clients come to counseling because they are in emotional turmoil and are not making good decisions about their lives, can they objectively decide that being a research participant is good for them?

In the context of evaluation research, which often takes place in business and industry, the counselor is acting in a social system composed of people who relate to each other in a hierarchial manner and who have a collective identity as an organization. One of the ethical responsibilities of the counselor is talking to clients about their rights, including the right not to be studied. In such an organizational setting, however, this is not possible because, according to Mirvis and Seashore (1979), these people cannot be approached as individuals. Employees are often required to participate in the evaluation project only because they are employees of the organization. The lower they rank in the hierarchy, the less likely they will be given a chance to agree to involvement.

The American Association for Counseling and Development (AACD, formerly the American Personnel and Guidance Association [APGA]) *Ethical Standards* (1981) state that AACD members should enhance the dignity, worth, potential, and uniqueness of each individual. Can this be done if the client is also a "subject" for study? The right to choose not to be involved is guaranteed by the U.S. Constitution, which protects people's autonomy over what happens to them. Without informed consent, autonomous decision making is compromised. Several court decisions have reinforced the protection of the right to give informed consent (e.g., *Merriken v. Cressman*, 1973; *Natanson v. Kline*, 1960). According to Bersoff, the following six elements of informed consent need to be adhered to:

1. Fair explanation of the procedures to be followed and their purposes, including identification of any procedures that are experimental

2. Description of any attendant discomforts and risks that can reasonably be expected
3. Description of any benefits that can reasonably be expected
4. Disclosure of any appropriate alternative procedures that may be advantageous to the participant
5. An offer to answer any inquiries concerning the procedure
6. An instruction that the person is free to withdraw consent and to discontinue participating in the project or activity without prejudice to the subject. (Bersoff, 1978, p. 380)

Coercion and Deception

Coercion and deception closely parallel the issues of informed consent. As Corey, Corey, and Callanan (1984) indicated, clients are often "unclear about what is expected of them" (p. 193). Therefore, they may be particularly vulnerable to allowing themselves to be manipulated into being research participants. Diener and Crandall (1978) stated that 19% to 44% of recent psychological research involves "direct lying to subjects" (p. 74). To arrive at a valid answer to a research question, often the researcher cannot totally disclose all aspects of the research to participants. In such cases the researcher needs to investigate all other possible methods for arriving at an answer to the question before employing deception. Bersoff (1978) advocated telling the participants that they may be deceived and then giving them an opportunity to not participate. In many cases the best choice may be not to do the research.

Counselor training research often uses another type of "captured participant"—students. One finds in the issues of *Counselor Education and Supervision* or the *Journal of Counseling Psychology* that the majority of research participants are students. Students in classes such as Introduction to Psychology or Introduction to Counseling frequently are chosen for study as "samples of convenience." Too often the research is conducted as part of training, so no consent is obtained. Counseling literature is replete with such phrases as "this research was part of required class training" or "students were given class credit for participation." These statements stretch the limits of ethical behavior and contain elements of coercion. Because the researcher is often the class instructor, students may fear that refusing to participate will negatively affect their class grades. The researcher-instructor must try to avoid dual roles and student manipulation while protecting student rights and freedoms, maintaining an effective research design, and adhering to principles of effective training.

In evaluation research, cooptation is possible because top management has tremendous power over lower-level employees (Robinson & Gross, 1985). Organizations are, by nature, systems of coercion, compliance, and accountability, and because of these characteristics employees are at risk if they refuse to participate (Gross & Robinson, 1985). Even though the information gathered from the research may help them and the organization to be more efficient and effective, the process is often "shoved down [their] throat" (Mirvis & Seashore, 1979, p. 767). The basic challenge for the counselor researcher is to protect the dignity and welfare of each participant while still achieving the objectives of the research. To meet this challenge, counselor researchers need to stipulate, during the initial contracting stages of the research, their need to protect the dignity and welfare of each participant. In so doing, they should make every effort to keep all participants informed about the nature and process of the research, explain participants' rights related to informed consent, keep deception to a minimum, and provide for debriefing at the conclusion of the research.

Coercion and manipulation also exist in the case of no-treatment controls. Some research is designed to help some participants and to leave others untreated. For instance, one group of college students in a college counseling center is given assertiveness training while another group receives no treatment. Because members of the latter group are not treated, their problems, presumably tied to a lack of assertive behaviors, persist. Is this practice ethical? Even if they had known they were on a waiting list, was their participation coerced and were they treated ethically?

Confidentiality and Privacy

All codes of ethics state that the counselor should hold confidential the disclosures of clients. Is the counselor breaching ethical standards if he or she uses client information in research even if the goal is to demonstrate the effectiveness of a treatment procedure? Not only are verbal disclosures confidential; so are tests, records, tape recordings, and other data. If counselors are to use any or all of these for research purposes, then the informed consent of clients must be obtained. Simply "changing the names to protect the innocent" is not sufficient protection of client privacy.

The concepts of confidentiality and privacy are also addressed by the question, "To whom do the data belong when research is being conducted for pay?" Many managers believe that because they hired the counselor, they should have access to all information. The counselor may not be able to guarantee confidentiality. An ethical dilemma is created by the tension between two powerful forces: (a) the employee, whose rights need to be protected and respected, and (b) the organization.

Security of test results and assessment instruments falls into the same problem area. Thus far, most of the court cases have focused on the issue of testing of employees (e.g., *Albermarle Paper Company v. Moody*, 1975; *Detroit Edison Company v. NLRB*, 1979; *Griggs v. Duke Power Company*, 1971). Several companies have taken positive steps to protect their employees' rights and freedoms by either limiting access to employee files or discontinuing the collection of large pools of information. Approximately one-half of the Fortune 500 companies have established strong rules of data confidentiality (Westin, 1978).

Solutions to these dilemmas are not simple. At the beginning of any paid research relationship, however, steps should be taken to establish a contract that provides answers to the following questions: (a) What types of data should be gathered and from whom? (b) What provisions will be made for nonparticipation? (c) Who owns the data? (d) What are the parameters of confidentiality? and (e) How will the data be reported?

Reporting of Results

Additional ethical dilemmas are connected with the reporting of findings. Limited generalizations must be made from small, nonrandom, or homogeneous samples. Too often psychometric properties of tests and instruments are never mentioned in the final report. Also, the researcher must give appropriate credit to everyone involved in the research. Establishing an alpha level that will allow for "practical significance" is just as important as "statistical significance" at the .05 or .01 probability level. Editors and editorial board members often reject research that has not reached these sacred probability levels. Perhaps if researchers made more eloquent arguments for the impact of their findings, regardless of statistical significance, editors would publish more research that has applied relevance.

According to Adair, Dushenko, and Lindsay (1985), another ethical dilemma in the reporting of results centers on the omission of information pertaining to such ethical procedures as informed consent, freedom to withdraw, use of deception, and procedures dealing with participant debriefing. These ethical practices, although stipulated in codes of ethics, are often not reported in published results. Blame for such oversights must be shared both by authors, who are not encouraged to report such information, and by editors, who, through their publication manuals, do not stress this type of information.

Conclusion

Counseling research is not clean and simple. If the field of counseling is to evolve professionally, counselors who also refer to themselves as scientists or researchers need to continue to avoid ethical pitfalls and to answer questions about human behavior that will improve their service to others. Regardless of the research domain, ethical issues such as informed consent, confidentiality and privacy, cooptation, manipulation, deception, participants' right to treatment, and honesty in reporting results need to be considered. The following safeguards are necessary for ethical research:

1. People conducting research for pay, whether in the private or public sector, should develop a contract at the beginning of the process that addresses the ethical issues discussed above.
2. People conducting research must be educated in the codes of ethical conduct related to both counseling and research as set forth by the professional associations.
3. People conducting research must evaluate their levels of knowledge and skill in the area to be researched and decide whether they have the expertise to design, conduct, and interpret results that are protective of participants.
4. People conducting research should establish "human subject committees" that would review, evaluate, and either approve or deny the conducting of the research based on its impact on the participants involved.

The ethical dilemma presented at the beginning of this article can be addressed by (a) presenting subliminal praise messages to each participant, (b) thoroughly debriefing each participant,

(c) arranging for participants to talk to a counselor if they so wish, and (d) seeking the approval of a "human subjects experimentation committee" (Mitchell, 1984).

References

Adair, J., Dushenko, T., & Lindsay, R. (1985). Ethical regulations and their impact on research practice. *American Psychologist, 40,* 59–72.

Albermarle Paper Company v. Moody, 422 U.S. 405 (1975).

American Association for Counseling and Development. (1981). *Ethical standards.* Alexandria, VA: Author. (Originally published by American Personnel and Guidance Association)

Bersoff, D.N. (1978). Legal and ethical concerns in research. In L. Goldman (Ed.), *Research methods for counselors* (pp. 363–400). New York: Wiley.

Corey, G., Corey, M.S., & Callanan, P. (1984). *Issues and ethics in the helping professions* (2nd ed.). Monterey, CA: Brooks/Cole.

Detroit Edison v. NLRB, 440 U.S. 301 (1979).

Diener, E., & Crandall, R. (1978). *Ethics in social and behavioral research.* Chicago: The University of Chicago Press.

Fox, R. (1975). Introduction to the cases. In *Experiments and research with humans: Values in conflict.* Washington, DC: National Academy of Sciences.

Griggs v. Duke Power Company, 401 U.S. 424 (1971).

Gross, D.R., & Robinson, S.E. (1985). Ethics: The neglected issue in consultation. *Journal of Counseling and Development, 64,* 38–41.

Merriken v. Cressman, 364 F. Supp. 913 (E.D. Pa. 1973).

Mirvis, P.H., & Seashore, S.S. (1979). Being ethical in organizational research. *American Psychologist, 34,* 766–780.

Mitchell, M. (1984). *The effects of subliminally presented praise and reprobation stimuli on willingness to self-disclose.* Unpublished doctoral dissertation, Arizona State University.

Natanson v. Kline, 186 Kan. 393, 350 P.2d 1093 (1960).

Remer, R. (1981). The counselor and research: Introduction. *Personnel and Guidance Journal, 59,* 567–572.

Robinson, S.E., & Gross, D.R. (1985). Ethics in consultation: The Canterville Ghost. *Counseling Psychologist, 13*(3), 444–465.

Schwitzgebel, R.L., & Schwitzgebel, R.K. (1980). *Law and psychological practice.* Toronto: Wiley.

Westin, A.F. (1978). A new move toward employee rights. *New York Times,* p. 18.

Boundaries of Sex and Intimacy Between Client and Counselor

Eli Coleman and *Susan Schaefer*

Numerous factors have contributed to increasing debate regarding sexual and intimacy boundaries between clients and therapists. Although having sexual contact with a client within a therapeutic relationship has been defined as unethical behavior, ways to deal with these potential situations have been less well defined. In addition, there are disputed areas of ethical behavior. The authors review these various ethical dilemmas and make some recommendations.

     Dilemma. A woman comes to see a male counselor and complains of anxiety and depression associated with her recent divorce. She is also deeply concerned about her attractiveness and ability to attract another partner. The thought of single life frightens her. After five or six sessions, she confesses to the counselor that she is deeply attracted to him. Although she finds him sexually attractive, she is equally or more attracted to his sensitivity, care, and support of her. Emotional intimacy is something her previous relationships have lacked. And, at times, those relationships have been abusive.

     The counselor does not know how to respond. He too is attracted and has already fantasized about a relationship with her. But because she is a client, he does not dare reveal his feelings. He knows that allowing a relationship to develop would be wrong. That, however, does not solve the problem.

Most people would agree with the counselor that sexual contact within a counseling relationship is unethical (e.g., Dahlberg, 1970; Edelwich & Brodsky, 1982). But few have offered suggestions on handling these types of situations. The dilemma is complex and dealing with it is difficult. In this case, the counselor determines that he has six options: (a) reveal his own feelings and suggest terminating the counseling relationship so they can have a relationship; (b) transfer her to another colleague, giving her the true reason for the referral; (c) deny his feelings and discuss the client's attractions as a natural part of transference that occurs in therapy; (d) discuss his ethical dilemma with his supervisor or supervision groups; (e) acknowledge the client's feelings and restate the professional boundaries of the counseling relationship; or (f) explore these feelings with the client while continuing the counseling relationship.

The complexity of this ethical dilemma increases when one' considers boundaries of other types of intimacy (e.g., affection, support) that are shared with a client. What types of intimacy are appropriate? What types are not? These dilemmas are faced by counselors at one time or another. Indeed, the entire range of sexual and intimacy boundaries between client and counselor is the subject of growing debate. Numerous factors have heightened the debate, including increased complaints against counselors, new ethical guidelines adopted by professional organizations and licensing boards, increased lawsuits against counselors, the creation of state task forces to consider legislation regarding sexual contact between clients and counselors, and the adoption of specific legislation governing counselor behavior.

For instance, in 1984 the Minnesota state legislature enacted a task force on sexual exploitation by psychotherapists after numerous complaints by victims who were clients that there was little effective recourse against abuse from counselors. The Minnesota state legislature passed several bills that now make it a felony if a counselor has sexual contact or intercourse with a client during the therapy session. Beyond the session itself, the counselor may still be found guilty of criminal sexual conduct under certain circumstances. In most cases, client consent cannot be used as a defense.

As a result of a similar task force, in May 1984 Wisconsin enacted a new law, which states, in part, that "any physician, psychotherapist, or any person who is, or holds him/herself out as a therapist is guilty of a Class A misdemeanor when he/she imposes sexual contact on a patient or a client during any treatment, consultation, interview or exam" (Criminal Code, State of Wisconsin, 1984). Laws similar to these will likely be enacted in other states but face constitutional challenge in the courts.

Professional licensing boards in recent years have also adopted rulings on sexual conduct. In addition to recognizing sexual activity between client and therapist as unethical and punishable, some licensing boards have established mandatory reporting guidelines. For instance, in 1982 the Minnesota Board of Psychology passed a ruling making it mandatory for all psychologists to report any knowledge of sexual exploitation by other psychologists unless that knowledge is gained during therapy with the abuser. Since then, the Minnesota Board reports that complaints have tripled.

Insurance companies, too, are concerned about the problem of sexual misconduct in therapy. According to Bill Burck, claims representative at Fred S. James and Company of Texas, Inc., one of the major insurers of members of the American Association for Counseling and Development (AACD), sexual misconduct claims have risen dramatically in recent years and are now second only to fee-dispute claims (B. Burck, personal communication, September 1985). We conjecture that this increase is responsible for the recent decision by the James Insurance affiliate, Interstate Insurance Group, to terminate malpractice insurance for AACD psychologist members. Whether AACD, in conjunction with James Insurance, will be able to find another insurance underwriter is in doubt at the time of this writing.

Claims can only suggest the extent of the problem. Feldman and Ward (1979), professors of law, suggested that even more malpractice cases are not brought against counselors because of the many legal and psychological obstacles that confront clients. These obstacles, however, are currently being reviewed.

As for the profession policing itself, the standards established by AACD are clear: Sexual activity between client and counselor is an ethical violation. Section A.8 of AACD's (formerly American Personnel and Guidance Association) *Ethical Standards* (1981) states: "In the counseling relationship the counselor is aware of the intimacy of the relationship and maintains respect for the client and avoids engaging in activities that seek to meet the counselor's personal needs at the expense of that client." More specifically, Section B.11 warns that "Dual relationships with clients that might impair the member's objectivity and professional judgment (e.g., as with close friends or relatives, sexual intimacies with any client) must be avoided and/or the counseling relationship terminated through referral to another competent professional."

But in reading these statements, one cannot be sure whether continuing or beginning an intimate or sexual relationship with a client after he or she has terminated the counseling relationship is an ethical violation. Without clear guidelines, counselors must make their own ethical decisions. It should be noted, however, that much of the testimony from clients at a recent task force hearing in Minnesota involved complaints against psychotherapists who became involved with clients after therapy had terminated (Task Force on Sexual Exploitation by Counselors and Therapists, 1985). Sentiment seems to be building that this is an ethical violation too.

The Extent of the Problem

The most commonly cited study of abuse in psychotherapist and client relationships was conducted by Kardener, Fuller, and Mensh (1973). They questioned various physicians about sexual involvement with their patients and found that 10% of psychiatrists admitted erotic contact with their patients (5% indicated that this contact included sexual intercourse).

A sample of 1,000 psychologists (500 men, 500 women) was asked similar questions by Holroyd and Brodsky (1977). They found that 10.9% of male psychologists acknowledged having erotic contact with their clients and 5.5% admitted having sexual intercourse. Significantly different statistics were found for female psychologists. Only 1.9% of the female sample admitted erotic contact with clients, and 0.6% admitted having sexual intercourse.

Although these studies show that only a small group of professionals have been involved with their clients, the occurrence of this erotic contact at all is disturbing. What may be most disturbing are findings that most professionals who admit having had erotic contact with their patients report more than one incident: 80% of Holroyd and Brodsky's (1977) sample and 75% in Butler's (1975) study.

Although the stereotypical notion of male counselors abusing female clients has been supported up until now, recent research has indicated that more abuse may involve the female counselor with a female client, a female counselor with a male client, or a male counselor with a male client than was previously indicated. In a study by Schoener and Milgrom (in press) of 350 clients reporting sexual abuse by a counselor, 10% of the cases involved a female client and a female therapist. Very few cases of abuse involving a male counselor and a male client (3%) or a female counselor and a male client (2%) were reported.

In another recent study by Bouhoutsos, Holroyd, Lerman, Forer, and Greenberg (1983), more male counselor and male client cases were found than female counselor and female client cases. Schoener and Milgrom (in press) and Bouhoutsos et al. (1983) cautioned that their results may simply reflect regional sampling differences. Schoener and Milgrom also warned that many homosexual types of abuses do not always involve a homosexual counselor. Many male and female counselors have become involved with same-sex clients as a result of experimentation with same-sex relationships and have not previously held a homosexual identity. Abuse, therefore, can occur with any combination of sex and sexual orientation of counselor and client.

The Abusing Counselor

Other than incidence statistics, very little is known about the abusing counselor. Dahlberg (1970) and Butler and Zelen (1977) have found these counselors to be lonely, vulnerable, and needy themselves. After reviewing nearly 400 complaints of sexual misconduct by counselors with their clients, Schoener (1984) labeled five levels of disturbance on the part of the offending counselor.

The first level is episodic. The offender has made an isolated decision to become involved with a client that reflects bad judgment, loss of control, or strong environmental factors. These offenders are usually remorseful about their actions and have a good prognosis for rehabilitation. Unfortunately, they represent a very small number of the cases Schoener reviewed.

The second level of disturbance is neurotic. These counselors are often socially isolated, lonely, and seek intimacy with their clients to satisfy their own intimacy needs. The types of affairs they have with their clients may not always be overtly sexual.

Compulsive character disorders represent the third level and one of the most common types of offending counselors. These offenders are similar to the chronic sexual offender. Layers of rationalizations, combined with a lack of control over their behavior, make these counselors very difficult to rehabilitate. They are often caught and disciplined, but this is not enough to prevent further abuses.

On the fourth level are those with narcissistic character disorders. These counselors are grandiose, deluded, and self-centered. In a delusional way, they believe that whatever they do is good for other people even if they are confronted with irrefutable evidence to the contrary. They usually have no remorse over their activity and justify their behavior without qualms.

Finally, on the fifth level are those who are schizophrenic or psychotic. Only a few counselors fit this category.

The Abused Client

Studies that have explored characteristics of clients who have been sexually abused by their counselors have found that the female victims were 12 to 16 years younger than their counselors (Belote, 1977; Bouhoutsos et al., 1983; Butler, 1975; D'Addarrio, 1978; Stone, 1981). These clients have been described as lonely, unhappy, and suffering from low self-esteem. Most are externally focused rather than internally directed. Many have a previous history of incestuous relationships or abuse by professionals. With their history of violations of their personal, psychological, and physical boundaries, which may or may not have been sexual, they are particularly vulnerable to this form of abuse.

A Continuum of Sexual and Intimacy Abuse of Clients

Although direct sexual contact is clearly abusive and unethical, it is important to broaden the framework of abuse to incorporate the psychological dynamics that underlie and set the stage for the occurrence of more blatant abuse as well as covert sexual behaviors that may be equally damaging. Conceptually, then, sexual and intimacy abuse of clients by counselors may best be viewed along a continuum consisting of psychological, covert, and overt abuse (see Table 1).

Psychological Abuse

Within this framework, the psychological column refers to aspects of the counseling relationship in which the client is put in the position of emotionally caretaking the needs of the counselor. This situation typically arises when poorly defined boundaries are set by the counselor as well as by the counselor's own "neediness." This constitutes an intimacy violation. The following is a case illustration:

> After a few counseling sessions, Dave asked his counselor to go have a cup of coffee, and he agreed. Initially, Dave was flattered that his counselor liked him enough to want to spend time with him outside of counseling. He enjoyed his counselor's company and thought it would be nice to have him as a friend.

Table 1

CONTINUUM OF SEXUAL AND INTIMACY ABUSE
BY COUNSELORS

Psychological	*Covert*	*Overt*
Therapist meeting own intimacies through client	Sexual hugs	Sexualizing remarks
	Professional voyeurism	Passionate kissing
Role reversal with client	Sexual gazes	Fondling
Self-disclosure with no therapeutic value	Over-attention to client's dress and appearance	Oral or anal sex
		Sexual intercourse
Loosely defined parameters of the therapeutic relationship	Therapist's seductiveness through dress or gestures	Sexual penetration with objects

Meeting in this setting, Dave's counselor told him much more about himself and that he was having marital problems. Again, Dave was flattered by this display of trust. It made him feel important. As time went on, Dave and his counselor began to see more of each other socially (e.g., having dinner together, playing racquetball, inviting each other to parties). At one point Dave's counselor called him, looking for support. The counselor had just learned that his wife had asked him for a divorce. At this point, Dave began to question the value of his counseling sessions.

In this case the therapist had reversed roles with the client and had engaged in a form of psychological intrusion. He failed to take responsibility for setting the boundaries of the relationship and met his own personal needs at the expense of the client.

Counselors who are experiencing grief or loss in their lives, such as Dave's counselor, are at greater risk for boundary violations and therefore should seek out additional outside support during these periods of vulnerability. In this way, such counselors are less likely to turn to their clients to meet these emotional needs. Counselors should be particularly watchful of their use of self-disclosure during these times. There is often a tendency to overindulge in self-sharing beyond the point of any therapeutic merit to the client. Before self-disclosing, counselors should consider whether the information is intended to broaden or deepen the client's understanding of his or her own issues.

Along with the content of therapy, the counselor should be cognizant of the importance of the structure of therapy and how this structure communicates boundaries of the counseling relationship. When a counselor ignores fees, fails to hold a client accountable for missed appointments, allows sessions to run overtime, accepts social invitations from clients, or interprets policies differently for certain clients, ambiguities in the professional relationship are communicated. These ambiguities often undermine a counselor's power and lead to more blatant forms of intrusion.

It is also important to realize that many clients are victims of boundary invasion (a physical or psychological intrusion that is experienced as unwanted and painful, e.g., emotional, psychological, physical, or sexual abuse) in relationships outside of counseling. Because of these experiences, many clients become confused and may misunderstand different forms of intimacy shown during counseling. They also may not be able to set appropriate boundaries for themselves. To avoid confusing the client, the counselor needs to establish clear boundaries by adhering to the principle of separation between a therapeutic relationship and other types of intimate relationships (e.g., with a friend or lover).

Covert Abuse

Moving along the continuum to the covert category (see Table 1), the counselor's boundary confusion with the client becomes more pronounced as the counselor displays behaviors with intended sexual connotations to the client, thus intruding further on the client's intimacy and sexual boundaries. The following are several common forms of covert sexual abuse that may occur in the counseling relationship:

Sexual hugs. These are hugs that are intended to arouse or satisfy the counselor's sexual needs rather than give support to the client.

Professional voyeurism. The counselor probes into the client's sexual history or practices to satisfy the counselor's curiosity rather than to produce any potential therapeutic gain for the client.

Sexual gazes. The counselor gives the client the "once over" while entering the room or stares at the client's sexual body parts during the session.

Although these behaviors are ambiguous in nature and their intent is somewhat camouflaged, they still possess sexual overtones. These behaviors confuse the client and cause him or her to wonder about the intent and how to respond. Again, these behaviors are damaging, abusive, and unethical.

Overt Abuse

Further along the continuum are examples of overt sexual behaviors, which may range from sexualizing remarks (e.g., propositions, sexual name calling, lascivious references to the client's sexual self) through some type of sexual contact or intercourse.

This category has been the most clearly recognized form of counselor abuse. Bouhoutsos et al. (1983) found that 90% of sexually abused clients experienced harm ranging from mistrust of opposite-sex relationships to hospitalization and, in some cases, suicide. Depression, emotional disturbances, impaired social adjustment, and increased use of alcohol and drugs were commonly reported symptoms. Clients typically found that their primary relationship worsened. Although their emotional problems increased, these clients found it more difficult to seek out further therapy because of their previous abusive situation.

For some clients, however, the psychological and covert forms of abuse may be the most damaging. When the behaviors have been made overt, the ethical violation is clear and the client can feel justified in his or her feelings of abuse. Psychological or covert forms of abuse, however, may provide more feelings of confusion, guilt, and shame.

Disputed Areas

Once counseling has ended, can intimacy be established? There are no ethical guidelines that seem to address this issue directly. Van Hoose and Kottler (1978) argued:

> If the therapist does genuinely believe that he is in love with his client, he has an ethical responsibility to terminate the therapy and refer the client to a colleague who can more appropriately be of service. Now, if that therapist decides to continue his personal feelings for the client, he may do so with clear conscience. (pp. 55–56)

The following case illustrates this issue:

> Mae was a 21-year-old woman who sought counseling at the small college she attended. She decided to see a school counselor because she was recently divorced and was having problems adjusting to being single again. Her relationship history included an abusive relationship with her ex-husband and physical, verbal, and sexual abuse from her father.
>
> It was unclear to her whether she or her counselor initiated the lengthy discussion about their mutual physical attraction to one another. Soon thereafter, the counselor abruptly ended the counseling and provided her with a referral to another counselor.
>
> They began to date one another 6 months after the counseling terminated. The counselor abruptly terminated the personal relationship 5 months later. Mae felt rejected and further victimized by this experience.

In this case, the counselor was faced with a variety of ethical dilemmas. Faced with the dilemma of providing professional care and serving his own romantic interests, he decided to terminate the counseling and make a referral. He thought he acted properly, but the result was a negative experience for the client. As in this case, it is probably unlikely that a counseling relationship can ever successfully evolve into a healthy intimate relationship and questionable whether this risk should ever be taken. Such an intimacy is negatively affected by the power imbalance implicit in the counseling relationship, the process in which counseling becomes internalized, and the continuation, in many ways, of the counseling relationship for years after counseling has ended.

There are several other disputed areas in defining the sexual boundaries between client and counselor. One is the use of sex surrogates. Most therapists agree that it is unethical for the therapist to function as a sex surrogate. Many sex therapists, however, believe that the use of sex surrogates in sex therapy is an ethically permissible way of establishing a therapeutic environment to facilitate sex therapy (see Masters, Johnson, & Kolodny, 1977, for further discussion). Ethical guidelines concerning the use of sex surrogates have been established by the American Association of Sex Educators, Counselors, and Therapists (1981). These guidelines state: "... it should be understood that the partner surrogate is not a sex therapist ... and sex therapists working with partner surrogates must exercise diligence and concern for protecting the dignity and welfare of both the surrogate and the client." These ethical guidelines are essentially the same as those of the International Professional Surrogates Association (n.d.).

Other disputed areas include the use of nudity in counseling, structured sexual fantasy exercises, and professionals' use of therapeutic massage as part of their practice. These areas need further exploration and ethical guidelines.

Recommendations

All counselors need to ask themselves how to responsibly set boundaries that deal with sexual and intimacy issues between themselves and their clients. Each counselor should ask the following questions:

1. In what ways do I behave differently toward my clients, in terms of time spent, intimacy, and touch? Can I back up these choices clinically?
2. How do I set boundaries for my sexual attraction to a client? For my client's sexual attraction to me?
3. Are there ways in which I am getting my intimacy needs met through my clients?
4. In what ways do I specifically state to my clients the parameters of the professional relationship?
5. How often have I raised ethical judgment calls, questions, and concerns to other professionals?

Conclusion

These questions may raise issues for all counselors. To resolve these ethical dilemmas, the counselor needs to discuss these issues with his or her colleagues in peer and other types of supervision. This is especially true when dealing with disputed areas in which licensing boards and professional organizations have provided little or conflicting ethical guidance. It is also important to keep up with changes occurring in state and national licensing boards, state legislation, and professional associations. Above all, in facing these ethical dilemmas, the counselor must take responsibility for setting appropriate sexual and intimacy boundaries for the client, communicating these boundaries, and keeping the relationship a professional rather than a personal one.

References

American Association for Counseling and Development. (1981). *Ethical standards*. Alexandria, VA: Author. (Originally published by the American Personnel and Guidance Association)

American Association of Sex Educators, Counselors, and Therapists. (1981). *Ethical standards*. Washington, DC: Author.

Belote, B. (1977). Sexual intimacy between female clients and male psychotherapists: Male sabotage (Doctoral dissertation, California School of Professional Psychology, Los Angeles, 1977). *Dissertation Abstracts International, 38*, 887B.

Bouhoutsos, J., Holroyd, J., Lerman, H., Forer, B., & Greenberg, M. (1983). Sexual intimacy between psychotherapists and patients. *Professional Psychology: Research and Practice, 14*, 185–196.

Butler, S.E. (1975). *Sexual contact between therapists and patients*. Unpublished doctoral dissertation, California School of Professional Psychology, Los Angeles.

Butler, S., & Zelen, S. (1977). Sexual intimacies between psychotherapists and their patients. *Psychotherapy: Theory, Research and Practice, 139*, 143–144.

D'Addarrio, L. (1978). Sexual relationship between female clients and male therapists. *Dissertation Abstracts International, 38*, 5077B. (University Microfilms No. 77-32429, 383)

Dahlberg, C.C. (1970). Sexual contact between patient and therapist. *Contemporary Psychoanalysis, 6*, 107–124.

Edelwich, J., & Brodsky, A. (1982). *Sexual dilemmas for the helping professional*. New York: Brunner/Mazel.

Feldman, S., & Ward, T. (1979). Psychotherapeutic injury: Reshaping the implied contract as an alternative to malpractice. *North Carolina Law Review, 58*, 63–96.

Holroyd, J., & Brodsky, A. (1977). Psychologists' attitudes and practices regarding erotic and non-erotic physical contact with patients. *American Psychologist, 32*, 843–849.

International Professional Surrogates Association. (n.d.). *Ethical standards*. Los Angeles, CA: Author.

Kardener, S., Fuller, M., & Mensh, I. (1973). A survery of physicians' attitudes and practices regarding erotic and non-erotic contact with patients. *American Journal of Psychiatry, 130*, 1077–1081.

Masters, W.H., Johnson, V.E., & Kolodny, R. (1977). *Ethical issues in sex therapy and research*. Boston: Little, Brown.

Minnesota Board of Psychology. (1982). *Adopted rules relating to rules of conduct and licensure of psychologists*. St. Paul: Author.

Schoener, G. (1984, September 25). *Report to Legislative Task Force on Sexual Exploitation of Clients by Therapists, Minneapolis.* (Available from G. Schoener, Walk-In Counseling Center, Minneapolis, MN)

Schoener, G., & Milgrom, J. (in press). Processing complaints of therapist misconduct. In A. Burgess (Ed.), *Sexual exploitation by health professionals.* New York: Praeger.

Stone, L.G. (1981). A study of the relationship among anxious attachment, ego functioning, and female patients' vulnerability to sexual involvement with their male psychotherapists. *Dissertation Abstracts International, 42,* 789B. (University Microfilms No. 81-14755, 1300)

Task Force on Sexual Exploitation by Counselors and Therapists. (1985). *Report to the Minnesota legislature.* St. Paul: Minnesota Department of Corrections.

Van Hoose, W.H., & Kottler, J.A. (1978). *Ethical and legal issues in counseling and psychotherapy.* San Francisco: Jossey-Bass.

APPENDIX A

Ethical Standards of the American Association for Counseling and Development

(As Revised by AACD Governing Council, March 1988)

Preamble

The Association is an educational, scientific, and professional organization whose members are dedicated to the enhancement of the worth, dignity, potential, and uniqueness of each individual and thus to the service of society.

The Association recognizes that the role definitions and work settings of its members include a wide variety of academic disciplines, levels of academic preparation, and agency services. This diversity reflects the breadth of the Association's interest and influence. It also poses challenging complexities in efforts to set standards for the performance of members, desired requisite preparation or practice, and supporting social, legal, and ethical controls.

The specification of ethical standards enables the Association to clarify to present and future members and to those served by members the nature of ethical responsibilities held in common by its members.

The existence of such standards serves to stimulate greater concern by members for their own professional functioning and for the conduct of fellow professionals such as counselors, guidance and student personnel workers, and others in the helping professions. As the ethical code of the Association, this document establishes principles that define the ethical behavior of Association members. Additional ethical guidelines developed by the Association's Divisions for their specialty areas may further define a member's ethical behavior.

Section A:
General

1. The member influences the development of the profession by continuous efforts to improve professional practices, teaching, services, and research. Professional growth is continuous throughout the member's career and is exemplified by the development of a philosophy that explains why and how a member functions in the helping relationship. Members must gather data on their effectiveness and be guided by the findings. Members recognize the need for continuing education to ensure competent service.

2. The member has a responsibility both to the individual who is served and to the institution within which the service is performed to maintain high standards of professional conduct. The member strives to maintain the highest levels of professional services offered to the individuals to be served. The member also strives to assist the agency, organization, or institution in providing the highest caliber of professional services. The acceptance of employment in an institution implies that the member is in agreement with the general policies and principles of the institution. Therefore the professional activities of the member are also in accord with the objectives of the institution. If, despite concerted efforts, the member cannot reach agreement with the employer as to acceptable standards of conduct that allow for changes in institutional policy conducive to the positive growth and development of clients, then terminating the affiliation should be seriously considered.

3. Ethical behavior among professional associates, both members and nonmembers, must be expected at all times. When information is possessed that raises doubt as to the ethical behavior of professional colleagues, whether Association members or not, the member must take action to attempt to rectify such a condition.

Such action shall use the institution's channels first and then use procedures established by the Association.

4. The member neither claims nor implies professional qualifications exceeding those possessed and is responsible for correcting any misrepresentations of these qualifications by others.

5. In establishing fees for professional counseling services, members must consider the financial status of clients and locality. In the event that the established fee structure is inappropriate for a client, assistance must be provided in finding comparable services of acceptable cost.

6. When members provide information to the public or to subordinates, peers, or supervisors, they have a responsibility to ensure that the content is general, unidentified client information that is accurate, unbiased, and consists of objective, factual data.

7. Members recognize their boundaries of competence and provide only those services and use only those techniques for which they are qualified by training or experience. Members should only accept those positions for which they are professionally qualified.

8. In the counseling relationship, the counselor is aware of the intimacy of the relationship and maintains respect for the client and avoids engaging in activities that seek to meet the counselor's personal needs at the expense of that client.

9. Members do not condone or engage in sexual harassment which is defined as deliberate or repeated comments, gestures, or physical contacts of a sexual nature.

10. The member avoids bringing personal issues into the counseling relationship, especially if the potential for harm is present. Through awareness of the negative impact of both racial and sexual stereotyping and discrimination, the counselor guards the individual rights and personal dignity of the client in the counseling relationship.

11. Products or services provided by the member by means of classroom instruction, public lectures, demonstrations, written articles, radio or television programs, or other types of media must meet the criteria cited in these standards.

Section B:
Counseling Relationship

This section refers to practices and procedures of individual and/or group counseling relationships.

The member must recognize the need for client freedom of choice. Under those circumstances where this is not possible, the member must apprise clients of restrictions that may limit their freedom of choice.

1. The member's primary obligation is to respect the integrity and promote the welfare of the client(s), whether the client(s) is (are) assisted individually or in a group relationship. In a group setting, the member is also responsible for taking reasonable precautions to protect individuals from physical and/or psychological trauma resulting from interaction within the group.

2. Members make provisions for maintaining confidentiality in the storage and disposal of records and follow an established record retention and disposition policy. The counseling relationship and information resulting therefrom must be kept confidential, consistent with the obligations of the member as a professional person. In a group counseling setting, the counselor must set a norm of confidentiality regarding all group participants' disclosures.

3. If an individual is already in a counseling relationship with another professional person, the member does not enter into a counseling relationship without first contacting and receiving the approval of that other professional. If the member discovers that the client is in another counseling relationship after the counseling relationship begins, the member must gain the consent of the other professional or terminate the relationship, unless the client elects to terminate the other relationship.

4. When the client's condition indicates that there is clear and imminent danger to the client or others, the member must take reasonable personal action or inform responsible authorities. Consultation with other professionals must be used where possible. The assumption of responsibility for the client's(s') behavior must be taken only after careful deliberation. The client must be involved in the resumption of responsibility as quickly as possible.

5. Records of the counseling relationship, including interview notes, test data, correspondence, tape recordings, electronic data storage, and other documents are to be considered professional information for use in counseling, and they should not be considered a part of the records of the institution or agency in which the counselor is employed unless specified by state statute or regulation. Revelation to others of counseling material must occur only upon the expressed consent of the client.

6. In view of the extensive data storage and processing capacities of the computer, the member must ensure that data maintained on a computer are: (a) limited to information that is appropriate

and necessary for the services being provided; (b) destroyed after it is determined that the information is no longer of any value in providing services; and (c) restricted in terms of access to appropriate staff members involved in the provision of services by using the best computer security methods available.

7. Use of data derived from a counseling relationship for purposes of counselor training or research shall be confined to content that can be disguised to ensure full protection of the identity of the subject client.

8. The member must inform the client of the purposes, goals, techniques, rules of procedure, and limitations that may affect the relationship at or before the time that the counseling relationship is entered. When working with minors or persons who are unable to give consent, the member protects these clients' best interests.

9. In view of common misconceptions related to the perceived inherent validity of computer-generated data and narrative reports, the member must ensure that the client is provided with information as part of the counseling relationship that adequately explains the limitations of computer technology.

10. The member must screen prospective group participants, especially when the emphasis is on self-understanding and growth through self-disclosure. The member must maintain an awareness of the group participants' compatibility throughout the life of the group.

11. The member may choose to consult with any other professionally competent person about a client. In choosing a consultant, the member must avoid placing the consultant in a conflict of interest situation that would preclude the consultant's being a proper party to the member's efforts to help the client.

12. If the member determines an inability to be of professional assistance to the client, the member must either avoid initiating the counseling relationship or immediately terminate that relationship. In either event, the member must suggest appropriate alternatives. (The member must be knowledgeable about referral resources so that a satisfactory referral can be initiated.) In the event the client declines the suggested referral, the member is not obligated to continue the relationship.

13. When the member has other relationships, particularly of an administrative, supervisory, and/or evaluative nature with an individual seeking counseling services, the member must not serve as the counselor but should refer the individual to another professional. Only in instances where such an alternative is unavailable and where the individual's situation warrants counseling interven-

tion should the member enter into and/or maintain a counseling relationship. Dual relationships with clients that might impair the member's objectivity and professional judgment (e.g., as with close friends or relatives) must be avoided and/or the counseling relationship terminated through referral to another competent professional.

14. The member will avoid any type of sexual intimacies with clients. Sexual relationships with clients are unethical.

15. All experimental methods of treatment must be clearly indicated to prospective recipients, and safety precautions are to be adhered to by the member.

16. When computer applications are used as a component of counseling services, the member must ensure that: (a) the client is intellectually, emotionally, and physically capable of using the computer application; (b) the computer application is appropriate for the needs of the client; (c) the client understands the purpose and operation of the computer application; and (d) a follow-up of client use of a computer application is provided to both correct possible problems (misconceptions or inappropriate use) and assess subsequent needs.

17. When the member is engaged in short-term group treatment/training programs (e.g., marathons and other encounter-type or growth groups), the member ensures that there is professional assistance available during and following the group experience.

18. Should the member be engaged in a work setting that calls for any variation from the above statements, the member is obligated to consult with other professionals whenever possible to consider justifiable alternatives.

19. The member must ensure that members of various ethnic, racial, religious, disability, and socioeconomic groups have equal access to computer applications used to support counseling services and that the content of available computer applications does not discriminate against the groups described above.

20. When computer applications are developed by the member for use by the general public as self-help/stand-alone computer software, the member must ensure that: (a) self-help computer applications are designed from the beginning to function in a stand-alone manner, as opposed to modifying software that was originally designed to require support from a counselor; (b) self-help computer applications will include within the program statements regarding intended user outcomes, suggestions for using the software, a description of the conditions under which self-help computer applications might not be appropriate, and a description of when

and how counseling services might be beneficial; and (c) the manual for such applications will include the qualifications of the developer, the development process, validation data, and operating procedures.

Section C:
Measurement & Evaluation

The primary purpose of educational and psychological testing is to provide descriptive measures that are objective and interpretable in either comparative or absolute terms. The member must recognize the need to interpret the statements that follow as applying to the whole range of appraisal techniques including test and nontest data. Test results constitute only one of a variety of pertinent sources of information for personnel, guidance, and counseling decisions.

1. The member must provide specific orientation or information to the examinee(s) prior to and following the test administration so that the results of testing may be placed in proper perspective with other relevant factors. In so doing, the member must recognize the effects of socioeconomic, ethnic, and cultural factors on test scores. It is the member's professional responsibility to use additional unvalidated information carefully in modifying interpretation of the test results.

2. In selecting tests for use in a given situation or with a particular client, the member must consider carefully the specific validity, reliability, and appropriateness of the test(s). General validity, reliability, and related issues may be questioned legally as well as ethically when tests are used for vocational and educational selection, placement, or counseling.

3. When making any statements to the public about tests and testing, the member must give accurate information and avoid false claims or misconceptions. Special efforts are often required to avoid unwarranted connotations of such terms as IQ and grade equivalent scores.

4. Different tests demand different levels of competence for administration, scoring, and interpretation. Members must recognize the limits of their competence and perform only those functions for which they are prepared. In particular, members using computer-based test interpretations must be trained in the construct being measured and the specific instrument being used prior to using this type of computer application.

5. In situations where a computer is used for test administration and scoring, the member is responsible for ensuring that administration and scoring programs function properly to provide clients with accurate test results.

6. Tests must be administered under the same conditions that were established in their standardization. When tests are not administered under standard conditions or when unusual behavior or irregularities occur during the testing session, those conditions must be noted and the results designated as invalid or of questionable validity. Unsupervised or inadequately supervised test-taking, such as the use of tests through the mails, is considered unethical. On the other hand, the use of instruments that are so designed or standardized to be self-administered and self-scored, such as interest inventories, is to be encouraged.

7. The meaningfulness of test results used in personnel, guidance, and counseling functions generally depends on the examinee's unfamiliarity with the specific items on the test. Any prior coaching or dissemination of the test materials can invalidate test results. Therefore, test security is one of the professional obligations of the member. Conditions that produce most favorable test results must be made known to the examinee.

8. The purpose of testing and the explicit use of the results must be made known to the examinee prior to testing. The counselor must ensure that instrument limitations are not exceeded and that periodic review and/or retesting is made to prevent client stereotyping.

9. The examinee's welfare and explicit prior understanding must be the criteria for determining the recipients of the test results. The member must see that specific interpretation accompanies any release of individual or group test data. The interpretation of test data must be related to the examinee's particular concerns.

10. Members responsible for making decisions based on test results have an understanding of educational and psychological measurement, validation criteria, and test research.

11. The member must be cautious when interpreting the results of research instruments possessing insufficient technical data. The specific purposes for the use of such instruments must be stated explicitly to examinees.

12. The member must proceed with caution when attempting to evaluate and interpret the performance of minority group members or other persons who are not represented in the norm group on which the instrument was standardized.

13. When computer-based test interpretations are developed by the member to support the assessment process, the member must ensure that the validity of such interpretations is established prior to the commerical distribution of such a computer application.

14. The member recognizes that test results may become obsolete. The member will avoid and prevent the misuse of obsolete test results.

15. The member must guard against the appropriation, reproduction, or modification of published tests or parts thereof without acknowledgement and permission from the previous publisher.

16. Regarding the preparation, publication, and distribution of tests, reference should be made to:
   a. "Standards for Educational and Psychological Testing," revised edition, 1985, published by the American Psychological Association on behalf of itself, the American Educational Research Association and the National Council of Measurement in Education.
   b. "The Responsible Use of Tests: A Position Paper of AMEG, APGA, and NCME," *Measurement and Evaluation in Guidance*, 1972, 5, 385–388.
   c. "Responsibilities of Users of Standardized Tests," APGA, *Guidepost*, October 5, 1978, pp. 5–8.

Section D:
Research and Publication

1. Guidelines on research with human subjects shall be adhered to, such as:
   a. *Ethical Principles in the Conduct of Research with Human Participants*, Washington, D.C.: American Psychological Association, Inc., 1982.
   b. Code of Federal Regulation, Title 45, Subtitle A, Part 46, as currently issued.
   c. *Ethical Principles of Psychologists*, American Psychological Association, Principle #9: Research with Human Participants.
   d. Family Educational Rights and Privacy Act (the Buckley Amendment).
   e. Current federal regulations and various state rights privacy acts.

2. In planning any research activity dealing with human subjects, the member must be aware of and responsive to all pertinent

ethical principles and ensure that the research problem, design, and execution are in full compliance with them.

3. Responsibility for ethical research practice lies with the principal researcher, while others involved in the research activities share ethical obligation and full responsibility for their own actions.

4. In research with human subjects, researchers are responsible for the subjects' welfare throughout the experiment, and they must take all reasonable precautions to avoid causing injurious psychological, physical, or social effects on their subjects.

5. All research subjects must be informed of the purpose of the study except when withholding information or providing misinformation to them is essential to the investigation. In such research the member must be responsible for corrective action as soon as possible following completion of the research.

6. Participation in research must be voluntary. Involuntary participation is appropriate only when it can be demonstrated that participation will have no harmful effects on subjects and is essential to the investigation.

7. When reporting research results, explicit mention must be made of all variables and conditions known to the investigator that might affect the outcome of the investigation or the interpretation of the data.

8. The member must be responsible for conducting and reporting investigations in a manner that minimizes the possibility that results will be misleading.

9. The member has an obligation to make available sufficient original research data to qualified others who may wish to replicate the study.

10. When supplying data, aiding in the research of another person, reporting research results, or making original data available, due care must be taken to disguise the identity of the subjects in the absence of specific authorization from such subjects to do otherwise.

11. When conducting and reporting research, the member must be familiar with and give recognition to previous work on the topic, as well as observe all copyright laws and follow the principles of giving full credit to all to whom credit is due.

12. The member must give due credit through joint authorship, acknowledgement, footnote statements, or other appropriate means to those who have contributed significantly to the research and/or publication, in accordance with such contributions.

13. The member must communicate to other members the results of any research judged to be of professional or scientific value. Results reflecting unfavorably on institutions, programs, services, or vested interests must not be withheld for such reasons.

14. If members agree to cooperate with another individual in research and/or publication, they incur an obligation to cooperate as promised in terms of punctuality of performance and with full regard to the completeness and accuracy of the information required.

15. Ethical practice requires that authors not submit the same manuscript or one essentially similar in content for simultaneous publication consideration by two or more journals. In addition, manuscripts published in whole or in substantial part in another journal or published work should not be submitted for publication without acknowledgement and permission from the previous publication.

Section E:
Consulting

Consultation refers to a voluntary relationship between a professional helper and help-needing individual, group, or social unit in which the consultant is providing help to the client(s) in defining and solving a work-related problem or potential problem with a client or client system.

1. The member acting as consultant must have a high degree of self-awareness of his/her own values, knowledge, skills, limitations, and needs in entering a helping relationship that involves human and/or organizational change and ensure that the focus of the relationship be on the issues to be resolved and not on the person(s) presenting the problem.

2. There must be understanding and agreement between member and client for the problem definition, change of goals, and prediction of consequences of interventions selected.

3. The member must be reasonably certain that she/he or the organization represented has the necessary competencies and resources for giving the kind of help that is needed now or may be needed later and that appropriate referral resources are available to the consultant.

4. The consulting relationship must be one in which client adaptability and growth toward self-direction are encouraged and

cultivated. The member must maintain this role consistently and not become a decision maker for the client or create a future dependency on the consultant.

5. When announcing consultant availability for services, the member conscientiously adheres to the Association's Ethical Standards.

6. The member must refuse a private fee or other remuneration for consultation with persons who are entitled to these services through the member's employing institution or agency. The policies of a particular agency may make explicit provisions for private practice with agency clients by members of its staff. In such instances, the clients must be apprised of other options open to them should they seek private counseling services.

Section F:
Private Practice

1. The member should assist the profession by facilitating the availability of counseling services in private as well as public settings.

2. In advertising services as a private practitioner, the member must advertise the services in a manner that accurately informs the public of professional services, expertise, and techniques of counseling available. A member who assumes an executive leadership role in the organization shall not permit his/her name to be used in professional notices during periods when he/she is not actively engaged in the private practice of counseling.

3. The member may list the following: highest relevant degree, type and level of certification and/or license, address, telephone number, office hours, type and/or description of services, and other relevant information. Such information must not contain false, inaccurate, misleading, partial, out-of-context, or deceptive material or statements.

4. Members do not present their affiliation with any organization in such a way that would imply inaccurate sponsorship or certification by that organization.

5. Members may join in partnership/corporation with other members and/or other professionals provided that each member of the partnership or corporation makes clear the separate specialties by name in compliance with the regulations of the locality.

6. A member has an obligation to withdraw from a counseling relationship if it is believed that employment will result in violation

of the Ethical Standards. If the mental or physical condition of the member renders it difficult to carry out an effective professional relationship or if the member is discharged by the client because the counseling relationship is no longer productive for the client, then the member is obligated to terminate the counseling relationship.

7. A member must adhere to the regulations for private practice of the locality where the services are offered.

8. It is unethical to use one's institutional affiliation to recruit clients for one's private practice.

Section G:
Personnel Administration

It is recognized that most members are employed in public or quasi-public institutions. The functioning of a member within an institution must contribute to the goals of the institution and vice versa if either is to accomplish their respective goals or objectives. It is therefore essential that the member and the institution function in ways to: (a) make the institutional goals specific; and public; (b) make the member's contribution to institutional goals specific; and (c) foster mutual accountability for goal achievement.

To accomplish these objectives, it is recognized that the member and the employer must share responsibilities in the formulation and implementation of personnel policies.

1. Members must define and describe the parameters and levels of their professional competency.

2. Members must establish interpersonal relations and working agreements with supervisors and subordinates regarding counseling or clinical relationships, confidentiality, distinction between public and private material, maintenance and dissemination of recorded information, work load, and accountability. Working agreeements in each instance must be specified and made known to those concerned.

3. Members must alert their employers to conditions that may be potentiallly disruptive or damaging.

4. Members must inform employers of conditions that may limit their effectiveness.

5. Members must submit regularly to professional review and evaluation.

6. Members must be responsible for inservice development of self and/or staff.

7. Members must inform their staff of goals and programs.

8. Members must provide personnel practices that guarantee and enhance the rights and welfare of each recipient of their service.

9. Members must select competent persons and assign responsibilities compatible with their skills and experiences.

10. The member, at the onset of a counseling relationship, will inform the client of the member's intended use of supervisors regarding the disclosure of information concerning this case. The member will clearly inform the client of the limits of confidentiality in the relationship.

11. Members, as either employers or employees, do not engage in or condone practices that are inhumane, illegal, or unjustifiable (such as considerations based on sex, handicap, age, race) in hiring, promotion, or training.

Section H:
Preparation Standards

Members who are responsible for training others must be guided by the preparation standards of the Association and relevant Division(s). The member who functions in the capacity of trainer assumes unique ethical responsibilities that frequently go beyond that of the member who does not function in a training capacity. These ethical responsibilities are outlined as follows:

1. Members must orient students to program expectations, basic skills development, and employment prospects prior to admission to the program.

2. Members in charge of learning experiences must establish programs that integrate academic study and supervised practice.

3. Members must establish a program directed toward developing students' skills, knowledge, and self-understanding, stated whenever possible in competency or performance terms.

4. Members must identify the levels of competencies of their students in compliance with relevant Division standards. These competencies must accommodate the paraprofessional as well as the professional.

5. Members, through continual student evaluation and appraisal, must be aware of the personal limitations of the learner that might impede future performance. The instructor must not only assist the learner in securing remedial assistance but also

screen from the program those individuals who are unable to provide competent services.

6. Members must provide a program that includes training in research commensurate with levels of role functioning. Paraprofessional and technician-level personnel must be trained as consumers of research. In addition, personnel must learn how to evaluate their own and their program's effectiveness. Graduate training, especially at the doctoral level, would include preparation for original research by the member.

7. Members must make students aware of the ethical responsibilities and standards of the profession.

8. Preparatory programs must encourage students to value the ideals of service to individuals and to society. In this regard, direct financial remuneration or lack thereof must not be allowed to overshadow professional and humanitarian needs.

9. Members responsible for educational programs must be skilled as teachers and practitioners.

10. Members must present thoroughly varied theoretical positions so that students may make comparisons and have the opportunity to select a position.

11. Members must develop clear policies within their educational institutions regarding field placement and the roles of the student and the instructor in such placement.

12. Members must ensure that forms of learning focusing on self-understanding or growth are voluntary, or if required as part of the educational program, are made known to prospective students prior to entering the program. When the educational program offers a growth experience with an emphasis on self-disclosure or other relatively intimate or personal involvement, the member must have no administrative, supervisory, or evaluating authority regarding the participant.

13. The member will at all times provide students with clear and equally acceptable alternatives for self-understanding or growth experiences. The member will assure students that they have a right to accept these alternatives without prejudice or penalty.

14. Members must conduct an educational program in keeping with the current relevant guidelines of the Association.

APPENDIX B

Ethical Standards for School Counselors

American School Counselor Association

Preamble

The American School Counselor Association (ASCA) is a professional organization whose members have a unique and distinctive preparation, grounded in the behavorial sciences, with training in counseling skills adapted to the school setting. The school counselor assists in the growth and development of each individual and uses his/her specialized skills to ensure that the rights of the counselee are properly protected within the structure of the school program. School counselors subscribe to the following basic tenets of the counseling process from which professional responsibilities are derived:

1. Each person has the right to respect and dignity as a unique human being and to counseling services without prejudice as to person, character, belief or practice.

2. Each person has the right to self-direction and self-development.

3. Each person has the right of choice and the responsibility for decisions reached.

4. Each person has the right to privacy and thereby the right

to expect the counselor-client relationship to comply with all laws, policies and ethical standards pertaining to confidentiality.

In this document, the American School Counselor Association has specified the principles of ethical behavior necessary to maintain and regulate the high standards of integrity and leadership among its members. The Association recognizes the basic commitment of its members to the *Ethical Standards* of its parent organization, the American Counseling Association (ACA), and nothing in this document shall be construed to supplant that code. *The Ethical Standards for School Counselors* was developed to complement the ACA standards by clarifying the nature of ethical responsibilities for present and future counselors in the school setting. The purposes of this document are to:

1. Serve as a guide for the ethical practices of all professional school counselors regardless of level, area, population served, or membership in this Association.

2. Provide benchmarks for both self-appraisal and peer evaluations regarding counselor responsibilities to students, parents, colleagues and professional associates, school and community, self, and the counseling profession.

3. Inform those served by the school counselor of acceptable counselor practices and expected professional deportment.

A. Responsibilities to Students

The school counselor:

1. Has a primary obligation and loyalty to the student, who is to be treated with respect as a unique individual, whether assisted individually or in a group setting.

2. Is concerned with the total needs of the student (educational, vocational, personal and social) and encourages the maximum growth and development of each counselee.

3. Informs the counselee of the purposes, goals, techniques and rules of procedure under which she/he may receive counseling assistance at or before the time when the counseling relationship is entered. Prior notice includes confidentiality issues such as the possible necessity for consulting with other professionals, privileged communication, and legal or authoritative restraints. The meaning and limits of confidentiality are clearly defined to counselees.

4. Refrains from consciously encouraging the counselee's ac-

ceptance of values, lifestyles, plans, decisions, and beliefs that represent only the counselor's personal orientation.

5. Is responsible for keeping abreast of laws relating to students and strives to ensure that the rights of students are adequately provided for and protected.

6. Avoids dual relationships which might impair his/her objectivity and/or increase the risk of harm to the client (e.g., counseling one's family members, close friends or associates). If a dual relationship is unavoidable, the counselor is responsible for taking action to eliminate or reduce the potential for harm. Such safeguards might include informed consent, consultation, supervision and documentation.

7. Makes appropriate referrals when professional assistance can no longer be adequately provided to the counselee. Appropriate referral requires knowledge of available resources.

8. Protects the confidentiality of student records and releases personal data only according to prescribed laws and school policies. Student information maintained through electronic data storage methods is treated with the same care as traditional student records.

9. Protects the confidentiality of information received in the counseling relationship as specified by law and ethical standards. Such information is only to be revealed to others with the informed consent of the counselee and consistent with the obligations of the counselor as a professional person. In a group setting, the counselor sets a norm of confidentiality and stresses its importance, yet clearly states that confidentiality in group counseling cannot be guaranteed.

10. Informs the appropriate authorities when the counselee's condition indicates a clear and imminent danger to the counselee or others. This is to be done after careful deliberation and, where possible, after consultation with other professionals. The counselor informs the counselee of actions to be taken so as to minimize confusion and clarify expectations.

11. Screens prospective group members and maintains an awareness of participants' compatibility throughout the life of the group, especially when the group emphasis is on self-disclosure and self-understanding. The counselor takes reasonable precautions to protect members from physical and/or psychological harm resulting from interaction within the group.

12. Provides explanations of the nature, purposes, and results of tests in language that is understandable to the client(s).

13. Adheres to relevant standards regarding selection, ad-

ministration, and interpretation of assessment techniques. The counselor recognizes that computer-based testing programs require specific training in administration, scoring and interpretation which may differ from that required in more traditional assessments.

14. Promotes the benefits of appropriate computer applications and clarifies the limitations of computer technology. The counselor ensures that (1) computer applications are appropriate for the individual needs of the counselee, (2) the counselee understands how to use the application, and (3) follow-up counseling assistance is provided. Members of underrepresented groups are assured of equal access to computer technologies and the absence of discriminatory information and values within computer applications.

15. Has unique ethical responsibilities in working with peer programs. In general, the school counselor is responsible for the welfare of students participating in peer programs under her/his direction. School counselors who function in training and supervisory capacities are referred to the preparation and supervision standards of professional counselor associations.

B. Responsibilities to Parents

The school counselor:

1. Respects the inherent rights and responsibilities of parents for their children and endeavors to establish a cooperative relationship with parents to facilitate the maximum development of the counselee.

2. Informs parents of the counselor's role, with emphasis on the confidential nature of the counseling relationship between the counselor and counselee.

3. Provides parents with accurate, comprehensive and relevant information in an objective and caring manner, as appropriate and consistent with ethical responsibilities to the counselee.

4. Treats information received from parents in a confidential and appropriate manner.

5. Shares information about a counselee only with those persons properly authorized to receive such information.

6. Adheres to laws and local guidelines when assisting parents experiencing family difficulties which interfere with the counselee's effectiveness and welfare.

7. Is sensitive to changes in the family and recognizes that all parents, custodial and noncustodial, are vested with certain rights

and responsibilities for the welfare of their children by virtue of their position and according to law.

C. Responsibilities to Colleagues and Professional Associates

The school counselor:

1. Establishes and maintains a cooperative relationship with faculty, staff and administration to facilitate the provision of optimal guidance and counseling programs and services.

2. Promotes awareness and adherence to appropriate guidelines regarding confidentiality, the distinction between public and private information, and staff consultation.

3. Treats colleagues with respect, courtesy, fairness and good faith. The qualifications, views and findings of colleagues are represented accurately and fairly to enhance the image of competent professionals.

4. Provides professional personnel with accurate, objective, concise and meaningful data necessary to adequately evaluate, counsel and assist the counselee.

5. Is aware of and fully utilizes related professions and organizations to whom the counselee may be referred.

D. Responsibilities to the School and Community

The school counselor:

1. Supports and protects the educational program against any infringement not in the best interest of students.

2. Informs appropriate officials of conditions that may be potentially disruptive or damaging to the school's mission, personnel and property.

3. Delineates and promotes the counselor's role and function in meeting the needs of those served. The counselor will notify appropriate school officials of conditions which may limit or curtail their effectiveness in providing programs and services.

4. Assists in the development of: (1) curricular and environmental conditions appropriate for the school and community, (2) educational procedures and programs to meet student needs, and (3) a systematic evaluation process for guidance and counseling programs, services and personnel. The counselor is guided by the findings of the evaluation data in planning programs and services.

5. Actively cooperates and collaborates with agencies, orga-

nizations, and individuals in the school and community in the best interest of counselees and without regard to personal reward or remuneration.

E. Responsibilities to Self

The school counselor:

1. Functions within the boundaries of individual professional competence and accepts responsibility for the consequences of his/her actions.

2. Is aware of the potential effects of her/his own personal characteristics on services to clients.

3. Monitors personal functioning and effectiveness and refrains from any activity likely to lead to inadequate professional services or harm to a client.

4. Recognizes that differences in clients relating to age, gender, race, religion, sexual orientation, socioeconomic and ethnic backgrounds may require specific training to ensure competent services.

5. Strives through personal initiative to maintain professional competence and keep abreast of innovations and trends in the profession. Professional and personal growth is continuous and ongoing throughout the counselor's career.

F. Responsibilities to the Profession

The school counselor:

1. Conducts herself/himself in such a manner as to bring credit to self and the profession.

2. Conducts appropriate research and reports findings in a manner consistent with acceptable educational and psychological research practices. When using client data for research, statistical or program planning purposes, the counselor ensures protection of the identity of the individual client(s).

3. Actively participates in local, state and national associations which foster the development and improvement of school counseling.

4. Adheres to ethical standards of the profession, other official policy statements pertaining to counseling, and relevant statutes established by federal, state and local governments.

5. Clearly distinguishes between statements and actions made

as a private individual and as a representative of the school counseling profession.

6. Contributes to the development of the profession through the sharing of skills, ideas and expertise with colleagues.

G. Maintenance of Standards

Ethical behavior among professional school counselors, Association members and nonmembers, is expected at all times. When there exists serious doubt as to the ethical behavior of colleagues, or if counselors are forced to work in situations or abide by policies which do not reflect the standards as outlined in these *Ethical Standards for School Counselors* or the ACA *Ethical Standards*, the counselor is obligated to take appropriate action to rectify the condition. The following procedure may serve as a guide:

1. If feasible, the counselor should consult with a professional colleague to confidentially discuss the nature of the complaint to see if she/he views the situation as an ethical violation.

2. Whenever possible, the counselor should directly approach the colleague whose behavior is in question to discuss the complaint and seek resolution.

3. If resolution is not forthcoming at the personal level, the counselor shall utilize the channels established within the school and/or school district. This may include both informal and formal procedures.

4. If the matter still remains unresolved, referral for review and appropriate action should be made to the Ethics Committees in the following sequence:
  —local counselor association
  —state counselor association
  —national counselor association

5. The ASCA Ethics Committee functions in an educative and consultative capacity and does not adjudicate complaints of ethical misconduct. Therefore, at the national level, complaints should be submitted in writing to the ACA Ethics Committee for review and appropriate action. The procedure for submitting complaints may be obtained by writing the ACA Ethics Committee, c/o The Executive Director, American Counseling Association, 5999 Stevenson Avenue, Alexandria, VA 22304.

H. Resources

School counselors are responsible for being aware of, and acting in accord with, the standards and positions of the counseling profession as represented in official documents such as those listed below.

Code of Ethics (1989). National Board for Certified Counselors. Alexandria, VA.

Code of Ethics for Peer Helping Professionals (1989). National Peer Helpers Association. Glendale, CA.

Ethical Guidelines for Group Counselors (1989). Association for Specialists in Group Work. Alexandria, VA.

Ethical Standards (1988). American Association for Counseling and Development. Alexandria, VA.

Position Statement: The School Counselor and Confidentiality (1986). American School Counselor Association. Alexandria, VA.

Position Statement: The School Counselor and Peer Facilitation (1984). American School Counselor Association. Alexandria, VA.

Position Statement: The School Counselor and Student Rights (1982). American School Counselor Association. Alexandria, VA.

Ethical Standards for School Counselors was adopted by the ASCA Delegate Assembly, March 19, 1984. This revision was approved by the ASCA Delegate Assembly, March 27, 1992.

As of July 1, 1992 the American Association for Counseling and Development (AACD) becomes the American Counseling Association (ACA).

APPENDIX C

Ethical Guidelines for Group Counselors

ASGW 1989 Revision

Association for Specialists in Group Work

Preamble

One characteristic of any professional group is the possession of a body of knowledge, skills, and voluntarily, self-professed standards for ethical practice. A Code of Ethics consists of those standards that have been formally and publicly acknowledged by the members of a profession to serve as the guidelines for professional conduct, discharge of duties, and the resolution of moral dilemmas. By this document, the Association for Specialists in Group Work (ASGW) has identified the standards of conduct appropriate for ethical behavior among its members.

The Association for Specialists in Group Work recognizes the basic commitment of its members to the Ethical Standards of its parent organization, the American Association for Counseling and Development (AACD) and nothing in this document shall be construed to supplant that code. These standards are intended to complement the AACD standards in the area of group work by clarifying

These guidelines were approved by the Association for Specialists in Group Work (ASGW) Executive Board, June 1, 1989.

the nature of ethical responsibility of the counselor in the group setting and by stimulating a greater concern for competent group leadership.

The group counselor is expected to be a professional agent and to take the processes of ethical responsibility seriously. ASGW views "ethical process" as being integral to group work and views group counselors as "ethical agents." Group counselors, by their very nature in being responsible and responsive to their group members, necessarily embrace a certain potential for ethical vulnerability. It is incumbent upon group counselors to give considerable attention to the intent and context of their actions because the attempts of counselors to influence human behavior through group work always have ethical implications.

The following ethical guidelines have been developed to encourage ethical behavior of group counselors. These guidelines are written for students and practitioners, and are meant to stimulate reflection, self-examination, and discussion of issues and practices. They address the group counselor's responsibility for providing information about group work to clients and the group counselor's responsibility for providing group counseling services to clients. A final section discusses the group counselor's responsibility for safeguarding ethical practice and procedures for reporting unethical behavior. Group counselors are expected to make known these standards to group members.

Ethical Guidelines

1. *Orientation and Providing Information:* Group counselors adequately prepare prospective or new group members by providing as much information about the existing or proposed group as necessary.

- Minimally, information related to each of the following areas should be provided.
- (a) Entrance procedures, time parameters of the group experience, group participation expectations, methods of payment (where appropriate), and termination procedures are explained by the group counselor as appropriate to the level of maturity of group members and the nature and purpose(s) of the group.
- (b) Group counselors have available for distribution, a professional disclosure statement that includes information on

the group counselor's qualifications and group services that can be provided, particularly as related to the nature and purpose(s) of the specific group.

(c) Group counselors communicate the role expectations, rights, and responsibilities of group members and group counselor(s).

(d) The group goals are stated as concisely as possible by the group counselor including "whose" goal it is (the group counselor's, the institution's, the parent's, the law's, society's, etc.) and the role of group members in influencing or determining the group's goal(s).

(e) Group counselors explore with group members the risks of potential life changes that may occur because of the group experience and help members explore their readiness to face these possibilities.

(f) Group members are informed by the group counselor of unusual or experimental procedures that might be expected in their group experience.

(g) Group counselors explain, as realistically as possible, what services can and cannot be provided within the particular group structure offered.

(h) Group counselors emphasize the need to promote full psychological functioning and presence among group members. They inquire from prospective group members whether they are using any kind of drug or medication that may affect functioning in the group. They do not permit any use of alcohol and/or illegal drugs during group sessions and they discourage the use of alcohol and/or drugs (legal or illegal) prior to group meetings which may affect the physical or emotional presence of the member or other group member.

(i) Group counselors inquire from prospective group members whether they have ever been a client in counseling or psychotherapy. If a prospective group member is already in a counseling relationship with another professional person, the group counselor advises the prospective group member to notify the other professional of their participation in the group.

(j) Group counselors clearly inform group members about the policies pertaining to the group counselor's willingness to consult with them between group sessions.

(k) In establishing fees for group counseling services, group counselors consider the financial status and the locality of prospective group members. Group members are not charged fees for group sessions where the group counselor is not present and the policy of charging for sessions missed by a group member is clearly communicated. Fees for participating as a group member are contracted between group counselor and group member for a specified period of time. Group counselors do not increase fees for group counseling services until the existing contracted fee structure has expired. In the event that the established fee structure is inappropriate for a prospective member, group counselors assist in finding comparable services of acceptable cost.

2. *Screening of Members:* The group counselor screens prospective group members (when appropriate to their theoretical orientation). Insofar as possible, the counselor selects group members whose needs and goals are compatible with the goals of the group, who will not impede the group process, and whose well-being will not be jeopardized by the group experience. An orientation to the group (i.e., ASGW Ethical Guideline #1), is included during the screening process.

- Screening may be accomplished in one or more ways, such as the following:
(a) Individual interview,
(b) Group interview of prospective group members,
(c) Interview as part of a team staffing, and,
(d) Completion of a written questionnaire by prospective group members.

3. *Confidentiality:* Group counselors protect members by defining clearly what confidentiality means, why it is important, and the difficulties involved in enforcement.
   (a) Group counselors take steps to protect members by defining confidentiality and the limits of confidentiality (i.e., when a group member's condition indicates that there is clear and imminent danger to the member, others, or physical property, the group counselor takes reasonable personal action and/or informs responsible authorities).
   (b) Group counselors stress the importance of confidentiality and set a norm of confidentiality regarding all group participants' disclosures. The importance of maintaining confidentiality is emphasized before the group begins and at various times in the group. The fact that confidentiality cannot be guaranteed is clearly stated.

(c) Members are made aware of the difficulties involved in enforcing and ensuring confidentiality in a group setting. The counselor provides examples of how confidentiality can non-maliciously be broken to increase members' awareness, and help to lessen the likelihood that this breach of confidence will occur. Group counselors inform group members about the potential consequences of intentionally breaching confidentiality.

(d) Group counselors can only ensure confidentiality on their part and not on the part of the members.

(e) Group counselors video or audio tape a group session only with the prior consent, and the members' knowledge of how the tape will be used.

(f) When working with minors, the group counselor specifies the limits of confidentiality.

(g) Participants in a mandatory group are made aware of any reporting procedures required of the group counselor.

(h) Group counselors store or dispose of group member records (written, audio, video, etc.) in ways that maintain confidentiality.

(i) Instructors of group counseling courses maintain the anonymity of group members whenever discussing group counseling cases.

4. *Voluntary/Involuntary Participation:* Group counselors inform members whether participation is voluntary or involuntary.

(a) Group counselors take steps to ensure informed consent procedures in both voluntary and involuntary groups.

(b) When working with minors in a group, counselors are expected to follow the procedures specified by the institution in which they are practicing.

(c) With involuntary groups, every attempt is made to enlist the cooperation of the members and their continuance in the group on a voluntary basis.

(d) Group counselors do not certify that group treatment has been received by members who merely attend sessions, but did not meet the defined group expectations. Group members are informed about the consequences for failing to participate in a group.

5. *Leaving a Group:* Provisions are made to assist a group member to terminate in an effective way.

(a) Procedures to be followed for a group member who chooses to exit a group prematurely are discussed by the counselor with all group members either before the group begins, during a pre-screening interview, or during the initial group session.

(b) In the case of legally mandated group counseling, group counselors inform members of the possible consequences for premature self-termination.

(c) Ideally, both the group counselor and the member can work cooperatively to determine the degree to which a group experience is productive or counterproductive for that individual.

(d) Members ultimately have a right to discontinue membership in the group, at a designated time, if the predetermined trial period proves to be unsatisfactory.

(e) Members have the right to exit a group, but it is important that they be made aware of the importance of informing the counselor and the group members prior to deciding to leave. The counselor discusses the possible risks of leaving the group prematurely with a member who is considering this option.

(f) Before leaving a group, the group counselor encourages members (if appropriate) to discuss their reasons for wanting to discontinue membership in the group. Counselors intervene if other members use undue pressure to force a member to remain in the group.

6. *Coercion and Pressure:* Group counselors protect member rights against physical threats, intimidation, coercion, and undue peer pressure insofar as is reasonably possible.

(a) It is essential to differentiate between "therapeutic pressure" that is part of any group and "undue pressure," which is not therapeutic.

(b) The purpose of a group is to help participants find their own answer, not to pressure them into doing what the group thinks is appropriate.

(c) Counselors exert care not to coerce participants to change in directions which they clearly state they do not choose.

(d) Counselors have a responsibility to intervene when others use undue pressure or attempt to persuade members against their will.

(e) Counselors intervene when any member attempts to act out aggression in a physical way that might harm another member or themselves.

(f) Counselors intervene when a member is verbally abusive or inappropriately confrontive to another member.

7. *Imposing Counselor Values:* Group counselors develop an

awareness of their own values and needs and the potential impact they have on the interventions likely to be made.

(a) Although group counselors take care to avoid imposing their values on members, it is appropriate that they expose their own beliefs, decisions, needs, and values, when concealing them would create problems for the members.

(b) There are values implicit in any group, and these are made clear to potential members before they join the group. (Examples of certain values include: expressing feelings, being direct and honest, sharing personal material with others, learning how to trust, improving interpersonal communication, and deciding for oneself.)

(c) Personal and professional needs of group counselors are not met at the members' expense.

(d) Group counselors avoid using the group for their own therapy.

(e) Group counselors are aware of their own values and assumptions and how these apply in a multicultural context.

(f) Group counselors take steps to increase their awareness of ways that their personal reactions to members might inhibit the group process and they monitor their countertransference. Through an awareness of the impact of stereotyping and discrimination (i.e., biases based on age, disability, ethnicity, gender, race, religion, or sexual preference), group counselors guard the individual rights and personal dignity of all group members.

8. *Equitable Treatment:* Group counselors make every reasonable effort to treat each member individually and equally.

(a) Group counselors recognize and respect differences (e.g., cultural, racial, religious, lifestyle, age, disability, gender) among group members.

(b) Group counselors maintain an awareness of their behavior toward individual group members and are alert to the potential detrimental effects of favoritism or partiality toward any particular group member to the exclusion or detriment of any other member(s). It is likely that group counselors will favor some members over others, yet all group members deserve to be treated equally.

(c) Group counselors ensure equitable use of group time for each member by inviting silent members to become involved, acknowledging nonverbal attempts to communicate, and discouraging rambling and monopolizing of time by members.

(d) If a large group is planned, counselors consider enlisting another qualified professional to serve as a co-leader for the group sessions.

9. *Dual Relationships:* Group counselors avoid dual relationships with group members that might impair their objectivity and professional judgment, as well as those which are likely to compromise a group member's ability to participate fully in the group.

(a) Group counselors do not misuse their professional role and power as group leader to advance personal or social contacts with members throughout the duration of the group.

(b) Group counselors do not use their professional relationship with group members to further their own interest either during the group or after the termination of the group.

(c) Sexual intimacies between group counselors and members are unethical.

(d) Group counselors do not barter (exchange) professional services with group members for services.

(e) Group counselors do not admit their own family members, relatives, employees, or personal friends as members to their groups.

(f) Group counselors discuss with group members the potential detrimental effects of group members engaging in intimate inter-member relationships outside of the group.

(g) Students who participate in a group as a partial course requirement for a group course are not evaluated for an academic grade based upon their degree of participation as a member in a group. Instructors of group counseling courses take steps to minimize the possible negative impact on students when they participate in a group course by separating course grades from participation in the group and by allowing students to decide what issues to explore and when to stop.

(h) It is inappropriate to solicit members from a class (or institutional affiliation) for one's private counseling or therapeutic groups.

10. *Use of Techniques:* Group counselors do not attempt any technique unless trained in its use or under supervision by a counselor familiar with the intervention.

(a) Group counselors are able to articulate a theoretical orientation that guides their practice, and they are able to provide a rationale for their interventions.

(b) Depending upon the type of an intervention, group counselors have training commensurate with the potential impact of a technique.

(c) Group counselors are aware of the necessity to modify their techniques to fit the unique needs of various cultural and ethnic groups.

(d) Group counselors assist members in translating in-group learnings to daily life.

11. *Goal Development:* Group counselors make every effort to assist members in developing their personal goals.

(a) Group counselors use their skills to assist members in making their goals specific so that others present in the group will understand the nature of the goals.

(b) Throughout the course of a group, group counselors assist members in assessing the degree to which personal goals are being met, and assist in revising any goals when it is appropriate.

(c) Group counselors help members clarify the degree to which the goals can be met within the context of a particular group.

12. *Consultation:* Group counselors develop and explain policies about between-session consultation to group members.

(a) Group counselors take care to make certain that members do not use between-session consultations to avoid dealing with issues pertaining to the group that would be dealt with best in the group.

(b) Group counselors urge members to bring the issues discussed during between-session consultations into the group if they pertain to the group.

(c) Group counselors seek out consultation and/or supervision regarding ethical concerns or when encountering difficulties which interfere with their effective functioning as group leaders.

(d) Group counselors seek appropriate professional assistance for their own personal problems or conflicts that are likely to impair their professional judgment and work performance.

(e) Group counselors discuss their group cases only for professional consultation and educational purposes.

(f) Group counselors inform members about policies regarding whether consultation will be held confidential.

13. *Termination from the Group:* Depending upon the purpose of participation in the group, counselors promote termination of members from the group in the most efficient period of time.

(a) Group counselors maintain a constant awareness of the progress made by each group member and periodically invite the group members to explore and reevaluate their experiences in the group. It is the responsibility of group counselors to help promote the independence of members from the group in a timely manner.

14. *Evaluation and Follow-up:* Group counselors make every attempt to engage in ongoing assessment and to design follow-up procedures for their groups.

(a) Group counselors recognize the importance of ongoing assessment of a group, and they assist members in evaluating their own progress.

(b) Group counselors conduct evaluation of the total group experience at the final meeting (or before termination), as well as ongoing evaluation.

(c) Group counselors monitor their own behavior and become aware of what they are modeling in the group.

(d) Follow-up procedures might take the form of personal contact, telephone contact, or written contact.

(e) Follow-up meetings might be with individuals, or groups, or both to determine the degree to which: (i) members have reached their goals, (ii) the group had a positive or negative effect on the participants, (iii) members could profit from some type of referral, and (iv) as information for possible modification of future groups. If there is no follow-up meeting, provisions are made available for individual follow-up meetings to any member who needs or requests such a contact.

15. *Referrals:* If the needs of a particular member cannot be met within the type of group being offered, the group counselor suggests other appropriate professional referrals.

(a) Group counselors are knowledgeable of local community resources for assisting group members regarding professional referrals.

(b) Group counselors help members seek further professional assistance, if needed.

16. *Professional Development:* Group counselors recognize that professional growth is a continuous, ongoing, developmental process throughout their career.

(a) Group counselors maintain and upgrade their knowledge and skill competencies through educational activities, clinical experiences, and participation in professional development activities.

(b) Group counselors keep abreast of research findings and new developments as applied to groups.

Safeguarding Ethical Practice and Procedures for Reporting Unethical Behavior

The preceding remarks have been advanced as guidelines which are generally representative of ethical and professional group practice. They have not been proposed as rigidly defined prescriptions. However, practitioners who are thought to be grossly unresponsive to the ethical concerns addressed in this document may be subject to a review of their practices by the AACD Ethics Committee and ASGW peers.

- For consultation and/or questions regarding these ASGW Ethical Guidelines or group ethical dilemmas, you may contact the Chairperson of the ASGW Ethics Committee. The name, address, and telephone number of the current ASGW Ethics Committee Chairperson may be acquired by telephoning the AACD office in Alexandria, Virginia at (703) 823-9800.
- If a group counselor's behavior is suspected as being unethical, the following procedures are to be followed:
- (a) Collect more information and investigate further to confirm the unethical practice as determined by the ASGW Ethical Guidelines.
- (b) Confront the individual with the apparent violation of ethical guidelines for the purposes of protecting the safety of any clients and to help the group counselor correct any inappropriate behaviors. If satisfactory resolution is not reached through this contact then:
- (c) A complaint should be made in writing, including the specific facts and dates of the alleged violation and all relevant supporting data. The complaint should be included in an envelope marked "CONFIDENTIAL" to ensure confidentiality for both the accuser(s) and the alleged violator(s) and forwarded to all of the following sources:

1. The name and address of the Chairperson of the state Counselor Licensure Board for the respective state, if in existence.

2. The Ethics Committee
c/o The President
American Association for Counseling
and Development
5999 Stevenson Avenue
Alexandria, Virginia 22304

3. The name and address of all private credentialing agencies

that the alleged violator maintains credentials or holds professional membership. Some of these include the following:

National Board for Certified Counselors, Inc.
3-D Terrace Way
Greensboro, NC 27403

National Council for Credentialing of Career Counselors
c/o NBCC
3-D Terrace Way
Greensboro, NC 27403

National Academy for Certified Clinical Mental Health Counselors
5999 Stevenson Avenue
Alexandria, Virginia 22304

Commission on Rehabilitation Counselor Certification
162 North State Street, Suite 317
Chicago, Illinois 60601

American Association for Marriage and Family Therapy
1717 K Street, N.W., Suite 407
Washington, D.C. 20006

American Psychological Association
1200 Seventeenth Street, N.W.
Washington, D.C. 20036

American Group Psychotherapy Association, Inc.
25 East 21st Street, 6th Floor
New York, New York 10010

APPENDIX D

Policies and Procedures for Processing Complaints of Ethical Violations

Approved March, 1990 - Amended December, 1991

Section A:
General

1. The American Association for Counseling and Development, hereinafter referred to as the "Association" or "AACD", as an educational, scientific, and charitable organization, is dedicated to enhancing the worth, dignity, potential, and uniqueness of each individual and rendering service to society.

2. The Association, in furthering its objectives, administers Ethical Standards that have been developed and approved by the AACD Governing Council.

3. The purpose of this document is to facilitate the work of the AACD Ethics Committee by specifying the procedures for processing cases of alleged violations of the AACD Ethical Standards, codifying options for sanctioning members, and stating appeal procedures. The intent of the Association is to monitor the professional conduct of its members to ensure sound ethical practices.

Section B:
Ethics Committee Members

1. The Ethics Committee is a standing committee of the Association. The Committee consists of six (6) appointed members, including the Chairperson. The editor of the *Ethical Standards Casebook* serves as an *ex officio* member of this Committee without vote. Two members are appointed annually for a three (3) year term by the President-Elect; appointments are subject to confirmation by the AACD Governing Council. Any vacancy occurring on the Committee will be filled by the President in the same manner, and the person appointed shall serve the unexpired term of the member whose place he or she took. Committee members may be reappointed to not more than one (1) additional consecutive term.

2. The Chairperson of the Committee is appointed annually by the incumbent President-Elect, subject to confirmation by the AACD Governing Council. A Chairperson may be reappointed to one additional term during any three (3) year period.

Section C:
Role and Function

1. The role of the Ethics Committee of the Association is to assist in the arbitration and conciliation of conflicts among members of the Association, except where appropriate client concerns may be expressed. The Committee also is responsible for:
   A. Educating the membership as to the Association's Ethical Standards,
   B. Periodically reviewing and recommending changes in the Ethical Standards of the Association as well as the Policies and Procedures for Processing Complaints of Ethical Violations,
   C. Receiving and processing complaints of alleged violations of the Ethical Standards of the Association, and
   D. Receiving and processing questions.

2. In processing complaints about alleged ethical misconduct, the Committee will compile an objective, factual account of the dispute in question and make the best possible recommendation for the resolution of the case. The Committee, in taking any action, shall do so only for cause, shall only take the degree of disciplinary

action that is reasonable, shall utilize these procedures with objectivity and fairness, and in general shall act only to further the interest and objectives of the Association and its membership.

3. The AACD Ethics Committee itself will not initiate any ethical violation charges against an AACD member.

4. Of the six (6) voting members of the Committee, a vote of four (4) is necessary to conduct business. In the event the Chair or any other member of the Committee has a personal interest in the case, he or she shall withdraw from reviewing the case. A unanimous vote of those members of the Committee who reviewed the case is necessary to expel a member from the Association.

5. The Chairperson of the AACD Ethics Committee and/or the AACD Executive Director (or his/her designee) may consult with AACD legal counsel at any time.

Section D:
Responsibilities of Committee Members

1. The members of the Ethics Committee must be conscious that their position is extremely important and sensitive and that their decisions involve the rights of many individuals, the reputation of the counseling and human development community, and the careers of the members. The Committee members have an obligation to act in an unbiased manner, to work expeditiously, to safeguard the confidentiality of the Committee's activities, and to follow procedures that protect the rights of all individuals involved.

Section E:
Responsibilities of the Chairperson

1. In addition to the above guidelines for members of the Committee, the Chairperson, in conjunction with Headquarters staff, has the responsibilities of:
   A. Receiving (via AACD Headquarters) complaints that have been certified for membership status of the accused,
   B. Notifying the complainant and the accused of receipt of the case,
   C. Notifying the members of the Ethics Committee of the case,
   D. Presiding over the meetings of the Committee,

E. Preparing and sending (by certified mail) communications to the complainant and accused member on the recommendations and decisions of the Committee, and

F. Arranging for legal advice with assistance and financial approval of the AACD Executive Director.

Section F:
Complaints

1. All correspondence, records, and activities of the AACD Ethics Committee will remain confidential.

2. The AACD Ethics Committee will not act on anonymous complaints, nor will it act on complaints currently under civil or criminal litigation.

3. The AACD Ethics Committee will act only on those cases where the accused is a current member of AACD or was a member of AACD at the time of the alleged violation. State Division and State Branch Ethics Committees may act only on those cases where the accused is a member of the State Division or State Branch and not a member of AACD.

Section G:
Submitting Complaints—Procedures for AACD Members

1. The procedures for submission of complaints to the Ethics Committee are as follows:

A. If feasible, the complainant should discuss with utmost confidentiality the nature of the complaint with a colleague to see if he or she views the situation as an ethical violation.

B. Whenever feasible, the complainant is to approach the accused directly to discuss and resolve the complaint.

C. In cases where a resolution is not forthcoming at the personal level, the complainant shall prepare a formal written statement of the complaint and shall submit it to the AACD Ethics Committee. Action or consideration by the AACD Ethics Committee may not be initiated until this requirement is satisfied.

D. Formal written complaints must include a statement indicating the behavior(s) that constituted the alleged violation(s), and the date(s) of the alleged violation(s). The written statement must also contain the accused member's full name and complete address. Any relevant supporting documentation may be included with the complaint.

E. All complaints that are directed to the AACD Ethics Committee should be mailed to the Ethics Committee, c/o The Executive Director, American Association for Counseling and Development, 5999 Stevenson Avenue, Alexandria, Virginia 22304. The envelope must be marked "CONFIDENTIAL." This procedure is necessary to ensure the confidentiality of the person submitting the complaint and the person accused in the complaint.

Section H:
Submitting Complaints—Procedures for Non-members

1. The AACD Ethics Committee recognizes the rights of non-AACD members to file grievances concerning a member. Ordinarily this non-member will be a client or student of an AACD member who believes that the AACD member has acted unethically.

2. In such cases, the complainant shall contact the AACD Executive Director (or his/her designee) and outline, in writing, those behaviors he or she feels were unethical in nature. Headquarters staff will delineate the complaint process to the complainant.

Section I:
Processing Complaints

1. When complaints are received at Headquarters, the AACD Executive Director (or his/her designee) shall: (a) check on the membership status of the accused, (b) acknowledge receipt of the complaint within ten (10) working days after it is received in AACD Headquarters, and (c) consult with the Chairperson of the AACD Ethics Committee within ten (10) working days after the complaint is received in AACD Headquarters to determine whether it is appropriate to proceed with the complaint. If the Director (or designee) and Chairperson determine it is inappropriate to proceed, the complainant shall be so notified. If the Director (or designee) and Chairperson determine it is appropriate to proceed with the complaint, they will identify which Ethical Standard(s) are applicable to the alleged violation. A formal statement con-

taining the Ethical Standard(s) that were allegedly violated will be forwarded to the complainant for his/her signature. This signed formal statement will then become a part of the formal complaint.

2. Once the formal complaint has been compiled (as indicated above), the Chairperson of the AACD Ethics Committee shall do the following:

   A. Inform the complainant in writing that the accused members has been notified of the charges,

   B. Direct a letter to the accused member informing the member of accusations lodged against him or her, including copies of all materials submitted by the complainant, asking for a response, and requesting that relevant information be submitted to the Chairperson within thirty (30) working days.

3. The accused is under no duty to respond to the allegations, but the Committee will not be obligated to delay or postpone its review of the case unless the accused so requests, with good cause, in advance. Failure of the accused to respond should not be viewed by the Committee as sufficient ground for taking disciplinary action.

4. Once the Chairperson has received the accused member's response or the thirty (30) days have elapsed, then the Chairperson shall forward to the members of the AACD Ethics Committee legal counsel's opinion (if applicable), staff verification of membership status, allegations, and responses, and direct the Committee to review the case and make recommendations for its disposition within two (2) weeks of receipt of the case.

5. The AACD Ethics Committee will review the case and make recommendations for its disposition and/or resolution within two hundred (200) working days following its receipt.

6. The AACD Ethics Committee Chairperson may ask the President of AACD to appoint an investigating committee at the local or state level to gather and submit relevant information concerning the case to the Committee.

Section J:
Options Available to the Ethics Committee

1. After reviewing the information forwarded by the Chairperson, the Ethics Committee shall have the power to:

   A. Dismiss the charges, find that no violation has occurred, and dismiss the complaint, or

B. Find that the practice(s) in which the member engages that is (are) the subject of the complaint, is (are) unethical, notify the accused of this determination, and request the member to voluntarily cease and desist in the practice(s) without impositions of further sanctions, or

C. Find that the practice(s) in which the member engages, that is (are) the subject of the complaint, is (are) unethical, notify the accused of this determination, and impose sanctions.

Section K:
Appropriate Sanctions

1. The Committee may consider extenuating circumstances before deciding on the penalty to be imposed. If the Committee finds the accused has violated the Ethical Standards and decides to impose sanctions, the Committee may take any of the following actions:

A. Issue a reprimand with recommendations for corrective action, subject to review by the Committee, or

B. Place the member on probation for a specified period of time, subject to review by the Committee, or

C. Suspend eligibility for membership in AACD for a specified period of time, subject to review by the Committee, or

D. Expel the member from AACD permanently.

Section L:
Consequences of Sanctions

1. Both a reprimand and probation carry with it no loss of membership rights or privileges.

2. A suspended member forfeits the rights and privileges of membership only for the period of his or her suspension.

3. In the event a member is expelled from AACD membership, he or she shall lose all rights and privileges of membership in AACD and its divisions permanently. The expelled member shall not be entitled to a refund of dues already paid.

4. If the member is suspended or expelled, and after any right to appeal has been exhausted, the Committee will notify the appropriate state licensing board(s) of the disciplined member's status

with AACD. Notice also will be given to the National Board for Certified Counselors, the AACD Divisions of which the disciplined party is a member, the State Branch of AACD in which the member resides, the members of AACD, the complainant, and other organizations as the Committee deems necessary. Such notice shall only state the sanctions imposed and the sections of the AACD Ethical Standards that were violated. Further elaboration shall not be disclosed.

5. Should a member resign from the Association after a complaint has been brought against him or her and before the Ethics Committee has completed its deliberations, that member is considered to have been expelled from the Association for failure to respond in a timely and complete manner to the Ethics Committee.

Section M:
Hearings

1. At the discretion of the Ethics Committee, a hearing may be conducted when the results of the Ethics Committee's preliminary determination indicate that additional information is needed. The Chairperson shall schedule a formal hearing on the case and notify both the complainant and the accused of their right to attend.

2. The hearing will be held before a panel made up of the Ethics Committee and, if the accused member chooses, a representative of the accused member's primary Division. This representative will be identified by the Division President and will have voting privileges.

Section N:
Recommended Hearing Procedures

1. Purposes of Hearings. The purposes for which hearings shall be conducted are: (a) to determine whether a breach of the Ethical Standards of AACD has occurred, and (b) if so, to determine what disciplinary action should be taken by the AACD. If a hearing is held, no disciplinary action will be taken by AACD until after the accused member has been given reasonable notice of the hearing and the specific charges raised against him or her and has had the opportunity to be heard and to present evidence in his or her behalf. The hearings will be formally conducted. The Committee will be guided in its deliberations by principles of basic fairness

and professionalism, and will keep its deliberations as confidential as possible, except as provided herein.

2. Notice. At least forty-five (45) working days before the hearing, the accused member should be advised in writing of the time and place of the hearing and of the charges involved. Notice shall be given either personally or by certified or registered mail and shall be signed by the Committee Chair. The notice should be addressed to the accused member at his or her address as it appears in the membership records of the AACD. The notice should include a brief statement of the complaints lodged against him or her, and should be supported by the evidence. The accused is under no duty to respond to the notice, but the Committee will not be obligated to delay or postpone its hearing unless the accused so requests in writing, with good cause, in advance. Failure of the accused to appear at the hearing should not be viewed by the Committee as sufficient ground for taking disciplinary action.

3. Conduct of the Hearing.

    A. Accommodations. The Committee shall provide a private room to conduct the hearings, and no observers shall be permitted. The location of the hearing shall be determined at the discretion of the Committee, taking into consideration the convenience of the Committee and the parties involved.

    B. Presiding Officer. The Chair of the Ethics Committee shall preside over the hearing and deliberations of the Committee. In the event the Chair or any other member of the Committee has a personal interest in the case, he or she shall withdraw from the hearing and deliberations and shall not participate therein. The Committee shall select from among its members a presiding officer for any case where the Chair has excused himself or herself. At the conclusion of the hearing and deliberation of the Committee, the Chair shall promptly notify the accused and complainant of the Committee's decision in writing.

    C. Record. A record of the hearing shall be made and preserved, together with any documents presented as evidence, at the AACD Headquarters for a period of three (3) years following the hearing decision. The record may consist of a summary of testimony received, or a verbatim transcript, at the discretion of the Committee.

    D. Right to Counsel. The parties shall be entitled to have counsel present to advise them throughout the hearing, but they may not participate beyond advising. Legal Counsel for AACD shall also be present at the hearing to advise the Committee and shall have the privilege of the floor.

E. Witnesses. Either party shall have the right to call witnesses to substantiate his or her version of the case. The Committee shall also have the right to call witnesses it believes may provide further insight into the matter before the Committee. Witnesses shall not be present during the hearings except when they are called upon to testify. The presiding officer shall allow questions to be asked of any witness by the opposition or members of the Committee and shall ensure that questions and testimony are relevant to the issues in the case. Should the hearing be disturbed by disparaging or irrelevant testimony or by the flareup of tempers, the presiding officer shall call a brief recess until order can be restored. Witnesses shall be excused upon completion of their testimony. All expenses associated with witnesses or counsel on behalf of the parties shall be borne by the respective parties.

F. Presentation of Evidence.

(1) A member of the Committee shall be called upon first to present the charge(s) made against the accused and to briefly describe the evidence supporting the charge(s).

(2) The complainant or a member of the Committee shall then be called upon to present the case against the accused. Witnesses who can substantiate the case shall be called upon to testify and answer questions of the accused and the Committee.

(3) If the accused has exercised the right to be present at the hearing, he or she shall be called upon last to present any evidence which refutes the charges against him or her. This includes the presentation of witnesses as in Subsection (E) above. The accused member has the right to refuse to make a statement in his or her behalf. The accused will not be found guilty simply for refusing to testify. Once the accused chooses to testify, however, he or she may be cross-examined by members of the Committee or the complainant.

(4) The Committee will endeavor to conclude the hearing within a period of approximately three (3) hours. The

parties will be requested to be considerate of this time frame in planning their testimony. Testimony that is merely cumulative or repetitious may, at the discretion of the presiding officer, be excluded.

(5) The accused has the right to be present at all times during the hearing and to challenge all of the evidence presented against him or her.

G. Relevancy of Evidence. The Hearing Committee is not a court of law and is not required to observe the rules of evidence that apply in the trial of lawsuits. Consequently, evidence that would be inadmissible in a court of law may be admissible in the hearing before the Committee, if it is relevant to the case. That is, if the evidence offered tends to explain, clarify, or refute any of the important facts of the case, it should generally be considered. The Committee will not receive evidence or testimony for the purpose of supporting any charge that was not set forth in the notice of the hearing or that is not relevant to the issues of the case.

4. Burden of Proof. The burden of proving a violation of the Ethical Standards is on the complainant and/or the Committee. It is not up to the accused to prove his or her innocence of any wrongdoing. Although the charge(s) need not be proved "beyond a reasonable doubt," the Committee will not find the accused guilty in the absence of substantial, objective, and believable evidence to sustain the charge(s).

5. Deliberation of the Committee. After the hearing with the parties is completed, the Committee shall meet in a closed session to review the evidence presented and reach a conclusion. The Committee shall be the sole trier of fact and shall weigh the evidence presented and judge the credibility of the witnesses. The act of a majority of the members of the Committee shall be the decision of the Committee and only those members of the Committee who were present throughout the entire hearing shall be eligible to vote.

6. Decision of the Committee. The Committee will first resolve the issue of the guilt or innocence of the accused. Applying the burden of proof in paragraph 4 above, the Committee will vote by secret ballot, unless the members of the Committee consent to an oral vote. In the event a majority of the members of the Committee do not find the accused guilty, the charges shall be dismissed and the parties notified. If the Committee finds the accused has

violated the Ethical Standards, it must then determine what sanctions to impose in accord with Section K: Appropriate Sanctions.

Section O:
Appeal Procedures

1. Appeals will be heard only in such cases wherein the appellant presents evidence that the sanction imposed by the Committee has been arbitrary or capricious or that the procedures outlined in the "Policy Document" have not been followed.

2. The complainant and accused shall be advised of the appeal procedure by the Chairperson of the AACD Ethics Committee. The following procedures shall govern appeals:

    A. A three (3) member review committee composed of the Executive Director of the AACD, the President of the AACD Division with which the accused member is most closely identified, and the immediate Past President of AACD. The AACD attorney shall serve as legal advisor and have the privilege of the floor.

    B. The appeal with supporting documentation must be made in writing within sixty (60) working days by certified mail to the AACD Executive Director and indicate the basis upon which it is made. If the member requires a time extension, he or she must request it in writing by certified mail within thirty (30) working days of receiving the decision by the AACD Ethics Committee. The extension will consist of ninety (90) working days beginning from that request.

    C. The review committee shall review all materials considered by the AACD Ethics Committee.

    D. Within thirty (30) working days of this review, the members on the review committee shall submit to the President of the AACD a written statement giving their opinion regarding the decision of the Ethics Committee. Each member shall concur with or dissent from the decision of the Ethics Committee.

    E. Within fifteen (15) working days of receiving this opinion, the President of AACD will reach a decision based on the considered opinions of the review committee from the following alternatives:

       (1) support the decision of the Ethics Committee, or

       (2) reverse the decision of the Ethics Committee.

3. The parties to the appeal shall be advised of the action in writing.

Section P:
Records

1. Records of the AACD Ethics Committee and the review committee shall remain at the AACD Headquarters.

Section Q:
Procedures for Submitting and Interpreting Questions of Ethical Conduct

1. The procedures for submitting questions to the Ethics Committee are as follows:
A. Whenever possible, the questioner is first advised to consult other colleagues seeking interpretation of questions.
B. If a national level resolution is deemed appropriate, the questioner shall prepare a written statement, which details the conduct in question. Statements should include the section or sections of the Ethical Standards to be interpreted relative to the conduct in question. All questions that are directed to the Ethics Committee should be mailed to: Ethics Committee, c/o AACD Executive Director.
C. The AACD Ethics Committee Chairperson or his/her designee:
(1) may confer with legal counsel, and
(2) shall direct a letter to the questioner acknowledging receipt of the question, informing the member that the questions will be interpreted by the Committee, and outlining the procedures to be involved in the interpretation.
D. The Ethics Committee will review and interpret the question and, if requested by the questioner, make recommendations for conduct.

APPENDIX E

ASCA Position Statement: The School Counselor and Confidentiality

(Adopted 1974; reviewed and reaffirmed 1980; revised 1986)

The members of the American School Counselor Association (ASCA) affirm their belief in the worth and dignity of the individual. It is the professional responsibility of school counselors to fully respect the right to privacy of those with whom they enter counseling relationships.

Confidentiality is an ethical term denoting a counseling practice relevant to privacy.

Privileged Communication is a legal term denoting a requirement to protect the privacy between counselor and student.

Counselors must keep abreast of and adhere to all laws, policies and ethical standards pertaining to confidentiality. It is the responsibility of the counselor to provide prior notice to students regarding the possible necessity for consulting with others.

Where confidentiality is provided, ASCA recognizes that a counseling relationship requires an atmosphere of trust and confidence between the student and the counselor. A student has the right to privacy and to expect confidentiality. This confidentiality must not be abridged by the counselor except where there is a clear and present danger to the student and to other persons.

The counselor reserves the right to consult with other professionally competent persons when this is in the interest of the student. Confidentiality assures that disclosures made will not be divulged to others except when authorized by the student. Counseling information used in research and training of counselors should be fully guaranteed the anonymity of the counselee.

In the event of possible judicial proceedings the counselor should initially advise the school administration as well as the counselee if available, and if necessary, consult legal counsel. When reports are required to be produced, every effort should be made to limit demands for information to those matters essential for the purposes of the legal proceedings.

Guidelines

1. The main purpose of confidentiality is to offer counselees a relationship in which they will be able to deal with what concerns them without fear of disclosure. Furthermore, counselors have a similar responsibility in protecting the privileged information received through confidential relationships with teachers and parents.

2. In reality, it is the student who is privileged. It is the student or student's parent or guardian in cases of minors who owns information and the student or guardian has the right to say who shall have access to it and who shall not.

3. The counselor and student should be provided with adequate physical facilities that guarantee the confidentiality of the counseling relationship.

4. With the enactment of P.L. 93-380 which speaks to the rights and privacy of parents and students, great care should be taken with recorded information.

5. Counselors must be concerned about individuals who have access to confidential information. Counselors must adhere to P.L. 93-380.

6. All faculty and administrative personnel should receive in-service training concerning the privacy rights of students. Counselors should assume the primary responsibility for educating school personnel in this area.

7. It should be the policy of each school to guarantee secretaries adequate working space so that students and school personnel will not come into contact with confidential information, even inadvertently.

8. Counselors should undertake a periodic review of information requested of their students. Only relevant information should be retained.

9. Counselors will adhere to ethical standards and local policies in relating student information over the telephone.

10. Counselors should be aware that it is much more difficult to guarantee confidentiality in group counseling than in individual counseling.

11. Communications made in good faith concerning a student may be classified as privileged by the courts and the communicating parties will be protected by law against legal action seeking damages for libel or slander. Generally, it may be said that an occasion of this particular privilege arises when one acts in the bona fide discharge of a public or private duty. This privilege may be abused or lost by malice, improper and unjustified motive, bad faith or excessive publication.

12. When a counselor is in doubt about what to release in a judicial proceeding, the counselor should arrange a conference with the judge to explain the counselor's dilemma and get advice as to how to proceed.

13. Counselors have a responsibility to encourage school administrators to develop written policies concerning the ethical handling of all records in their school system. The development of additional guidelines relevant to the local situation are encouraged.

14. Finally, it is strongly recommended that state and local counselor associations implement these principles and guidelines with appropriate legislation.

With the passage of the Family Educational Rights and Privacy Act, P.L. 93-380 (The Buckley Amendment), great care must be taken with recorded information. It is essential that counselors familiarize themselves with this Law which is a part of the omnibus Education Amendments of 1974 and support its intent to all their publics.

Provisions of this law on parent and student rights and privacy:

1. Deny federal funds to any educational institution that refuses a student's parents access to their child's school record. Parents also have the right to challenge the accuracy of any records.

2. Deny federal funds if records are released to outside groups without parent consent with exception of other school court orders and financial aid applications, with clearance procedures of parents even on the exceptions.

All counselors should have a copy of the complete law.

APPENDIX F

ASCA Position Statement: The School Counselor and Child Abuse/Neglect Prevention

(Adopted 1981; revised 1985)

Introduction:

The incidence of reported child abuse and child neglect has increased significantly, both nationally and statewide, during the past several years. Generally, state laws require people in the helping professions, who have reasonable cause to believe that a child is suffering serious physical or emotional injury, to report this situation to the appropriate authorities. School counselors are mandated reporters and need policies, referral procedures, and information. However, it is not simply a legal issue of reporting child abuse, but also a moral and ethical responsibility of school counselors to help children and adults cope with abusive behavior, facilitate behavioral changes, and prepare for parenting styles and positive interpersonal relationships. Counselors must commit themselves to providing strategies to help break the cycle of child abuse.

Rationale:

There are societal beliefs and values that parents have the right to discipline their children as they choose. The consequence of such beliefs, to some individuals, is physical and/or emotional harm and lowered self-esteem. The cycle of abuse seems to be self-perpetuating. Research shows that a large percentage of abusive parents were abused children. Counselors having an understanding of the dynamics of child abuse can aid in early recognition and detection of families with the potential for child abuse. School counselors are often in a unique position to identify potential and actual cases of abuse/neglect of children. Responsible action by the counselor can be achieved through the recognition and understanding of the problem, knowing the reporting procedures, and participating in available child abuse information programs.

The American School Counselor Association recognizes that it is the absolute responsibility of school counselors to report suspected cases of child abuse/neglect to the proper authorities.

We also recognize that the abuse of children is not limited to the home and that corporal punishment by school authorities might well be considered child abuse. The American School Counselor Association supports any legislation which specifically bans the use of corporal punishment as a disciplinary tool within the schools.

Definitions:

Abuse: The infliction by other than accidental means of physical harm upon the body of a child, continual psychological damage or denial of emotional needs.

Corporal Punishment: Any act of physical force upon a pupil for the purpose of punishing that pupil.

This definition specifically excludes any reasonable force exercised by a school employee which is used in self-defense, in defense of other persons or property or to restrain or remove a pupil who is disrupting school functions and who refuses to comply with a request to stop.

Some examples of child abuse are:
1. Extensive bruises or patterns of bruises.
2. Burns or burn patterns.
3. Lacerations, welts or abrasions.
4. Injuries inconsistent with information offered.

5. Sexual abuse is any act or acts involving sexual molestation or exploitation, including but not limited to rape, carnal knowledge, sodomy, or unnatural sexual practices.

6. Emotional disturbance caused by continuous friction in the home, marital discord, or mentally ill parents.

7. Cruel treatment.

Neglect: the failure to provide necessary food, care, clothing, shelter, supervision, or medical attention for a child.

Examples of child neglect are:

1. Malnourished, ill clad, dirty, without proper shelter or sleeping arrangements, lacking appropriate health care.

2. Unattended, lacking adequate supervision.

3. Ill and lacking essential medical attention.

4. Irregular/illegal absences from school.

5. Exploited, overworked.

6. Lacking essential psychological/emotional nurturance.

7. Abandonment.

Endorsements:

The American School Counselor Association strongly endorses, supports and encourages incorporation into the counselor's role the following:

—The awareness that all state statutes make school counselors immune from both civil and criminal liability when reporting suspected cases of child abuse/neglect cases in good faith. Failure to report may result in legal penalties. Thorough knowledge of local child abuse policy and procedures is essential.

—It is not the responsibility of the school counselor to prove that the child has been abused/neglected, or to determine the cause of suspected abuse/neglect, or to determine whether the child is in need of protection.

—The protection of confidentiality and the child's right to privacy with discussion of the situation limited to school staff members who have a need to know or authorized personnel from appropriate agencies. Counselors should develop their position as a liaison between the school, child, and the appropriate agency.

Counselor Role:

The American School Counselor Association encourages its members to participate in the implementation of the following guidance and counseling activities:

—Coordinate team efforts involving the principal, teacher, counselor, school nurse, protective services worker, and the child.

—Serve as a support to teachers, and other school personnel, especially if the child was abused as a result of a report sent home about the child from school.

—Emphasize the non-punitive role of protective services and allay fears that the child will be removed immediately from the home.

—Facilitate the contact between the child and the social worker. The issue of confidentiality and re-establishing the trust of the child after the report is made is critical to the child-counselor relationship.

—Provide on-going counseling services to the child and/or family after the crisis is over, or refer to an appropriate community agency.

—Provide programs designed to help prevent child abuse. Counselors can help children with coping skills and ways to prevent their own abuse by improving their self-concepts, being able to recognize stress in their parents, and being sensitive to cues that abuse may occur if their own behavior is not changed.

—Help teachers and administrators in understanding the dynamics of abuse and abusive parents, and in developing a non-judgmental attitude so they can react more appropriately in crisis situations.

—Provide developmental workshops and/or support groups for parents focusing upon alternative methods of discipline, handling anger and frustration, and enhancing parenting skills.

Summary:

School counselors are key people in the child abuse prevention network. The school counselor must be able to guide and help, and provide all appropriate services during a crisis situation. Up-to-date information can sometimes mean a turning point in the life and behavior of an abusive family.

Reprint Sources by Chapter

Chapter 1

Huey, W.C. (1987). "Ethical standards for school counselors": Test your knowledge. *The School Counselor, 34,* 331–335.

Mabe, A.R., & Rollin, S.A. (1986). The role of a code of ethical standards in counseling. *Journal of Counseling and Development, 64,* 294–297.

Ferris, P.A., & Linville, M.E. (1985). The child's rights: Whose responsibility? *Elementary School Guidance and Counseling, 19,* 172–180.

Klenowski, J.R. (1983). Adolescents' rights of access to counseling. *Personnel and Guidance Journal, 61,* 365–367.

DePauw, M.E. (1986). Avoiding ethical violations: A timeline perspective for individual counseling. *Journal of Counseling and Development, 64,* 303–305.

Levenson, J.L. (1986). When a colleague practices unethically: Guidelines for intervention. *Journal of Counseling and Development, 64,* 315–317.

Marchant, W. (1987). Reporting unethical practices: Revised guidelines. *Journal of Counseling and Development, 65,* 573–574.

Huey, W.C. (1986). Ethical concerns in school counseling. *Journal of Counseling and Development, 64,* 321–322.

Chapter 2

Zingaro, J.C. (1983). Confidentiality: To tell or not to tell. *Elementary School Guidance and Counseling, 17,* 261–267.

Walker, M.M., & Larrabee, M.J. (1985). Ethics and school records. *Elementary School Guidance and Counseling, 19,* 210–216.

Sheeley, V.L., & Herlihy, B. (1987). Privileged communication in school counseling: Status update. *The School Counselor, 34,* 268–272.

Chapter 3

Remley, T.P., Jr. (1985). The law and ethical practices in elementary and middle schools. *Elementary School Guidance and Counseling, 19,* 181–189.

Aiello, H., & Humes, C.W. (1987). Counselor contact of the noncustodial parent: A point of law. *Elementary School Guidance and Counseling, 21,* 177–182.

Kaplan, L.S., & Geoffroy, K. (1987). The Hatch Amendment: A primer for counselors. Part II: Protective legislation and recommendations for action. *The School Counselor, 35,* 88–95.

Talbutt, L.C. (1983). The counselor and testing: Some legal concerns. *The School Counselor, 30,* 245–250.

Talbutt, L.C. (1983). Libel and slander: A potential problem for the 1980s. *The School Counselor, 30,* 164–168.

Talbutt, L.C. (1983). Current legal trends regarding abortions for minors: A dilemma for counselors. *The School Counselor, 31,* 120–124.

Herlihy, B., & Sheeley, V.L. (1988). Counselor liability and the duty to warn: Selected cases, statutory trends, and implications for practice. *Counselor Education and Supervision, 27,* 203–215.

Chapter 4

Camblin, L.D., Jr., & Prout, H.T. (1983). School counselors and the reporting of child abuse: A survey of state laws and practices. *The School Counselor, 30,* 358–367.

Sandberg, D.N., Crabbs, S.K., & Crabbs, M.A. (1988). Legal issues in child abuse: Questions and answers for counselors. *Elementary School Guidance and Counseling, 22,* 268–274.

Spiegel, L.D. (1988). Child abuse hysteria and the elementary school counselor. *Elementary School Guidance and Counseling, 22,* 275–283.

Krugman, R.D. (1988). Overstating the issue: A reaction to Spiegel. *Elementary School Guidance and Counseling, 22,* 284–286.

Ferris, P.A. (1988). Counselors need to be knowledgeable and sensitive: A reaction to Spiegel. *Elementary School Guidance and Counseling, 22,* 287–288.

Howell-Nigrelli, J. (1988). Shared responsibility for reporting child abuse cases: A reaction to Spiegel. *Elementary School Guidance and Counseling, 22,* 289–290.

Gerler, E.R., Jr. (1988). Recent research on child abuse: A brief review. *Elementary School Guidance and Counseling, 22,* 325–327.

Chapter 5

Kottler, J.A. (1982). Ethics comes of age: Introduction to the special issue. *Journal for Specialists in Group Work, 7,* 138–139.

Corey, G., Corey, M.S., Callanan, P., & Russell, J.M. (1982). Ethical considerations in using group techniques. *Journal for Specialists in Group Work, 7,* 140–148.

Davis, K.L., & Meara, N.M. (1982). So you think it is a secret. *Journal for Specialists in Group Work, 7,* 149–153.

Terres, C.K., & Larrabee, M.J. (1985). Ethical issues and group work with children. *Elementary School Guidance and Counseling, 19,* 190–197.

Kottler, J.A. (1982). Unethical behaviors we all do and pretend we do not. *Journal for Specialists in Group Work, 7,* 182–186.

Chapter 6

Sampson, J.P., Jr., & Pyle, K.R. (1983). Ethical issues involved with the use of computer-assisted counseling, testing, and guidance systems. *Personnel and Guidance Journal, 61,* 283–287.

Childers, J.H., Jr. (1985). The counselor's use of microcomputers: Problems and ethical issues. *The School Counselor, 33,* 26–31.

Cayleff, S.E. (1986). Ethical issues in counseling gender, race, and culturally distinct groups. *Journal of Counseling and Development, 64,* 345–347.

Robinson, S.E., & Gross, D.R. (1986). Counseling research: Ethics and issues. *Journal of Counseling and Development, 64,* 331–333.

Coleman, E., & Schaefer, S. (1986). Boundaries of sex and intimacy between client and counselor. *Journal of Counseling and Development, 64,* 341–344.